Russia Confronts Chechnya

Roots of a Separatist Conflict

In this book John Dunlop provides an understanding of the background to the Russian invasion of Chechnya in December 1994, tracing events from 4,000 BC to the time of the invasion. The historic encounter between Chechens and Russians, first during pre-Petrine and then with imperial Russia, is carefully examined. The genocide and oppression endured by the Chechens under the communists are discussed in detail. The convulsive "Chechen Revolution" of 1991, which brought General Dzhokhar Dudaev to power, is described, as are developments within Chechnya during 1992–94. The author traces the negotiation process between the Russian Federation and secessionist Chechnya, elucidating the reasons for the breakdown of the quest for a peaceful resolution of the conflict.

JOHN B. DUNLOP is Senior Fellow at the Hoover Institution, and a member of the Steering Committee of the Center for Russian and East European Studies at Stanford University. He is the author, editor, or co-editor of eight books, including *The Rise of Russia and the Fall of the Soviet Union* (1993).

Russia Confronts Chechnya

Roots of a Separatist Conflict

John B. Dunlop

CAMBRIDGE
UNIVERSITY PRESS

PUBLISHED BY THE PRESS SYNDICATE OF THE UNIVERSITY OF CAMBRIDGE
The Pitt Building, Trumpington Street, Cambridge CB2 1RP, United Kingdom

CAMBRIDGE UNIVERSITY PRESS
The Edinburgh Building, Cambridge CB2 2RU, United Kingdom
http://www.cup.cam.ac.uk
40 West 20th Street, New York, NY 10011-4211, USA   http://www.cup.org
10 Stamford Road, Oakleigh, Melbourne 3166, Australia

© John B. Dunlop 1998

First published 1998

Printed in the United Kingdom at the University Press, Cambridge

Typeset in Plantin   [CE]

A catalogue record for this book is available from the British Library

Library of Congress Cataloguing in Publication data

Dunlop, John B.
Russia confronts Chechnya : roots of a separatist conflict / John B. Dunlop.
  p. cm.
Includes index.
ISBN 0 521 63184 X – ISBN 521 63619 1 (pbk.)
1. Chechnia (Russia) – History.
2. Chechnia (Russia) – History – Civil War, 1994–1996 – Causes.
I. Title.
DK511.C37B86   1998
947.5'2 – dc21   97–51840   CIP

ISBN 0 521 63184 X hardback
ISBN 0 521 63619 1 paperback

To Maria, John, Olga, Catherine, Bea,
Jan-Nicholas, and Peter

Contents

Preface

> There is no more important question in Russia than that of Chechnya.
> It is an open bleeding wound.   Lt. General Aleksandr Lebed'[1]

The Russian military invasion of Chechnya, which was launched on 11 December 1994, triggered a harsh, 21-month-long war which constituted, at the least, a serious setback for nascent Russian democracy. How did this bloody war come about, and could it have been avoided? And how did Russia come to find itself facing such a motivated and implacable opponent? Finding answers to these questions will be a major aim of this book.

Russia Confronts Chechnya – the first of two projected volumes on the war – traces events from 4,000 BC, when the ancestors of present-day Chechens began to emerge in the North Caucasus region, to the end of November 1994, when the Russian Federation, in the person of its president and his top advisers, set an irrevocable course toward war. Our focus in this study will, rather narrowly, be upon Russian–Chechen relations; the larger geopolitical context of the encounter of these two peoples will be touched upon only briefly.

My intention in this study, which is an essay in contemporary history, has been to cast as wide a net as possible in order to bring together the available source material concerning the decisions and the events which led up to the war. I would have liked to have had greater access to pro-secessionist Chechen sources, but they were not available; interviews with General Dudaev and other Chechen nationalist leaders appearing in the Russian press have been utilized, as have two detailed volumes of memoirs by Dudaev's acting vice president, Zelimkhan (Zelimkha) Yandarbiev. The present book necessarily represents a pioneering effort; I hope that, by taking a first cut through the available source material, I will attract other specialists into looking more closely at the multifaceted causes of a bloody and unnecessary war.

[1] Press conference given by Aleksandr Lebed' in August 1996, in Discussion List about Chechnya, Chechnya@Plearn.EDU.PL, 13 August 1996.

The book's opening chapter treats the fate of the Chechens over the course of their historic encounter first with pre-Petrine and then with imperial Russia, focusing especially upon the hundred years of contact extending from 1817 through 1917. Chapter 2 examines the oppression and genocide endured by the Chechens during the communist period up until the year 1989, in the middle of the Gorbachev years. Over the course of the lengthy Soviet era, the Chechens, as we shall see, lost a quarter of their population and suffered the shock of deportation as a people to remote regions of Central Asia.

Chapter 3 looks at the convulsive "Chechen Revolution" of 1991, which brought the obdurate and intrepid General Dzhokhar Dudaev to power in Chechnya. Chapter 4, entitled "Dudaev in power," scrutinizes largely internal events taking place in separatist Chechnya during the years 1992–94. Dudaev's failed attempt to create a new "Mountain Republic" uniting the Muslim peoples of the North Caucasus is also analyzed. The emergence of a significant political opposition within Chechnya, increasingly aided and abetted by the Russian Federation, is treated as well.

The closing fifth chapter takes a close look at the negotiation process between the Russian Federation and secessionist Chechnya during the years 1992–94. I attempt to discern the key reasons for the breakdown in the quest for a peaceful resolution of the conflict. The roles of minister for nationalities and regional policy, Sergei Shakhrai, and of President Boris Yeltsin with respect to the collapse of the negotiations are examined both in this chapter and in the ensuing conclusion section. The conclusion attempts to identify salient lessons to be learned both from the breakdown of the negotiation process and from the outbreak of war in December 1994.

From chapter 3 onwards, I cite and reflect upon the opinions of three leading Moscow-based specialists on ethnic affairs: Valerii Tishkov, director of the Institute of Ethnology of the Russian Academy of Sciences, and, briefly, in 1992, chairman of the Russian State Committee on Nationality Affairs (Goskomnats); Sergei Arutyunov (Arutiunov), professor of anthropology and director of the Caucasus Department at the same Institute of Ethnology; and Emil' Pain (Payin), a member of the Russian Presidential Council, who, in September 1996, was appointed Yeltsin's adviser on Chechnya. (A number of Pain's publications were coauthored with another specialist, Arkadii Popov.)

The views of these three scholars – arguably the best-informed specialists in Russia working on the thorny and intractable issue of Russian–Chechen relations – are often cited in this book; in instances where they disagree among themselves, I seek to determine which of them has the

more persuasive arguments. Their criticisms of the views and actions of
Nationalities Minister Shakhrai are also a subject of analysis. (It should
be noted that while Professor Arutyunov is a "pure scholar," Tishkov
and Pain – and especially the latter – represent what might be called
"scholar-politicians.")

I am indebted to two Bay Area colleagues who cheerfully undertook
to read the manuscript in draft form. Norman Naimark, chairman of the
Stanford University History Department, took time away from his
immensely busy schedule to read through a draft of chapters 1 and 2,
and then offered trenchant and helpful comments. Edward ("Ned")
Walker, director of the Berkeley Program in Soviet/Post-Soviet Studies
at the University of California at Berkeley, generously read through a
draft of chapters 3 through 5, as well as the conclusion, and made a
number of pertinent suggestions.

I am also grateful to Fiona Hill, associate director of the Strengthening Democratic Institutions Project at Harvard University's John F.
Kennedy School of Government, and to a second reader who wished to
remain anonymous, both of whom evaluated the manuscript for Cambridge University Press. It should be underlined that none of the four
specialists mentioned should be held responsible for any failings remaining in the text.

Warm thanks are also due to Lee Schwartz, chief of the Global Issues
Division, Office of the Geographer and Global Issues, Bureau of
Intelligence and Research, US Department of State, for granting me
and the Press permission to use two excellent maps produced by the
Office of the Geographer and Global Issues: "The Caucasus Region,"
2762 6-94 STATE (INR/GGI); and "Chechnya and Ingushetia," 3201
5-95 STATE (INR/GGI).

A debt of thanks is also owed to a number of colleagues at the Hoover
Institution. First, I would like most warmly to single out and to thank
John Raisian, director of the institution, for his unflagging support and
for his continued encouragement of this project. I would also like to
acknowledge the unremitting assistance which I have received from my
secretary and de facto research assistant, Joyce Cerwin, whose fluent
knowledge of Russian and administrative skills were important factors
enabling me to finish this study on schedule. I should like, further, to
express my gratitude to the talented staff of the Hoover Institution
Library for frequent assistance; special thanks, in this regard, are due to
Joseph Dwyer, Molly Molloy, and Edward Jajko.

This book is dedicated to my children and to their spouses. A number
of them have had the temerity to embark upon teaching and academic
careers. May they all flourish, "rightly dividing the word of truth."

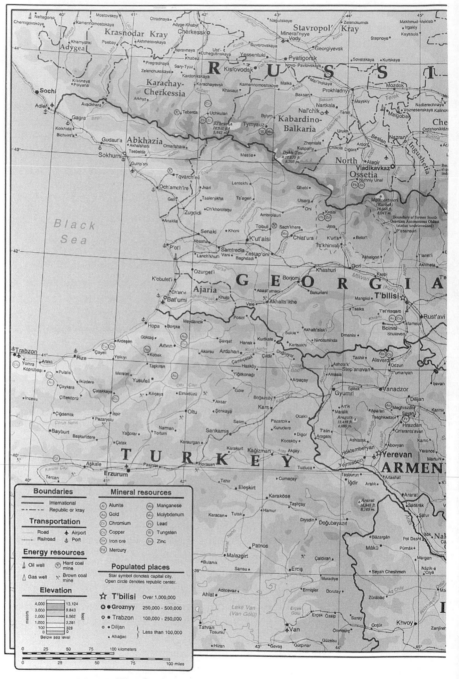

Map 1 The Caucasus region (from 2762 6-94 STATE [INR/GGI]
Bureau of Intelligence and Research,

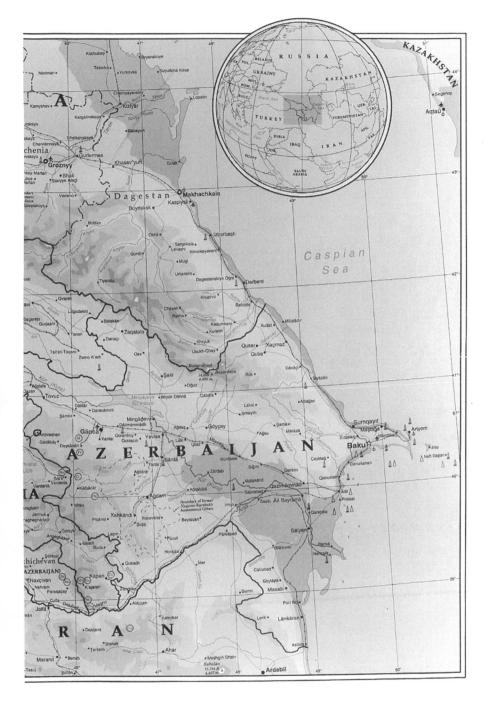

produced by the Office of the Geographer and Global Issues,
US Department of State)

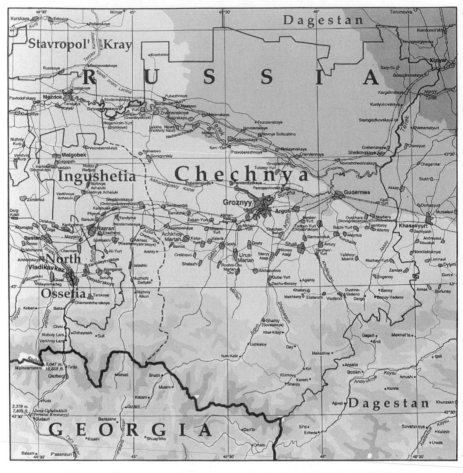

Map 2 Chechnya and Ingushetiya (3201 5-95 STATE [INR/GGI]
produced by the Office of the Geographer and Global Issues,
Bureau of Intelligence and Research, US Department of State)

1   The Chechens' encounter with Russia

[E]verywhere there are mountains, everywhere forests, and the Chechens are fierce and tireless fighters.
John F. Baddeley, *The Russian Conquest of the Caucasus* (1908)[1]

The sun had risen and its spreading rays were lighting up the dewy grass. Near by the Terek murmured in the awakening forest . . . The Cossacks, still and silent, stood round the dead [Chechen] . . . The brown body . . . was well-proportioned and comely. "He, too, were a man," [the Cossack who had killed him] muttered, evidently admiring the corpse.   Lev Tolstoi, *The Cossacks* (1863)[2]

The Caucasus, a chain of high mountains which extends across an isthmus separating the Caspian and Black Seas, have traditionally been recognized as a key natural frontier dividing Europe from Asia. The range stretches a total of 650 miles, of which 400 miles constitute the truly mountainous part; the chain's width averages about 100 miles, except in the middle, the site of the Daryal Pass and the Georgian Military Highway, where it narrows significantly, and at the tapering extremities. The two natural routes for traversing the mountains are through the Daryal Pass and along the Caspian coast in the present-day autonomous republic of Dagestan.[3]

   The word "Chechen," which entered Russian from a Turkish tongue, is taken from the name of a lowland Chechen village where the Russians first encountered them. The Chechens, it should be noted, do not refer to themselves by this name; rather they call themselves "Nokhchii" (singular "Nokhchuo"). The Chechens have lived in or near their present territory for at least 6,000 years. Their language belongs to the so-called Nakh branch of the Caucasian group of languages (the two

[1] John F. Baddeley, *The Russian Conquest of the Caucasus* (London: Longmans, Green & Co., 1908), p. 268.
[2] Leo Tolstoy, *The Cossacks; The Death of Ivan Ilych; Happy Ever After* (Harmondsworth, UK: Penguin, 1960), pp. 203–04.
[3] Baddeley, *Russian Conquest*, pp. xxii–xxiii.

other Nakh languages are Ingush and Batsbi, a moribund language found in Georgia). The Nakh branch split off from the Caucasian family of languages some 5,000–6,000 years ago, thus rendering it comparable in age to Indo-European, the language family ancestral to English, Russian, and many other modern languages. The Caucasian family of languages is entirely indigenous to the Caucasus mountains.[4]

The area which tsarist Russia named Chechnya – and which present-day Chechens refer to as "Checheniya" – constituted a quadrangle located between the Terek and Sunzha Rivers in the west and north; the Andi mountain range in the east, separating it from adjacent Dagestan; and the main Caucasus range to the south.[5] Most of Chechnya lay within the forest zone of the Caucasus. Writing in 1908, before the environmental devastation of the Soviet and post-Soviet periods, British author John Baddeley observed that Chechnya "was, and for the most part still is, covered with dense forests interspersed by numberless streams, deep-set and rapid, having their sources in the mountains that rise range upon range, higher and ever higher, to the south."[6] What the Russians called Chechnya was largely populated by ethnic Chechens, but the western and southwestern part of the region was inhabited by the Ingush, the name a Russian ethnonym based on the place-name Angusht; the Ingush, who refer to themselves as "Ghalghaaj," speak a related but distinct Nakh language. The Chechens and Ingush together are said to speak "Vainakh" (or "Veinakh") languages – the word means "our people" – and the term "Vainakh" is frequently used to refer to the two peoples taken together.

---

[4] See Johanna Nichols, "Chechen," and "Ingush," in Rieks Smeets, ed., *The Indigenous Languages of the Caucasus* (Delmar, NY: Caravan Books, 1994), vol. IV, pp. 1–77, 79–145; and Johanna Nichols, "Who Are the Chechen?," Discussion List about Chechnya, Chechnya@Plearn.EDU.PL, 15 January 1995, and the same author's "Ingush and Chechen," Discussion List about Chechnya, 7 November 1996. See also Paul B. Henze, *Islam in the North Caucasus: The Example of Chechnya*, P-7935 (Santa Monica, CA: RAND, 1995), pp. 1–7. On the unrecorded and early recorded history of the forebears of the Chechens, see Zaindi Shakhbiev, *Sud'ba checheno-ingushskogo naroda* (Moscow: Rossiya molodaya, 1996), pp. 7–63.

[5] Moshe Gammer, *Muslim Resistance to the Tsar: Shamil and the Conquest of Chechnia and Daghestan* (London, UK: Frank Cass, 1994), p. 12. For an example of the use of the word "Checheniya," see the book by former Chechen acting president Zelimkhan (Zelimkha) Yandarbiev, *Checheniya – bitva za svobodu* (L'vov, Ukraine: Svoboda narodiv [sic] and Antibol'shevitskii blok narodov, 1996).

[6] In Baddeley, *Russian Conquest*, p. xxxv. On the geography of Chechnya, see Yu. A. Aidaev, ed., *Chechentsy: istoriya i sovremennost'* (Moscow: Mir domu tvoemu, 1996), pp. 71–110.

Chechnya before the Russians

From the seventh to the seventeenth centuries, there took place a slow penetration of Sunni Islam into the Caucasus region. During the eighth century, the Arabs began actively to convert the peoples of the Caucasus to Islam. When their advance was checked by the Turks, they turned into the mountains, where they spread their religion among the ancestors of the Chechens and of the Avars, who were centered in mountain Dagestan. Many pagan beliefs, however, persisted among the forebears of the Chechens, so the religion of their region before the nineteenth century is best described as mixed Islamic–animist.[7] Orthodox Christianity, it should be noted, had also begun to spread into the mountains, particularly in the area adjacent to the Daryal Pass; it was disseminated from the territories that today compose the Republic of Georgia.[8] The conversion of the Golden Horde between the thirteenth and fourteenth centuries sparked a second penetration of Islam into the North Caucasus and halted the inroads being made into the area by Orthodox Christianity.

In ancient times, the highland regions of the Caucasus had been populous and self-sufficient. From the period of the late Middle Ages until the nineteenth century, however, a worldwide cooling phase known as the Little Ice Age ensued, which resulted in glacial advances and in shortened growing seasons in the alpine areas of the Caucasus. This development had major repercussions for the Chechens, since it served to weaken highland economies and virtually to force their migration down from the mountains into the lowlands; for many Chechens this economically forced descent from the mountains occurred just as the Cossacks were beginning to migrate into the region in large numbers. There was thus a likelihood attaching to the historic encounter of Chechens and Russians, which ensued in the second half of the sixteenth century.[9]

The Russians move south

The ancestors of present-day Russians and Ukrainians had been making periodic appearances in the Caucasus region for a millennium. The

---

[7] Ronald Wixman, *Language Aspects of Ethnic Patterns and Processes in the North Caucasus* (Chicago: University of Chicago Department of Geography Research Series, no. 191, 1980), pp. 70–71.

[8] Baddeley, *Russian Conquest*, p. 263.

[9] Nichols, "Who Are the Chechen?," and V. A. Tishkov, E. L. Belyaeva, and G. V. Marchenko, *Chechenskii krizis* (Moscow: Tsentr kompleksnykh sotsial'nykh issledovanii i marketinga, 1995), p. 6.

"Rus'" or Varangians passed through the Caspian region en route to invading Persia in the tenth century. Prince Mikhail of Tver' was assassinated in the year 1319 near Derbent on the Caspian Sea in what is today Dagestan.[10] The first stage of concerted Russian penetration into the North Caucasus extends for over a century and a half, from the 1550s to the early 1720s. In 1556, when Tsar Ivan the Terrible succeeded in conquering the khanates of Kazan' and Astrakhan' and thus in entering into the Caspian orbit, the North Caucasus region – which had previously been a geopolitical backwater – became the object of a competition involving Muscovy, the Ottoman Empire, Iran, the Crimean Khanate, and other lesser powers. The strategic importance of the region for trade and military routes became clear.

Ivan the Terrible's thrust southward coincided with a largely un-planned and elemental movement south by two discrete groups of Cossacks. These two groups had settled in the Terek delta and in the foothills of Chechnya and subsequently became known as the Terek and Greben Cossacks. When the Chechens began to come down from the mountains in large numbers beginning in the sixteenth century, they found Greben Cossacks already residing in the Caucasus foot-hills.[11] In the sixteenth century, the Cossacks represented free and lawless communities, who conducted plundering raids on their Muslim neighbors and, on occasion, on the states of Poland and Muscovy as well. Many of them were by origin runaway serfs. While living a freebooting existence, the Cossacks clung tenaciously to the Orthodox Christian religion. Ethnically, the Cossacks were of mixed race, many of them having taken native women as wives, some of them in raids. A number of the Cossack wives were ethnic Chechens, while others were Kumyks.[12]

The first Russian fort in the North Caucasus region was erected at Tarki on the Sunzha River in 1559.[13] Ivan the Terrible had agreed to pardon the Greben Cossacks for various misdeeds in exchange for their agreeing to build a fort on the Sunzha. Due to fierce and repeated attacks by tribesmen, the fort had to be relocated four times.[14]

In the year 1559, emissaries from the Adygei, a people of the western North Caucasus region, appeared in Moscow with a request that

---

[10] Baddeley, *Russian Conquest*, pp. 1–2.   [11] Gammer, *Muslim Resistance*, p. 1.

[12] Baddeley, *Russian Conquest*, p. 11. For a discussion of the Kumyks and the other peoples of the North Caucasus region, see Ronald Wixman, *The Peoples of the USSR: An Ethnographic Handbook* (Armonk, NY: M. E. Sharpe, 1988).

[13] Alexandre Bennigsen, "Un mouvement populaire au Caucase à XVIIIe siècle," *Cahiers du monde russe et soviétique*, April–June (1964), 168.

[14] Baddeley, *Russian Conquest*, pp. 7–8.

Orthodox priests be sent to them to baptize the populace.[15] Russia, however, at the time lacked the will and the organizational strength to undertake a major missionary effort in the region. The triumph within the Russian Church of the ritualistic "Josephite" tendency, which led directly to the Old Believer schism of the following century, was a key reason for this weakness. It would be another two hundred years, during the time of Empress Catherine the Great, before Russia would undertake such a proselytizing effort, but by then Islam would have begun to be firmly rooted throughout most of the North Caucasus region.

As Muscovy slowly penetrated the North Caucasus, the rulers of Kakheti (a part of present-day Georgia) began increasingly to look to their powerful Orthodox Christian neighbors to the north for assistance against Muslim powers. The first contacts with Russia were made by King Levan I in 1558, but it was during the reign of Levan's son, Alexandre II, that Moscow sent a number of embassies to Kakheti. Alexandre wanted Russia to assist him in his conflicts with Iran and against the powerful Shamkhal of Targhu in Dagestan. After an exchange of ambassadors in 1586–87, Tsar Fedor of Muscovy, in 1589, told envoys from Kakheti that he was prepared to take their king under his protection, and he pledged to fight the Shamkhal.[16]

In 1594, Fedor sent a force of 7,000 men to Alexandre's aid. The force captured the Shamkhal's capital but was then annihilated on the banks of the Sulak River in present-day Dagestan. In 1590, the Russians had built a fortress on the lower Sunzha River and were thus poised for breakthrough into the North Caucasus. By the following year, they had reached the banks of the Sulak in Dagestan. In the year 1604, Tsar Boris Godunov sent out a force from Kazan' and Astrakhan' to avenge the 1594 massacre suffered under Tsar Fedor, but his force was driven back by Dagestanis, aided by Ottoman Turks.[17]

In 1615, the Georgian kings of Kakheti and Imereti sent a letter to the newly enthroned Tsar Mikhail Romanov asking him for aid and informing him of their opposition to the Persian shah. No assistance was forthcoming. In 1624, the request was repeated, but "Russia, recovering

---

[15] See *Kavkazskaya voina: uroki istorii i sovremennosti* (Krasnodar: Kubanskii gosudarstvennyi universitet, 1995), p. 256. This volume contains papers presented at a scholarly conference held on 16–18 May 1994.

[16] Ronald Grigor Suny, *The Making of the Georgian Nation*, 2nd edn., (Bloomington, IN: Indiana University Press, 1994), p. 49.

[17] See Gammer, *Muslim Resistance*, p. 1; Daddeley, *Russian Conquest*, pp. 8–9; Marie Bennigsen Broxup, "Introduction," in Marie Bennigsen Broxup, ed., *The North Caucasus Barrier* (New York: St. Martin's Press, 1992), p. 2.

from its Time of Troubles, was not prepared to intervene in the Caucasian maelstrom."[18]

In hindsight, we can see that Muscovy of the late sixteenth and early seventeenth century had overreached. Expansionist élan, combined with a desire to help Orthodox co-religionists in proto-Georgia, had brought the Russians to the Mountain (as they were wont to refer to the Caucasus range). But Russia was revealed as militarily too weak to challenge the Ottoman Turks, Persia, and the numerous Muslim princes of the region. For more than a century – from 1604 until 1722 – Russia was forced to abandon its thrust into the Caucasus region. During the seventeenth century, Muscovy entered a period of great turmoil, which witnessed the Time of Troubles, the Old Believer Schism, and the rebellion of Sten'ka Razin, among other travails.

Peter the Great

"The conquest of the Caucasus, as distinct from the Cossack approach," John Baddeley has observed, "begins with Peter the Great's [1722] campaign."[19] Having succeeded in strengthening the institutions and military prowess of the Russian state, and having recently defeated Sweden, Peter felt ready to head an expedition against much-weakened Persia down the Caspian coast, during which he captured the strategically located city of Derbent, as well as Baku, the capital of today's Republic of Azerbaijan. On his way back from Derbent, Peter founded the Holy Cross fort on the Sulak River. It should be noted that in the course of preparing for this campaign Peter had in essence integrated the "hosts" (voiska) of the Terek and Greben Cossacks into the Russian state. In 1721, the Terek Cossacks were withdrawn from the authority of the Foreign Office and put under the command of the War College.[20] Henceforth the Cossacks would be seen by the Russian state as its servants, required to provide military, courier, construction, and other services.[21] Peter's 1722 campaign proved to be a major but temporary success. In the Treaty of St. Petersburg (September 1723), Persia ceded key Caspian territories to Peter, and for the next ten years the Dagestan plain was placed under the direct administration of Russia.[22]

---

[18] Suny, *Making*, p. 51.   [19] Baddeley, *Russian Conquest*, p. 23.
[20] Thomas M. Barrett, "Lives of Uncertainty: The Frontiers of the North Caucasus," *Slavic Review*, Fall (1995), 591.
[21] Gammer, *Muslim Resistance*, p. 2; Baddeley, *Russian Conquest*, p. 10.
[22] Bennigsen, "Un mouvement populaire," 172.

First major clash with the Chechens

It was during the course of Peter's 1722 thrust into the Caucasus that the Russians had their first serious encounter with the Chechens. Earlier, in 1707, Chechens had joined with other tribes and with Cossack Old Believers in destroying the Russian fort at Tarki.[23] In 1722, Russian cavalry were sent by Peter to occupy the village of Enderi, located on the Aktash River in eastern Chechnya, and that force suffered a serious reversal at the hands of the local Chechens. "This was the first time that Russian regular troops had come in contact with that tribe in their native forests, and the result was ominous."[24] Ominous indeed.

Peter died in 1725, and his expansionist project was put on hold for nearly half a century. Empress Anna soon abandoned Peter's conquests of Persian territory, and Russia withdrew to its old line on the Terek River. Under Empress Elizabeth, Russia's sole concern in the eastern regions of the North Caucasus became to defend its line of forts near the Terek. In 1735, a new fort was founded at Kizlyar on the Terek, in present-day Dagestan, which until the year 1763 remained the Russian capital of the Caucasus.[25] (In January 1996, 160 years later, Kizlyar would become the site of a bloody battle between Russians and Chechens.)

Russia's military presence in the North Caucasus region was significantly weakened by the growth of the Old Believer schism among the Cossacks. By 1768, fully half of the Greben Cossacks adhered to the Schism.[26] Before the coming to power of Empress Catherine the Great, it appeared possible that Russia might settle on the Terek River as its "natural" southern boundary in the North Caucasus region.

Catherine the Great

It was under Catherine the Great (ruled 1762–96), like Peter I a protean state-builder, that a major conflict between Russia and the Muslim peoples of the North Caucasus became increasingly likely. In 1762, in an aggressive and portentous move, she constructed a fort at Mozdok on the Terek, in what is today North Ossetiya. Mozdok has aptly been called "the cornerstone of the Russian conquest" of the Caucasus.[27] This fort brought Russia close to the Daryal Pass, the natural passageway through the mountains to Georgia. The construction of this fort sparked a fourteen-year struggle with the Kabardintsy

---

[23] Ibid., 171, n. 1.   [24] Baddeley, *Russian Conquest*, p. 25.
[25] Gammer, *Muslim Resistance*, p. 2.   [26] Baddeley, *Russian Conquest*, p. 14.
[27] Ibid., p. 33.

(1765–79), as well as a war with the Ottoman Empire (1768–74). During this latter conflict, in 1769, a Russian force of 400 men was sent through the Daryal Pass to Tbilisi.[28] Mozdok also came to serve as a center of Russian Orthodox missionary efforts in the region; in 1746, through a ruling of the Holy Synod, and with the participation of the Russian government, a decision was taken to reestablish Orthodoxy in the North Caucasus, especially among the Ossetians, who played a central role in controlling transit through the Daryal Pass.[29]

Catherine's political and military successes encouraged the embattled kings of Georgia to renew their pleas for protection and assistance. In 1769, Solomon I of Imereti and Erekle II of Kartli–Kakheti requested that Russia send five regiments to the region. In 1773, Erekle's son, Levan, together with the Georgian catholicos, traveled to St. Petersburg to petition Catherine to take Kartli–Kakheti under her protection. Instead, however, the empress, not wishing to overextend her forces, withdrew her troops from Transcaucasia.[30]

In 1783, the town of Azaq fell to the Russians, and the Crimean khanate was eliminated. The Crimea was then directly absorbed by Russia, whose boundaries were thus automatically pushed to the frontiers of the Mountain. This development significantly increased the likelihood of an eventual confrontation between Orthodox Russia and the Muslim peoples of the North Caucasus.

As in the second half of the sixteenth century, it was Georgia which continued to beckon its powerful northern neighbor to come south. In 1783 – the same year that the Crimea was absorbed by Russia – King Erekle of Kartli–Kakheti appealed for help to Russia. Catherine the Great responded positively to this appeal, and by the Treaty of Georgievsk of 1783, a Russian protectorate was established over Kartli–Kakheti. The path through the Daryal Pass was transformed into a military road, and the construction of a major fort called Vladikavkaz ("Ruler of the Caucasus") near the Pass was begun. These moves understandably concerned the Ottoman Turks, who, in 1782, had begun construction of a fort at Anapa on the Black Sea, north of the present-day Russian city of Novorossiisk.[31] In 1787, however, during a Russo-Turkish war, and following Sheikh Mansur's insurrection (to be discussed shortly), Catherine once again ordered her troops to evacuate Georgia.

To dilute the impact of Islam in the region, the Russian Empire settled Christian peoples from the Transcaucasus at key forts in the

---

[28] Gammer, *Muslim Resistance*, pp. 2–3; Baddeley, *Russian Conquest*, p. 19.
[29] In *Kavkazskaya voina*, pp. 256–58.   [30] Suny, *Making*, p. 58.
[31] Bennigsen, "Un mouvement populaire," 173.

North Caucasus. In 1796, there were 2,800 Armenians and only 1,000 Russians at Kizlyar; in 1789, 55.6 percent of the population of Mozdok was Armenian or Georgian.[32]

The rebellion of Sheikh Mansur

At the time of the Russian invasion of Chechnya in December 1994, it was observed by journalists that a painting of Sheikh Mansur, the son of a Chechen shepherd who had led a major resistance movement against the Russian Empire from 1785 to 1791, hung in a prominent place in the office of Chechen president Dzhokhar Dudaev.[33] To return to the eighteenth century, as we have seen, given the rapidity and the pervasiveness of the Russian move into the Caucasus and Transcaucasia, a counterthrust by Muslim tribes had become a near certainty. Especially worrisome for the Muslims was the solidifying of Russian ties with Kartli–Kakheti following the signing of the Treaty of Georgievsk in 1783.

Mansur Ushurma hailed from the Chechen *aul* (i.e., Muslim village) of Aldi, located near the present-day capital of Groznyi, an area which was at the time coming under heavy Russian pressure. As Alexandre Bennigsen has observed in an excellent study devoted to Mansur, there were strong economic and social factors underlying the Mansur uprising.[34] The North Caucasus had been preserving its traditional economic equilibrium with great difficulty. The poor soil of the region did not offer sufficient resources to support a relatively dense population. The local agriculture was primitive and, since the alpine pastures were inadequate, flocks and herds had to be moved long distances in the winter. By contrast, the adjacent lowlands (the Kuban', the Terek plains, and the steppes along the Caspian) represented fertile areas capable of sustaining the needs not only of the local populace but of the mountaineers (in Russian: *gortsy*) as well. An interchange between mountain and plain was thus necessary for the continued survival of the mountain peoples of the North Caucasus. Unfortunately, with the arrival of the Russians to the region, access to the steppes had become "precarious."[35]

In the late eighteenth century, the mountaineers of the North Caucasus numbered about a million and a half persons, divided into some twenty groups. With the exception of the Ossetians, who had been converted by the Russians to Orthodox Christianity, all of them were at

---

[32] Barrett, "Lives of Uncertainty," 593.
[33] See *Moscow Times*, 18 December 1994, pp. 22–23.
[34] Bennigsen, "Un mouvement populaire," 167.   [35] Ibid., 167–68.

least nominally Muslim, though some, such as the Chechens, were at the time only superficially so. It would take perceived massive aggression on the part of "infidel" Russians to transform them into observant Muslims.

Like the mountain Dagestani tribes, the Chechens were largely isolated from the outside world and maintained rudimentary ethnic and social structures. The Chechens and the mountain Dagestanis had preserved the patriarchal structure of large extended families (*teipy* or *taipy*) in which all members were both free and equal (*uzden*).[36]

In their initial contacts with the indigenous peoples of the North Caucasus, the Russian authorities sought to deal, as much as possible, with the feudal nobility of the region. (The Ottoman Turks, too, chose to focus on the feudal nobility, and this was one reason that they refused to take Mansur and his movement seriously.) But the Chechens and the mountain Dagestanis completely lacked feudal structures, being grouped in "free societies." The struggle against the Russians in these regions was rooted in the very poorest areas of the eastern North Caucasus, those which had preserved the most archaic political, social, and economic forms. The most archaic of all of these peoples were the economically destitute Chechens, who "first raised the banner of revolt."[37]

In 1784, Mansur proclaimed himself sheikh (i.e., elder) and then, more boldly, imam (i.e., chief of a Sufi Muslim order), and the following year he began his public preaching. In his sermons, Mansur called for a return to an ascetical and purified Islam and vilified the use of tobacco and alcohol (both of which had been introduced into the region by the Russians). He also criticized certain practices which were widespread among his semi-pagan fellow Chechens: theft, the cult of the dead, and the practice of vendetta. Mansur fought for the replacement of corrupt customary law (*adat*) by Islamic religious law (*sharia*). In the name of Islamic unity, Mansur declared a three-day fast in the settlements of Chechnya. As he traveled about the villages of Chechnya, he demanded "faith in God" and "order."[38] The *gazavat*, or holy war, he declared was directed first of all against corrupt Muslims, who held to the *adat* and allowed themselves to be assimilated by infidels. It seems wisest to see Mansur as a forerunner or precursor of the great religious revival led by Naqshbandi Sufi imams – the most renowned of whom was, of course, the legendary Shamil' – in the following century.[39]

---

[36] Ibid., 169–70. On the development of the clan system in Chechnya, see Aidaev, *Chechentsy*, pp. 185–90.

[37] Bennigsen, "Un mouvement populaire," 171.

[38] In M. M. Bliev and V. V. Degoev, *Kavkazskaya voina* (Moscow: Roset, 1994), p. 134.

[39] Bennigsen, "Un mouvement populaire," 178.

In March 1785, the Russians became aware of Mansur's activities, and a native spy was sent to his home base of Aldi, where he learned that the sheikh was planning a campaign against neighboring Kabarda to the west in order to submit its populace to Islam, and that he had established contact with the Avar khan in Dagestan. The Russian commandant of the Vladikavkaz fortress reported that the fame of the "false prophet" had already penetrated to Kabarda and that the mountaineers there were beginning to adopt a menacing attitude toward the Russians. Chechens, Dagestanis, Kumyks, and people from as far away as Kabarda and the Kuban' were flocking to Mansur's banner. During the course of 1785, Mansur also tried to enter into contact with the Ottoman Turks, who rebuffed his advances.[40]

The Russian military leaders in the Caucasus appear to have seen Mansur as a Chechen Emel'yan Pugachev, the leader of a great Cossack and peasant revolt which had broken out a few years earlier in Catherine's reign. Mansur's destitute followers were dismissed contemptuously by the Russian military command as "scoundrels," "ignorant people," "ragamuffins," and "serfs."[41] (President Yeltsin and his entourage would revive such demeaning language in late 1994, excoriating their Chechen opponents as "bandits" and "terrorists.")

A Russian colonel, Pieri, received an order to lead a force into Chechnya and to occupy Mansur's home base of Aldi. Pieri accomplished this mission – though the village was deserted when he arrived – and burned Aldi to the ground. On his way back from this successful raid, however, Pieri and his men were trapped on the banks of the Sunzha River by a force led by Mansur and annihilated. Colonel Pieri, seven other officers, and more than 600 men were killed; 200 soldiers were captured, and only 100 escaped the massacre.[42] This major victory by Mansur constituted "the worst-ever defeat inflicted on the armies of Catherine II."[43]

From the summer until December 1785, the *gazavat*, originally issued in Chechnya, spread throughout Dagestan and Kabarda and became more intense. Virtually the whole of the North Caucasus became embroiled in the revolt. Mansur's force grew to number 12,000 men, most of them Chechens and Dagestanis. His decisive victory over the Russians on the Sunzha led Mansur into overconfidence and prompted him to undertake certain ill-advised military actions. In July 1785, Mansur came down from the mountains and marched upon the Russian fortress of Kizlyar near the Terek. Despite three days of furious

[40] Ibid., 184.   [41] Ibid., 185.
[42] Ibid., 185 86, and Baddeley, *Russian Conquest*, p. 49.
[43] Broxup, "Introduction," p. 3.

assault, during 19–21 August, Mansur failed to capture the garrison, whose artillery was a decisive factor in repelling the invaders. On 22 August, he was forced to retreat back into the mountains. This constituted one of the few attempts by the mountaineers in the eighteenth and nineteenth centuries to take the war to their enemy.[44] (In 1995 and 1996, however, it might be noted, the embattled Chechens revived Mansur's tactic, attacking the Russian city of Budennovsk in Stavropol' krai as well as the settlement of Kizlyar in Dagestan.) Following Mansur's rising, the Russians were forced to regroup to their fortresses at Mozdok, Kizlyar, and Ekaterinodar, while troops were withdrawn from Georgia to the Terek Line. The fortress of Vladikavkaz, built in 1784, had to be abandoned in 1786; it was not reconstructed until 1803.[45]

In September 1785, Mansur marched on Kabarda, at that time "the richest and most populated" region of the Mountain.[46] General Pavel Potemkin led out a well-trained force of 5,700 men against Mansur and, in November, completely routed the mountaineers. It was a turning point in the conflict. After this defeat suffered by Mansur, feudal princes in Kabarda, Dagestan, and elsewhere began to withdraw their support for him. Eventually Mansur's fellow Chechens also turned cool toward his costly *gazavat*. By the spring of 1786, his movement was very much on the wane.

During the Russo-Turkish war of 1787–91, Mansur moved from his home territory of Chechnya to that of the Adygei in the western North Caucasus. Here he had spectacular success in converting the Adygei, who had hitherto been only nominal Muslims, to a devout adherence to Islam. "The Islamization of the Northwest Caucasus is the most durable work of Sheikh Mansur."[47] As a military leader, Mansur proved to be much less successful. In September 1787, he led a large force of Adygei and Nogai against Russian positions but was repelled; the following month he was repulsed once again. It seems clear that Mansur's gifts lay primarily in the sphere of religious preaching, not in politics or military leadership. He was no Shamil'.

In June 1791, the Russians under General Gudovich seized the Turkish fortress of Anapa on the Black Sea. An unexpected prize was the capture by the invaders of the much-sought-after Mansur. Treated as a dangerous rebel, he was sent to Petersburg and incarcerated for life in the Schlusselburg Fortress "for having raised the people of the

[44] Bennigsen, "Un mouvement populaire," 188.
[45] Barrett, "Lives of Uncertainty," 590.
[46] Bennigsen, "Un mouvement populaire," 188–89.   [47] Ibid., 195.

Mountain against Russia and for having caused great harm to the Empire."[48] He died in captivity in 1794.

Russia absorbs Georgia

Following the defeat of Mansur and the capture of Anapa on the Black Sea in 1791, Russia moved to solidify its ties with Georgia. As he lay dying of dropsy in Tbilisi in December 1800, King Giorgi XII of Kartli–Kakheti saw no hope, except in the protecting hand of Russia, for the future of a country largely surrounded by Muslims. He sent an emissary to St. Petersburg begging Emperor Paul to accept direct authority over his country. Just days before the king's death, Paul signed a manifesto in which he declared Kartli–Kakheti annexed to the Russian Empire. Paul's successor, Alexander I, confirmed this action in a manifesto issued on 24 September 1801; Alexander declared the kingdom of Kartli–Kakheti abolished.

The annexation of Georgia by Russia had major geopolitical repercussions. The road through the Daryal Pass from Vladikavkaz to Tbilisi was now regarded as indefensible without further conquests. This meant further conflict with the Muslim tribes of the North Caucasus, as well as with the Ottomans and Persia. By 1804, Russia was at war with Iran and, by 1807, with Turkey.[49]

As aptly described by John Baddeley, Russia's imperial strategy in the Caucasus had now become apparent: "Russia's task should now be clear – in the Caucasus proper, to subdue, on the one hand, the Western tribes, who looked for support to Turkey; on the other, the peoples of Dagestan and Chechnya; in Transcaucasia, to reunite the Georgian race, defend it against Persian and Turk, and enlarge and make safe its boundaries at their expense."[50]

General Yermolov

The effort by imperial Russia to subdue the Caucasus is associated above all with the name of General Aleksei Yermolov (1777–1861), who, in 1816, was appointed commander-in-chief in Georgia with jurisdiction over the entire Caucasus region. Even a century after Yermolov's death, his name is capable of eliciting strong passions among Muslim mountaineers. In 1969, for example, during the early years of

[48] Ibid.
[49] Baddeley, *Russian Conquest*, pp. 76, 87; Gammer, *Muslim Resistance*, pp. 4–7; Suny, *Making*, p. 59.
[50] Baddeley, *Russian Conquest*, pp. xxiii–xxiv.

Brezhnev's reign, two attempts were made by Chechens to blow up a statue of Yermolov in Groznyi, the capital of Checheno-Ingushetiya, the site of a fort founded in 1818 by the general.[51]

"Yermolov's central idea," John Baddeley has noted, "was that the whole of the Caucasus must, and should, become an integral part of the Russian empire."[52] Given these strongly held beliefs of Yermolov, it was certain that there would be a clash with the freedom-minded Chechens. Compounding the conflict would be the general's militant and what we might today call racist view of the mountaineers: "I desire," Yermolov affirmed in an oft-cited statement, "that the terror of my name should guard our frontiers more potently than chains or fortresses, that my word should be for the natives a law more inevitable than death. Condescension in the eyes of Asiatics is a sign of weakness and out of pure humanity I am inexorably severe."[53]

It was not long before Yermolov began to put these harsh convictions into effect. In November 1817 and again in May 1818, he sent Emperor Alexander I detailed plans for subduing the region. Significantly, he singled out the Chechens, whom he termed "a bold and dangerous people," for special attention and animus. Yermolov's ire had been raised by the unceasing raids conducted by the Chechens against Russian and Cossack outposts and settlements and by their patent determination never to submit to Russian rule.

General Yermolov's plan was to build a new fortified line along the Lower Sunzha and then to settle Cossacks between that river and the Terek, thus bringing the Empire closer to Dagestan.[54] In 1817, Yermolov had given orders to build a small fort in Chechnya at Pregradnyi Stan, an action viewed with alarm by the local Chechens. On 10 June 1818, he founded the major fortress of Groznaya (the name means "Menacing" or "Dread") on the banks of the Sunzha, a direct challenge to the Chechens. Other forts followed: Vnezapnaya ("Sudden") in 1819, and Burnaya ("Stormy") in 1821 in Dagestan.[55] The very names of these forts were intended to strike awe and fear in the imaginations of the natives.

A hard line toward the Chechens

Since Yermolov was convinced that the Chechens were implacable enemies of Russia, he advocated the harshest policies toward them.

---

[51] See Robert Conquest, *The Nation Killers*, 2nd edn. (New York: Macmillan, 1970), p. 158, n.
[52] Baddeley, *Russian Conquest*, p. 99.   [53] Ibid., p. 97.
[54] Gammer, *Muslim Resistance*, p. 30.   [55] Baddeley, *Russian Conquest*, pp. 107–08.

According to his program, they were to be "constrained within their mountains" and were also to lose the "agricultural land and pastures in which they shelter their flocks in winter from the severe cold in the mountains."[56] Reduced to semi-starvation and economic desperation, they would then have no choice other than to submit to Russian rule. Yermolov's chief-of-staff, General Vel'yaminov, held similarly rigid views. It would, he wrote, take thirty years for an extension of forts and Cossack settlements to subdue the North Caucasus. "The enemy," Vel'yaminov wrote, "is absolutely dependent on his crops for the means of sustaining life. Let the standing corn be destroyed each autumn as it ripens, and in five years they would be starved into submission."[57]

Under General Yermolov, the previous tsarist system of offering bribes and subsidies to the natives was replaced by one of severe punishments. Yermolov advocated economic warfare against those mountaineers who would not submit – their crops were to be devastated and their villages sacked. On occasion, his men carried out massacres and raped native women.[58] Some native women were sold as slaves or distributed as property to Russian officers.[59]

The Chechens fought back relentlessly against Russian expansion into their home territory and the accompanying depredations. While the fortress of Groznaya was being constructed, Chechen snipers were active every night. At the time that Fort Vnezapnaya was being built in 1819 in eastern Chechnya, the Chechens succeeded in driving off a number of horses belonging to the Russians. Yermolov vowed to teach them an indelible lesson.

The prosperous lowland Chechen *aul* of Dadi-Yurt on the banks of the Terek was singled out for retribution. On 15 September 1819, Russian forces arrived and demanded that the village surrender; this demand was refused, and a fearful massacre ensued. Each house in the village was surrounded by a high stone wall and constituted a kind of fortress which had to be first battered by artillery and then taken by storm: "Some of the natives, seeing defeat to be inevitable, slaughtered their wives and children under the eyes of the [Russian] soldiers; many of the women threw themselves on the latter knife in hand, or in despair leaped into the burning buildings and perished in the flames."[60]

When the *aul* was finally taken, only fourteen Chechen men remained alive, all of them severely wounded. One hundred and forty women and children were taken prisoner, with many of the women and some of the children also being wounded. The exultant Russian soldiers proceeded

---

[56] Gammer, *Muslim Resistance*, p. 30.   [57] Baddeley, *Russian Conquest*, pp. 121–22.
[58] Ibid., p. 97.   [59] Gammer, *Muslim Resistance*, p. 34.
[60] Baddeley, *Russian Conquest*, p. 131.

to loot the village. Such were Yermolov's methods, which set the tone for the Russian–Chechen conflict during the Caucasus War.

In similar fashion, under Yermolov, if it was established that an individual Chechen had taken part in a raid on a Russian or Cossack settlement, then the village where he lived was required to surrender both the culprit and his family. If the village community failed to do so, then the settlement was burned to the ground.[61]

The first deportation of the Chechens

In addition to conducting punitive expeditions and practicing economic warfare, Yermolov sought aggressively to push the Chechens out of the populated zone lying between the Terek and Sunzha Rivers. Yermolov regarded it as a serious error of previous Russian administrations that they had permitted mountaineers and, especially, Chechens to move down from the mountains to the plains.[62] Yermolov's deportation policy reversed the natural migration pattern of Chechens from the mountains to the lowlands and deprived them of a great deal of fertile land. In their book on the nineteenth-century Caucasus War, M. M. Bliev and V. V. Degoev, who generally tend to be pro-Russian in their views (Bliev is a well-known and controversial North Ossetian historian), label the decision to deport the Chechens "one of [Yermolov's] greatest mistakes."[63]

Yermolov's deportation policy, Bliev and Degoev argue, arrested two progressive economic tendencies prevalent among the Chechens, namely, "the transition from a livestock-raising to an agricultural economy, and the decay of patrimonial relations and the formation of feudal ones."[64] By forcing the Chechens back up into the inhospitable mountains, Yermolov returned them to an economically and socially primitive state, thereby ensuring the existence of a fierce and dedicated opponent for the Russian Empire over the next half century (and beyond).

Another form of deportation practiced by Yermolov and his men was to send captured Chechens off to Siberian exile. "They are seized and kept prisoners," one contemporary account reports, "till a significant number is collected, and then they are transported to the East for life."[65] No figures are provided for the number of Chechens so banished from their homeland.

[61] Bliev and Degoev, *Kavkazskaya voina*, p. 177.
[62] Ibid., p. 153.   [63] Ibid.   [64] Ibid., p. 154.
[65] From Robert Lyall, *Travels in Russia, the Krimea [sic] and the Caucasus and Georgia*, 2 vols. (London: T. Cadell, 1825), vol. I, p. 459.

Assessments of General Yermolov and his policies

While Yermolov's brutal methods were applauded by Russian imperialists among his contemporaries, thoughtful and educated Russians were less enthusiastic. In a letter written in 1822 to P. A. Vyazemskii, Aleksandr Turgenev, for example, asked indignantly: "[W]hat kind of a hero is . . . Yermolov? . . . That sort of notoriety makes your blood run cold and your hair stand on end."[66] In similar vein, Decembrist Mikhail Orlov affirmed: "It is just as hard to subjugate the Chechens and other peoples of this region as to level the Caucasian range. This is something to achieve not with bayonets but with time and enlightenment."[67]

Western commentators past and present have tended to agree with the sentiments expressed by Turgenev and Orlov. An English visitor to the Caucasus during Yermolov's viceregency there, Robert Lyall, commented in 1825: "General Yermolov's severe policy may suit the ambitious spirit of Russia but it is not calculated to unite the virtues of humanity and bravery, the highest meed of praise a warrior can receive. He may delude himself with the propriety of the most cruel measures to narrow the range of the predatory excursions of the mountain tribes, but he may rest assured that public opinion will brand his name with infamy for his deeds, as well as that of the monarch who permits them, now that they are fully exposed."[68]

Almost a hundred years later, another English visitor to the Caucasus, John Baddeley, expressed himself in similar fashion: "[F]rom the Christian and moral point of view," he wrote, "there is no justification of such a ruthless policy as Yermolov's."[69] Elsewhere in his book, Baddeley concludes that the harsh policy advocated and implemented by Yermolov in effect "aroused that fierce spirit of fanaticism and independence which alone made political union possible amongst the turbulent tribesmen of Dagestan and Chechnya."[70] "[I]t may be argued," historian Hugh Seton-Watson has observed, "that [Yermolov's] methods won Russia more bitter enemies than reliable subjects."[71] Yermolov's "extreme brutality," Moshe Gammer has concluded, "achieved results opposite to his intentions."[72]

A more positive assessment of Yermolov is provided in the book by M. M. Bliev and V. V. Degoev. General Yermolov, they argue, was no

---

[66] In Susan Layton, *Russian Literature and Empire: Conquest of the Caucasus from Pushkin to Tolstoy* (Cambridge, UK: Cambridge University Press, 1994), p. 107.
[67] Ibid., p. 108.   [68] Lyall, *Travels in Russia*, vol. II, p. 51.
[69] Baddeley, *Russian Conquest*, p. 163.   [70] Ibid., p. 138.
[71] Hugh Seton-Watson, *The Russian Empire, 1801–1917* (Oxford, UK: Clarendon Press, 1967), p. 183.
[72] Gammer, *Muslim Resistance*, p. 37.

conscious genocidist, and, while his actions in the Caucasus were unquestionably cruel, they were no worse than, say, those of Persia and Turkey in that region. In the final analysis, Bliev and Degoev believe that Yermolov's methods actually worked, since they served to "weaken the mass character of the raid system [of the mountaineers]."[73] As has been noted, Bliev and Degoev condemn Yermolov's deportation policy as a mistake.

Yermolov's work continued

In 1827, General Yermolov was replaced as viceroy of the Caucasus by an order of the newly enthroned Emperor Nicholas I (ruled 1825–55). Though the general had been replaced, the "Yermolov system" vis-à-vis the Chechens and other mountaineers was largely retained. In 1829, immediately following the conclusion of war with Turkey, Nicholas I wrote to Yermolov's successor, Field Marshal I. F. Paskevich: "Having completed one glorious task, you are confronted with another . . . the suppression once and for all of the mountaineers or the extermination of the recalcitrant."[74] Writing in 1834, a Russian civil servant and specialist on the Caucasus, Platon Zubov, put it more bluntly: "The only way to deal with this ill-intentioned people [i.e., the Chechens] is to destroy it to the last."[75] Words can become deeds; the brutal Caucasus War did indeed lead to the "extermination" of many.

If the Russian state and its servants had few apparent qualms concerning the proposed annihilation of the mountain tribes, Russia's classical literature, which began to glow brightly in the 1820s and 1830s, expressed gnawings of conscience and a visceral rejection of that country's imperial project in the Caucasus. A gifted young officer who served in the Caucasus, the poet Mikhail Lermontov, dealt repeatedly in his poems and prose with the ambiguities of imperial expansion and the suppression of the natives. Especially in his later works, Lermontov "conveyed a suspicion that the conquest [of the Caucasus] was a spiritually losing proposition for Russia."[76] In his eyes, Russia had become a kind of brutal "Roman" state whose goal was to subjugate a primitive world of harmonious relation to nature.[77] "To a greater extent than any other Russian writer," literary critic Susan Layton has concluded, "Lermontov went to the heart of the paradox of genocidal warfare as the route to terrestrial paradise."[78]

---

[73] Bliev and Degoev, *Kavkazskaya voina*, p. 179.   [74] Cited ibid., p. 264.
[75] Cited by Broxup, "Introduction," p. 10.
[76] Layton, *Russian Literature and Empire*, p. 212.
[77] Ibid., p. 213.   [78] Ibid., p. 230.

Another major Russian writer who returned repeatedly to the theme of Russia's armed struggle with the recalcitrant mountaineers was Lev Tolstoi who, like Lermontov, had served as an officer in the Caucasus region. In his earlier works, such as *The Cossacks* (1863), Tolstoi focused upon the mutual relations of Russians, Cossacks, and the Chechens and other mountaineers. However, in his last great work of literature, the anti-imperialist *Hadji Murat*, Tolstoi vehemently rejected the hypocrisy and brutality behind Russia's supposed "civilizing mission" in the North Caucasus.

In a passage contained in a draft version of the work, the authorial voice asserts that what occurred in the North Caucasus region was "what always happens when a state, having large-scale military strength, enters into relations with primitive, small peoples, living their own independent life. Under the pretext of self-defense (even though attacks are always provoked by the powerful neighbor), or the pretext of civilizing the ways of a savage people (even though the savage people is living a life incomparably better and more peaceable than the civilizers'), or else under some other pretext, the servants of large military states commit all sorts of villainy against small peoples, while maintaining that one cannot deal with them otherwise."[79] Classical Russian literature, the "conscience" of nineteenth-century Russia, expressed painful doubts concerning the Russian state's imperial project.

The Chechens on the eve of the Caucasus War

At the time of the outbreak of the Caucasus War, for which the conventional dates are 1817–64, the Chechens lived chiefly in isolated *auls*, which could number as many as hundreds of houses, all of them single-storied, flat-roofed structures built of sun-baked mud. Each house had its own garden, or orchard, and, in a forest clearing nearby, there were cultivated fields sown with maize, oats, barley, rye, or millet, whichever best suited the locale. At the first indication of danger, the Chechen women and children would seize all moveable wealth and conceal themselves in the surrounding forest, which consisted largely of giant beech trees.[80] "As long as these forests stood, the Chechens were unconquerable. The Russians made no permanent impression on them save when and where they cut the beech trees down; and it is literally the fact that they were beaten in the long run not by the sword but by the axe."[81]

Chechen males constituted a "martial race," raised from childhood to

---

[79] Ibid., pp. 284–85
[80] Baddeley, *Russian Conquest*, p. xxxv.   [81] Ibid.

be warriors.[82] Each male claimed equality with his neighbor by birth-right, and there were no class distinctions among them. Household and agricultural work was left to the women or to slaves, the latter being mainly prisoners of war. "In person the Chechens were tall, lithe, well (though slenderly) built, and often handsome; alert in mind, brave and cruel, treacherous and cunning; yet . . . honorable according to their own peculiar code, to a degree little known to more civilized tribes. Hospitality [was] . . . a most sacred duty."[83]

General Vel'yaminov, Yermolov's chief-of-staff, who remained in the Caucasus until his death in 1838, wrote that as horsemen the Chechens, like the other mountaineers, "are very superior in many ways both to our regular [Russian] cavalry and the Cossacks. They are all but born on horseback." The nineteenth-century Cossack, Vel'yaminov noted, func-tioned "as an agriculturist as well as a soldier," putting him at a disadvantage compared to the mountaineers.[84]

Another Russian officer, Torneau, wrote in 1832: "As opponents the Chechens merited the fullest respect, and amidst their forests and mountains no troops in the world could afford to despise them. Good shots, fiercely brave, intelligent in military affairs, they, like other inhabitants of the Caucasus, were quick to take advantage of local conditions."[85] The mountaineers' moves in combat were invariably swift, whether on foot or on horseback, and their military tactics were characterized by adaptability and flexibility.[86]

Clan and tribal identities

The Chechen population was divided along patrilineal lines into ex-tended families, clans, and tribes. These communities were "free," i.e., fully independent of outside control. Important decisions in the com-munity were taken by a gathering of the elders or by a general assembly of all the males.[87]

Tribal identities and loyalties were important among the Chechens, hindering the development of a larger ethnic identity. Among the Chechen tribes there were, for example, the Ichkeri, a highland tribe after which General Dudaev, in 1994, named his "independent re-public" of Chechnya; other tribes were the Aukh and the Kist. Unlike, say, the Kabardintsy, the Nogai, and Kumyks – all of them Muslim peoples of the North Caucasus – the Chechens had not developed a differentiated feudal system but had remained in a purely clannic state,

---

[82] Gammer, *Muslim Resistance*, p. 21.   [83] Baddeley, *Russian Conquest*, p. xxxvii.
[84] Ibid., pp. 114–15.   [85] Ibid., p. 266.
[86] Gammer, *Muslim Resistance*, pp. 21–22.   [87] Ibid., p. 20.

like, say, the Ingush, Balkars, Karachai, and the mountain Dagestanis.[88] As Ronald Wixman and other specialists have stressed, the Chechens did not, in the nineteenth century, possess a national identity. Rather they had a sense of being "Caucasian," based on a geographical concept of their home region, and on a culture, religion, and way of life which they shared with the other Muslim peoples of the North Caucasus.[89]

Religion

Before the coming of General Yermolov to the Caucasus, the Chechens were Muslims, but of a variety heavily admixed with paganism. Civil and criminal affairs were usually decided in the Chechen language according to the *adat*, or customary law, which coexisted with and effectively sanctioned an elaborate system of vendetta or blood-feud. In the principal villages, mullahs expounded the Koran, with Arabic being the only accepted language of religion and the only written tongue.[90]

As Bernard Lewis has observed, Western and Christian penetration of the world of Islam forced Muslims at various points on the globe to focus concern upon "problems of the faith and of the community overwhelmed by infidels."[91] Among Muslims in India in the seventeenth and eighteenth centuries, for example, there was a religious revival sparked by the Naqshbandi order, a Sufi brotherhood of Central Asian origin which became the vanguard of Islamic orthodoxy in an India threatened by the return of Hinduism and by the militant Catholicism of the Portuguese. The revivalism promoted by the Naqshbandi order later spread from India to the Middle East.

The Naqshbandi *tariqat* (the word, usually translated as "brother-hood," means "the path") came to Chechnya from neighboring Dage-stan in the decade following Yermolov's appointment to the Caucasus. In a direct sense, Yermolov prepared the way for the triumph of this orthodox Muslim tendency in Dagestan and Chechnya.

Beibulat's rebellion

In the 1780s, as has been noted, Chechnya already knew the first stage of what Russian specialists call "the ideology of Muridism."[92] The Arabic word *miurid* means "one who desires," i.e., one who strives to

---

[88] Wixman, *Language Aspects*, p. 105.   [89] Ibid., pp. 101, 107.
[90] Baddeley, *Russian Conquest*, p. xxxvii.
[91] Bernard Lewis, *The Middle East and the West* (Bloomington, IN: Indiana University Press, 1964), pp. 95–96.
[92] Bliev and Degoev, *Kavkazskaya voina*, p. 220.

find the way or the true path. Muridism and Sufism are in essence the same thing.[93]

The military and economic blockade of Chechnya carried out by General Yermolov had led gradually to a consolidation of Chechen society, which previously had been separated into tribes and clans. The key figure in this initial consolidation process was Beibulat Taimazov. General Yermolov, it should be noted, was wont to behave haughtily and arrogantly in the presence of the mountaineers, terming them "scoundrels" and "robbers," and this intolerant posture was often emulated by his subordinates. One of them, General Grekov, mortally offended Beibulat, a leading figure among the Chechens, when he refused to shake his hand and behaved contemptuously toward him. In 1822, Beibulat, who had earlier allied himself with the Russians, began to conduct raids against them.[94]

Beibulat began to cast about for an "ideology" to support his movement. At one point Abdul-Kadyr, a preacher of Islam, had supplied him with such support, but Abdul soon died from wounds suffered in battle. In 1823, in northern Dagestan, Beibulat found what he was looking for.

Founded in the twelfth century, the Naqshbandiya is named after Mohammed Baha al-Din al-Naqshbandi (1318–89), who gave the brotherhood its final structure. The *tariqat* took root in the Shirvan khanate in present-day Azerbaijan during the second decade of the nineteenth century. Following the annexation of this khanate in 1820, the Russian authorities began to persecute the brotherhood, which it regarded as seditious. From Shirvan it moved to Dagestan, where Mohammed Yaragskii emerged as its chief leader and spokesman. The chief concern of Yaragskii and his followers was to enforce the *sharia* and to do away with the *adat*. Only after Muslims had cleansed themselves and turned to the right path could *gazavat* be declared to free them from foreign rule. The knowledge of Arabic language and culture was promoted by Yaragskii, and that knowledge spread from Dagestan to Chechnya.[95]

The exasperation of the Chechens with the Russians began to acquire a religious dimension after the arrival in Chechnya of Mullah Mohammed Mayurtupi from Dagestan in 1824. Mohammed proclaimed a certain Avko from Germenchuk to be the long-awaited imam chosen by God to lead the struggle against the Russians. The rebels' key military leader, however, was Beibulat. The revolt soon spread throughout Chechnya and to the Ingush lands as well. On the night of 20 July 1825,

[93] Baddeley, *Russian Conquest*, pp. 231–33.
[94] Bliev and Degoev, *Kavkazskaya voina*, pp. 222–24.
[95] Gammer, *Muslim Resistance*, pp. 39–40.

the mountaineers stormed and destroyed a Russian fort at Amir-Haji-Yurt. Ninety-eight defenders were killed and thirteen taken prisoner. Soon after this victory, however, the revolt collapsed from within due to poor leadership.

The three imams

Though they played a key role in the Caucasus War and suffered more from it than any other people of the North Caucasus, the Chechens did not provide the inspiration or the leadership for the Muslim side in the conflict. That role was filled by three imams, all of them Avars from Dagestan: Kazi (Gazi) Mullah, Gamzat-Bek, and Shamil'. As we shall see, the Chechens did not even become deeply involved in the war until 1839–40, and then only due to monumental errors committed by the Russian authorities.

Kazi Mullah, the first of the three Avar imams, was born in the village of Gimri in the Dagestan highlands. During the 1820s he was initiated into the Naqshbandi brotherhood by the Sheikh Mohammed Yaragskii.[96] With Yaragskii's blessing, Kazi was proclaimed imam in Dagestan late in 1829, and he then proceeded to travel around the villages "in order to return sinners to the right path."[97] By April 1830, Kazi's influence had begun to spread throughout Chechnya. From the beginning, Kazi enjoyed the support of the leaders of the earlier 1824–26 revolt. In May 1830, Kazi sent one of his deputies, Sheikh Abdallah of Ashilti, to Chechnya, and he proved to be an excellent organizer. Later that same year, Kazi made a personal tour of Chechnya, where he learned of Ashilti's success in that region. One reason for Abdallah's success was General Vel'yaminov's winter campaigns, in which he destroyed some thirty or thirty-five Chechen villages. These harsh punitive actions drove many Chechens into the arms of the imam. The Russians also created enemies by demanding that Muslim villages abandon the *sharia*.[98]

In October 1831, Kazi made a daring and successful raid on Fort Kizlyar on the Terek, and, in October–November, he threatened the fortress of Groznaya. In 1832, Kazi attempted to raise Kabarda (as Mansur had tried to do in the late eighteenth century), besieged Nazran' – the capital of the present-day Ingush Republic – and threatened the fortress of Vladikavkaz. In August of that year, Kazi attacked Fort Vnezapnaya in eastern Chechnya and ambushed a 500-man Cossack

---

[96] Bliev and Degoev, *Kavkasskaya voina*, pp. 240–41; Gammer, *Muslim Resistance*, p. 50.
[97] Gammer, *Muslim Resistance*, p. 50.
[98] Ibid., pp. 50–51.

force, causing 155 casualties. The imam also threatened the key town of Derbent along the Caspian Sea in Dagestan, as well as areas of proto-Georgia. Kazi's professed goal was to fuse the Muslim peoples of the North Caucasus into one potent force. At the height of his power, he reportedly commanded 6,000 footsoldiers and 2,000 cavalry.[99]

Like Sheikh Mansur before him, Kazi soon found himself outgunned and outmanned by superior Russian forces. During 1831–32, the Russians repeatedly attempted to arrange for Kazi's assassination. In August 1832, General Rosen led into Chechnya a force of 15,000–20,000 men, who systematically pillaged and destroyed gardens, fields, and villages. In October, General Vel'yaminov invaded Kazi's home territory in the highlands with 10,000 troops and succeeded in capturing his mountain strongholds of Dargo in Chechnya and Gimri in Dagestan. On 29 October 1832, the Russians stormed Kazi's fortified position at Gimri, and the imam was killed in battle; Kazi's eventual successor, Shamil', was severely wounded in the fighting.[100]

Gamzat-Bek

Following Kazi's death in battle, he was succeeded by another Avar from Dagestan, Gamzat-Bek. Gamzat's rule lasted a mere two years, as he was killed in September 1834 (while entering a mosque) as part of a vendetta proclaimed against him by fellow Avars. During his brief rule, Gamzat had offered to reconcile with the Russians "on condition that it causes no harm to our *sharia*."[101] But the Russians had offered no response to this offer, and General Rosen had put pressure on the Avar ruling house to arrest Gamzat and extradite him.

Imam Shamil'

Perhaps the most outstanding political and military leader ever to emerge in the North Caucasus region, Shamil' (1796/97–1871), also an Avar from Dagestan, is described as having been an exceptionally tall, strong, and athletic man, an unrivaled horseman, highly intelligent, and well educated in the Arabic language and Muslim religious literature. "Shamil'," Moshe Gammer has written, "was a born leader, commander, diplomat, and politician. He repeatedly outmaneuvered the

---

[99] Seton-Watson, *Russian Empire*, pp. 292–93; Baddeley, *Russian Conquest*, pp. 256–63; Bliev and Degoev, *Kavkazskaya voina*, p. 296, Gammer, *Muslim Resistance*, p. 56.

[100] Seton-Watson, *Russian Empire*, p. 293; Bliev and Degoev, *Kavkazskaya voina*, p. 313; Gammer, *Muslim Resistance*, p. 56.

[101] Gammer, *Muslim Resistance*, p. 61.

Russians in battles, intrigues, and negotiations. Contrary to Russian propaganda, he was far from extremism or blind fanaticism."[102] Shamil' had been introduced to religious instruction by Kazi Mullah, who initiated him into the Naqshbandiya.[103] Following Gamzat's death in 1834, Shamil' was selected imam.

Like Gamzat-Bek before him, Shamil' sought initially to come to an arrangement with the powerful Russians; he formally accepted Russian sovereignty and undertook not to raid the lowlands. All of this, however, was conditional on the Russians agreeing to the "implementation of the *sharia.*" General Rosen did not trust Shamil' and, instead of an agreement, in 1836 he demanded the imam's unconditional surrender. In the summer of 1836, Rosen resolved "once and for all" to eliminate Shamil', Shamil''s representative in Chechnya, Tashov Haji, and "Muridism" in general. Shamil' was offered the choice of complete surrender willingly or by force.[104]

In 1839, the fortunes of Shamil' and his movement looked bleak. During that year, he had even been forced to suffer the humiliation of surrendering his son, Jemaluddin, aged twelve, to the Russians as a hostage. (Like the mountaineers, the Russians adhered to the practice of taking native hostages [*amanaty*] and of procuring ransom for them.)[105] Also in 1839, the Russian General Pavel Grabbe expressed certainty that the spirit of the mountaineers had finally been broken. The subjugation of the North Caucasus appeared to be imminent. But it was at this juncture that the Russian authorities made a series of key blunders involving the Chechens.

The Russian leadership resolved to introduce direct rule into Chechnya. So-called inspectors (*pristavy*), many of them natives from the region serving the Russians, were appointed to various communities. Under the pretext of collecting taxes and fines, these "inspectors" seized the best belongings of the Chechens and had innocent people arrested. Detainees and hostages were treated in inhumane fashion. During expeditions into Chechnya by the Russian military, forced collections of food and seizure of livestock were permitted. These arbitrary acts served to enrage the Chechens.[106]

These mistakes were serious ones, but the pivotal error occurred when the Russians began to attempt to confiscate the Chechens' firearms. As Timur Muzaev has written: "The mass participation of

[102] Ibid., p. 292.
[103] Seton-Watson, *Russian Empire*, pp. 292–93; Gammer, *Muslim Resistance*, p. 69.
[104] Gammer, *Muslim Resistance*, pp. 81–83.
[105] Barrett, "Lives of Uncertainty," 588.
[106] Gammer, *Muslim Resistance*, pp. 113–14.

Chechens in Shamil''s movement began from the winter of 1839–40, when the Russian troops attempted to disarm the Chechen people."[107] For the Chechens, their daggers and muskets were regarded as family heirlooms, handed down from generation to generation. Those mountain villages which could not be easily reached by the Russian army refused to accept the venal "inspectors." Lowland Chechen villages were then forbidden by the Russians to have any contact with the rebellious highlanders and were forbidden to sell them grain or to let them use their pastures; it was clearly an attempt to starve out those who would not voluntarily surrender their weapons.[108]

Incensed by this treatment, the Chechens had become tinder awaiting a spark, and that spark was provided by Shamil', who arrived in Ichkeriya, in mountain Chechnya, with a mere seven followers. He was repeatedly approached by delegations of Chechens, who asked him to be their leader. Shamil' "reluctantly" agreed to these requests and then moved from village to village, where he was uniformly welcomed with delight. The imam's forces grew by leaps and bounds, and by 1840 he had begun to think in terms of reviving the strategies of Sheikh Mansur and Imam Kazi before him, i.e., unifying all the mountain tribes in a struggle against the Russians.[109] In 1841, the Russian general Golovin warned solemnly: "We have never had in the Caucasus an enemy so savage and dangerous as Shamil'."[110]

Spreading Islam among the Chechens

In his activities in Chechnya, Shamil' sought – like Mansur and Kazi before him – to convert the Chechens from semi-paganism to a strict form of Muslim orthodoxy. The ideas of the *sharia* and *gazavat* were disseminated by him throughout "clan Chechnya."[111] Referring to Shamil''s work, Alexandre Bennigsen and S. Enders Wimbush have concluded: "The [Naqshbandiya] brotherhood achieved [a] deep and long-lasting result: it transformed the half-pagan mountaineers into strict Orthodox Muslims and introduced Islam into the animist areas of upper Chechnya."[112]

Implementation and enforcement of the *sharia* was Shamil''s primary religious goal in Chechnya, and he sought persistently to uproot the *adat*. Smoking and drinking were strictly prohibited by him, and women

---

[107] Timur Muzaev, *Chechenskaya respublika* (Moscow: Panorama, 1995), p. 151.
[108] Gammer, *Muslim Resistance*, p. 114.   [109] Ibid., pp. 118, 163.
[110] Ibid., p. 121.   [111] Bliev and Degoev, *Kavkazskaya voina*, p. 372.
[112] Alexandre Bennigsen and S. Enders Wimbush, *Mystics and Commissars* (Berkeley, CA: University of California Press, 1985), p. 19.

were required to dress modestly. Dances and music were limited to weddings and circumcisions. Traditional Muslim schools were set up at the mosques. Due to the high bride-money customary among the Chechens, many young men and women were unable to marry; Shamil' imposed a maximum bride-money limit of twenty silver rubles for a virgin (ten for a widow or divorcee). As early as 1842–43, even Russian sources began to attest to significant improvements which had taken place in the morals of the mountaineers, particularly among the Chechens.[113]

Shamil' versus the "whole strength of the Empire"

A detailed discussion of the Caucasus War, which raged in the eastern North Caucasus from 1840 until 1859 – when Shamil' surrendered to General Baratynskii at the imam's mountain retreat of Mount Gunib in Dagestan – lies beyond the scope of this study. Readers are directed to the useful historical investigations by Baddeley and Gammer, as well as to the often-helpful book by Bliev and Degoev, all of which have been frequently cited in the notes.[114]

As Moshe Gammer has observed, the eventual defeat of Shamil' was due to the "basic imbalance of power" between Shamil' and his Russian enemy. In the final analysis, he concludes, neither "Russian mistakes" nor "the mountaineers' steadfastness and Shamil''s talents" were sufficient to prevent the Russian conquest. However, as Gammer goes on to note, "it should not be forgotten [that] it took the support of the 'whole strength of the Empire' finally to subdue Chechnya and Dagestan."[115] Following the Paris Peace Conference of 1856, which brought an end to the Crimean War, the Russian military possessed a huge 200,000-man army in the Caucasus region, and a decision was taken to use it first to crush Shamil''s movement and then that of the Circassians in the western regions. By 1864, both goals had been accomplished.

A second deportation of the Chechens

As part of their strategy against Shamil', the Russian military authorities resurrected General Yermolov's policy of mass deportation of Chechens. In 1844, the Russians had erected Fort Vozdvizhenskoe ("Elevation [of

---

[113] Gammer, *Muslim Resistance*, pp. 232–35.
[114] Note that Bliev and Degoev tend to be pro-Russian. I have chosen not to utilize V. A. Potto's five-volume "popular history," *Kavkazskaya voina* (Stavropol': Kavkazskii krai, 1994), since this work contains neither footnotes nor scholarly apparatus, and hence cannot be cited with any degree of confidence.
[115] Gammer, *Muslim Resistance*, p. 293.

the Cross]'") near the Argun River, deep within Chechnya. A fortified line, dubbed "the Great Russian Highway," was then extended from this new fort to the settlement of Achkoi. Chechens living between this new line and the Sunzha River were then forcibly expelled from the region. Most of the Chechens migrated south toward the "Black Mountains" and beyond. A number of them, however, continued to attempt to slip back into the area between the Sunzha and the Great Russian Highway. On 13 October 1850, the Russian forces rounded up this populace and expelled it beyond the Terek, i.e., to a territory not traditionally settled by Chechens. The struggle for the lowlands of western or Lesser Chechnya had been won.[116]

In 1856, following the end of the Crimean War, the Russian authorities began to contemplate expelling the Chechens from the Caucasus region altogether, a kind of foreshadowing of Stalin's genocidal action of 1944. At a council held in Stavropol', it was decided to deport all the Chechens to the town of Manych. This information soon reached the ears of the Chechen elders, and Shamil''s flagging fortunes were temporarily revived. "This is God's finger," Shamil' angrily told the wavering Chechens, who had been contemplating coming to terms with the Russians.[117] The Russians soon abandoned the deportation plan.

Shamil' and the Chechens

Shamil', a Dagestani Avar, never fully trusted the Chechens – though they constituted an integral part of his military machine – and once in Russian captivity was to complain bitterly about their obdurate "disobedience." He considered them politically less reliable than his fellow Dagestanis and religiously less orthodox. He resisted their persistent attempts to obtain more self-rule through the appointment of a Chechen *naib* (deputy).[118] Once his movement began to come under insuperable Russian pressure following the Crimean War, and especially during 1858 and 1859, Shamil' saw one Chechen community after another approach the Russians with declarations of submission.[119] Nevertheless, as Moshe Gammer has stressed, "the majority of the mountaineers, and especially the Chechens, who suffered most, stayed with their imam to the end, despite great deprivations and suffering."[120]

That the Chechens suffered the most from a Caucasus War which had been sparked by Yermolov's policies seems incontestable. As Timur Muzaev has written: "During the time of this war, the territory of

---

[116] Ibid., pp. 179–81.   [117] Ibid., pp. 277–78.   [118] Ibid., p. 244.
[119] Bliev and Degoev, *Kavkazskaya voina*, pp. 515–16.
[120] Gammer, *Muslim Resistance*, p. 245.

Chechnya was a locus of de facto unceasing battles, as a result of which the economy was destroyed and almost half the populace was exterminated."[121]

Ethnic cleansing – the third deportation

While Shamil' was accorded the honors of a captured head of state and offered residence, together with his two wives, in a "gilded cage," first in the city of Kaluga and then in Kiev – and was eventually permitted to make the *hajj* to Mecca – the rank-and-file mountaineers received less generous treatment. At the conclusion of the Crimean War in 1856, Emperor Alexander II had made it clear that he believed that the Crimean Tatars had behaved disgracefully during the war and that they probably continued to constitute a security risk. He suggested that they might be happier living in a Muslim-dominated state, i.e., in Ottoman Turkey. In May 1856, Count Kiselev, minister of state domains, informed officials in the Crimea that Alexander was interested in "cleansing" (Kiselev used the verb *ochishchat'*) Crimea of as many Tatars as possible.[122]

Following the defeat of the Chechens and Dagestanis in 1859, and of the Circassians in the western regions of the North Caucasus in 1864, the tsarist authorities decided that these recalcitrant mountaineers, too, should be "cleansed." "[T]he exodus of Crimean Tatars after 1856 and of Caucasians after 1859," Alan Fisher has written, "were two branches of essentially the same phenomenon."[123] In both instances, Fisher notes, "the Russian government, which had precipitated the exodus, achieved its objectives, that is, vast unpopulated areas in the south which it could fill with settlers more congenial to its interests."[124] Among these "congenial" settlers were to be Russians, Ukrainians and Cossacks, Georgians, and Armenians. "The tsarist government," historian Aleksandr Nekrich has written, "not only did not try to prevent this movement [to Turkey] but even encouraged it, hoping to use the Mountaineers' lands as endowments for the Cossack villages it was establishing in the region."[125]

Between 1856 and 1864, approximately 600,000 Muslim peoples of the Caucasus quit that region for the Ottoman Empire.[126] According to some sources, the Circassian migration alone had reached one million

[121] Muzaev, *Chechenskaya respublika*, p. 152.
[122] Alan W. Fisher, "Emigration of Muslims from the Russian Empire in the Years After the Crimean War," *Jahrbücher für Geschichte Osteuropas*, 35, 3 (1987), 359.
[123] Ibid., 361.   [124] Ibid., 361.
[125] Aleksandr M. Nekrich, *The Punished Peoples* (New York: W. W. Norton, 1978), p. 107.
[126] Fisher, "Emigration of Muslims," 362.

by the end of 1866.[127] In 1860, according to Soviet-era figures, 81,360 Chechens left for Turkey; a second emigration took place in 1865, when an additional 22,500 Chechens left.[128] More than 100,000 Chechens were thus ethnically "cleansed" during this process. This was perhaps a majority of their total population; more than thirty years later, in 1897, the Chechens were reported by the imperial census to have a total population of only 226,171.[129]

The fate of the participants in this mass exodus was singularly painful. The Ottoman Empire was in no position to cope with such a massive influx. Death from infectious diseases was widespread. Thus, for example – as the Russian consul in Trabzon coldly observed – of 24,700 Circassians who had arrived in that city, a total of 19,000 had died. An 1864 report described the landing of 80,000 Circassians in Varna, "suffering from fever, smallpox, and dysentery."[130] According to one source, the peoples of the Caucasus who left for Turkey suffered a 33 percent mortality rate over the course of migrating there.[131] It was, as Marie Bennigsen Broxup, has put it, "genocide through forced exodus, a crude but efficient policy."[132]

The Chechens return from Turkey

The tsarist Empire thought that it had rid itself once and for all of 100,000 troublesome Chechens. But it was not long before many of the Chechens who had emigrated to Turkey realized that they had made a grievous mistake. Many had died, and women and children had been sold into slavery; the Chechens yearned for their mountain homeland, where they had lived for millennia. They petitioned the tsarist government for permission to return and even offered "to accept the Orthodox faith as long as they could live in their homeland."[133] It is interesting to contemplate what might have occurred if the Russians had acquiesced to this offer. An Orthodox "wedge" would have been created among the Chechens, who had at the time become disillusioned with the Naqsh-bandiya brand of Islam.

Whatever the case, the tsarist authorities spurned these advances, and

[127] Paul B. Henze, "Circassian Resistance to Russia," in Broxup, *North Caucasus Barrier*, p. 103.
[128] Fisher, "Emigration of Muslims," 363.
[129] See *Naselenie imperii po perepisi 28-go yanvarya 1897 goda: po uezdam*, 1 and 7 (St. Petersburg: S. P. Yakovlev, 1897 and 1905). The overwhelming majority (202,273) of Chechens were reported as residing in Groznenskii okrug, Terskaya guberniya.
[130] Fisher, "Emigration of Muslims," 367.
[131] Henze, "Circassian Resistance,' p. 104.
[132] Broxup, "Introduction," p. 9.   [133] Nekrich, *Punished Peoples*, p. 107.

the Chechens eventually returned anyway, after the Russo-Turkish war of 1877–78. "From then on, the tsarist administration promoted the image of the Chechens not only as 'savages' (something constantly reiterated even earlier by General Yermolov . . .) but also as traitors who had sold themselves to Turkey."[134]

The rise of the Qadiriya

Following Russia's crushing victory over Shamil' in 1859 and over the Circassians in 1864, the Empire appeared invincible to the demoralized mountaineers. In their discouragement, they cast about for a new religious orientation to replace the Naqshbandiya, which had brought about such widespread devastation in the region. The quest ended with the appearance on the scene of a new Sufi order, the Qadiriya, brought to the Caucasus by a Kumyk shepherd named Kunta Kishiev (better known as Kunta Haji), a native of northern Dagestan living in the Chechen *aul* of Eliskhan-Yurt.[135]

The Qadiriya *tariqat* had been founded by Abd Al-Qadir al-Ghiliani of Baghdad in the twelfth century AD. Following the defeat of the Naqshbandiya adepts in the Caucasus War, the Qadiriya came to enjoy spectacular success in the eastern North Caucasus region, especially in Chechnya and in the Avar part of Dagestan. Kunta Haji had begun his missionary activity in the region in 1849 but had been forced to leave the Caucasus due to the Naqshbandiya hostility to his pacifist sermons. He returned in 1861 after Shamil'²s defeat and began preaching a mystical asceticism and detachment from worldly affairs. Kunta's message of non-violence and "non-resistance to evil" found broad acceptance among the exhausted mountaineers.[136] The Qadiriya order practiced the loud *zikr*, with ecstatic dances, songs, and music, all practices strictly forbidden by the purist Naqshbandiya order.[137]

Soon, however, the Qadiriya was confronted with the same dilemma that had faced the Naqshbandiya in the 1820s: what to do about the Russian infidels who dominated the Muslim lands of the North Caucasus. In 1862 and 1863, unrest swept over Chechnya, and in 1864 the Russian authorities, frightened at the success of the Qadiriya and fearing a new uprising, arrested Kunta Haji and his followers. Kunta was not tried but, rather (in anticipation of Soviet practices under Brezhnev),

[134] Ibid.
[135] Broxup, "The Last Ghazawat: The 1920–1921 Uprising," in Broxup, *North Caucasus Barrier*, p. 118.
[136] Bennigsen and Wimbush, *Mystics and Commissars*, pp. 20–21; Broxup, "The Last Ghazawat," p. 118.
[137] Bennigsen and Wimbush, *Mystics and Commissars*, pp. 20–21.

was declared insane and incarcerated in a prison hospital, where he died in 1867. His associates were accused of planning rebellion and deported to hard-labor camps in Siberia.[138]

The Qadiriya was not outlawed, but some of its practices, such as the loud *zikr*, were forbidden, and the Russian authorities strongly encouraged its adherents among the Chechens and Ingush to emigrate to the Ottoman Empire. (This explains the 22,500 Chechens who left the region for Turkey in 1865.) Tsarist repressive measures and harassment failed to impede the growth of the *tariqat*, and the order continued to make new converts among the still pagan Ingush.[139]

The rebellion of 1877

In 1877, there took place a major rebellion in Chechnya and Dagestan which lasted for a year into 1878. The leader of the uprising in Dagestan was a certain Haji Mohammed and, in Chechnya, Ali-Bek Haji. In Chechnya, most of the insurgents were Qadiri, who on this occasion fully cooperated with the Naqshbandi. The tsarist regime cracked down harshly on the rebellion, with overwhelming force. Under the command of General Svistunov, the tsarist military force numbered some fifteen soldiers for every inhabitant of Chechnya.[140]

Those leaders of the rebellion who were not killed in battle were nearly all hanged – twenty-three out of twenty-eight – and thousands of participants in the revolt were deported to Siberia. In his address to a court-martial prior to his execution, the young leader of the Chechens, Ali-Bek Haji, aged twenty-three, is reported to have declared: "It is only before God and the Chechen people that we consider ourselves guilty because, in spite of all the sacrifices, we were not able to reconquer the freedom that God gave us!"[141] The failure of this attempted rebellion marked a key turning point in the tactics of the Sufi brotherhoods. Henceforward, until the February and October Revolutions of 1917, they would eschew the tactic of *gazavat*, given the imbalance of forces between the mountaineers and the Empire. During this period of 1877–1917, however, it may safely be said that virtually the entire population of Chechnya and Ingushetiya belonged to either the Naqshbandi or Qadiri brotherhood.[142]

Following the bloody suppression of the 1877–78 revolt, the tsarist administration generally behaved with outward tolerance toward both

---

[138] Broxup, "The Last Ghazawat," p. 118.   [139] Ibid.
[140] Abdurakhman Avtorkhanov, "The Chechens and Ingush During the Soviet Period and Its Antecedents" in Broxup, ed., *North Caucasus Barrier*, pp. 150–51.
[141] Ibid., p. 151.   [142] Broxup, "The Last Ghazawat," p. 119.

national schools and the Islamic religion in Chechnya; the Orthodox Church was even forbidden to proselytize in Chechnya and in Dagestan. (Attempts were, however, made to counter the spread of the Arabic language in the region.) In 1913, it was reported that in Chechnya alone there were 806 mosques and 427 medressehs (religious schools).[143] This spirit of religious tolerance exhibited by the tsarist authorities, however circumscribed, is still recalled with favor by present-day Chechens.

To cite one example of such sentiment, when, in early 1996, an American journalist had occasion to talk with Shirvani Basaev, commander of the Chechen forces in Vedeno district and brother of a leading Chechen guerrilla fighter, Shirvani commented: "Russia would be a different and better country today if the Romanov dynasty were still in power." "[T]he Romanovs," he explained to an intrigued listener, were religious people and "therefore Russia under their rule included a 'divine factor' which is now absent." "People without faith," Shirvani concluded, "are more dangerous than those who accept God as a higher power."[144] For the Chechens of 1996, Boris Yeltsin and the leadership of the Russian Federation were regarded as atheists, people far worse than the Romanov dynasty.

The "land question" and the military courts

During the period separating the suppression of Shamil' in 1859 and the Bolshevik Revolution of 1917, the "land question" served to put perhaps the most strain on relations between Russia and the mountaineers. The commander-in-chief of Russian military forces in the Caucasus for 1863–65 issued a report in which he noted that "there were seven Cossacks per square verst of land and 12.6 mountaineers – in fact 600,000 Cossacks had nearly twice as much land per head as 948,000 mountaineers."[145] By 1912, this imbalance had worsened further: "The Ingush and the Chechens, with average land allotments of 5.8 and 3.0 desiatinas, were the poorest people in the [North Caucasus] area. Their hatred was concentrated on the Cossacks."[146] By 1912, the Terek Cossacks already possessed more than twice as much land per person

---

[143] Wixman, *Language Aspects*, p. 119, n. 1.

[144] Lawrence A. Uzzell, Keston News Service Report, Keston@gn.apc.org, 5 February 1996.

[145] Seton-Watson, *Russian Empire*, p. 291, n. 1. A verst is 0.66 miles.

[146] Richard Pipes, *The Formation of the Soviet Union: Communism and Nationalism, 1917–1923* (Cambridge, MA: Harvard University Press, 1957), p. 96. A desiatina is 2.7 acres.

(13.57 desiatinas) as did the native peoples of the mountains (6.05 desiatinas).[147]

Hundreds and thousands of hectares of fertile land and also the best wooded land had been given to the Cossacks by the tsarist authorities. Retired Russian soldiers and peasant settlers – some of whom had themselves renamed "Cossacks" and were treated as such – were also beneficiaries of this tsarist largesse, at the expense of the mountaineers. In 1864, Emperor Alexander II had issued a decree concerning the "inviolability of their [i.e., the mountaineers'] religion, adats, lands, and woods," which were to be "preserved unshakably and in perpetuity for the peoples of the North Caucasus."[148] This solemn pledge by the emperor was, however, soon violated and "hundreds of thousands of hectares of fine land and vast stretches of untouched forest were either given to 'highly placed persons' and settlers or declared to be state property. Consequently, all the North Caucasian tribes lacked arable land."[149]

A second perceived injustice which rankled the Chechens and other mountaineers during the period 1859–1917 was the trial system. If a Russian or Cossack was accused of a crime, he or she would normally be handed over to the civil authorities. For identical or similar crimes, however, the Chechens "came under the sole jurisdiction of the military authorities and were judged by the military district courts."[150] Often the Chechens who stood before these courts were sentenced to death. Thus, a dual system of justice prevailed – one system for the Russians and Cossacks, and another for the Chechens and other mountaineers.

Economic development

The discovery of oil in Chechnya served as a powerful stimulus for economic development, and during the 1880s and 1890s the region experienced an economic boom connected with the expansion of the oil industry in the vicinity of the principal city, Groznyi. That city also became a major industrial and transport center, and a railroad and oil pipeline began to be constructed. The opening of the New Groznyi petroleum industries in 1913 sparked "oil fever" in the region. The strong development of industry, trade, and transport in the last years of tsarist Russia led to the formation of a national bourgeoisie in

---

[147] Ibid., p. 94.
[148] P. Kosok, "Revolution and Sovietization in the North Caucasus," *Caucasian Review*, 1 (1955), 49.
[149] Ibid.   [150] Ibid., 48.

Chechnya; there also emerged a national intelligentsia, relatively few in number, consisting largely of military officers and teachers.[151]

The Chechens under the tsars – a summary

Summing up the painful fate of the Chechens and Ingush under the tsarist system, Russian ethnographer Galina Soldatova has written: "In the process of association with Russia, these nationalities received a series of powerful 'vaccinations' against any potential Russification. The start of their close mutual relations with Russia coincided with the beginning of the Caucasus war, which lasted nearly half a century and was fought under the banner of *gazavat* on the part of indigenous Muslim nationalities of the Caucasus. This was followed by another half-century of colonization of the Caucasus by tsarist Russia and by the troubled times of revolution . . . It hardly needs stating that the Soviet period is associated with Russian rule."[152] The "vaccinations" to which Soldatova refers explain, to a degree, the upsurge of Chechen secessionist sentiment in 1990 and 1991, though the deportation of 1944 undoubtedly served as a significantly stronger factor.

As Soldatova has rightly noted, the historical encounter of Chechens with Russians was scarcely a felicitous one. During the nineteenth-century Caucasus War, the Chechens lost close to half of their population and saw their economy uprooted and destroyed. They were incorporated against their will and by naked force into the Russian Empire. Despite explicit pledges made to them by Emperor Alexander II and by other high-ranking Russian officials following the surrender of Shamil' in 1859, they did not come to receive equal treatment with other peoples of the Empire but were instead reduced to a condition of harsh poverty and of "land hunger" and, in contrast with ethnic Russians, saw justice meted out to them by military rather than civilian courts.

Particularly galling to the Chechens was the Russian government's visible preference for and lavish treatment of the Cossacks, their historic neighbors and frequent rivals. Traditional Chechen lands were taken away from them and awarded in large swaths to the Cossacks. Despite being the victims of clear-cut discrimination under the tsars, the Chechens, as we have seen, remain to a degree ambivalent about the imperial period, recalling with favor the religious liberties they came to

---

[151] Muzaev, *Chechenskaya respublika*, p. 152.
[152] Galina U. Soldatova, "The Former Checheno-Ingushetiya," in Leokadia Drobizheva, Rose Gottemoeller, Catherine McArdle Kelleher, and Lee Walker, eds., *Ethnic Conflict in the Post-Soviet World* (Armonk, NY: M. E. Sharpe, 1996), pp. 224–25.

enjoy in the years after 1859. They also recall, to take one other example, that they were permitted to form their own national units as part of the so-called Wild Division of the imperial army at the time of the First World War.[153]

Moving from the realm of perceptions to that of objective processes, we can see that, beginning with General Aleksei Yermolov, the tsarist military and political leadership were unwittingly engaged in accelerating the national formation and religious self-identification of the Chechen people. In response to the aggressive policies and depredations of Yermolov and his successors in the North Caucasus, the various Chechen tribes and clans, frequently feuding among themselves, underwent the beginnings of a slow process of national consolidation, though in the main they continued to conceive of themselves as *gortsy*, part of a larger supra-ethnic Caucasus-wide Muslim entity.

Similarly, in the religious sphere, the aggression of Yermolov and his successors effectively forced the Chechens into the arms of Naqshbandi Sufi imams from neighboring Dagestan, who provided the ideological underpinning for the long Caucasus War. Following their devastating defeat in this war, some Chechens sought, with heavy-handed tsarist encouragement, to emigrate to Ottoman Turkey, with catastrophic results for those who left. Others turned to the Qadiriya, the Sufi brotherhood which today remains one of the two most influential Muslim *tariqats* among Chechens (the other being the Naqshbandiya).

Revolution and civil war

The period which began with the February ("bourgeois") Revolution of 1917 and concluded with the Red Army's investing of Chechnya in the summer of 1920 saw the Chechens, like all the peoples of the Empire, pitched into chaos and tumult. Exploiting the loosening of controls brought about by the February Revolution, a group of educated mountaineers meeting in May 1917 in Vladikavkaz convoked a "First North Caucasus Congress" and established a "Central Committee of the North Caucasus and Dagestan." This new Central Committee was to act as a provisional government for an independent North Caucasus state.

In September 1917, the organization's Second Congress ratified a provisional constitution for the newly formed state. At first, the leadership behind this initiative, who were political moderates, appear to have seen their state as being autonomous within Russia. And when, in

---

[153] On the "Wild Division," see Shakhbiev, *Sud'ba checheno-ingushskogo naroda*, pp. 193–95.

October 1917, the new Military Government of the Terek Cossacks offered the mountaineers an alliance, they proved receptive. These overtures, however, were soon brought to nothing by the Chechens and Ingush who, having waited for nearly a year to regain the lands which they had lost to the Russians, "in December 1917 . . . swooped down from the mountains and attacked the cities and Cossack settlements," rendering further cooperation among Cossacks and mountaineers impossible. The cities of Vladikavkaz, Groznyi, and the entire Cossack Line along the Sunzha were attacked.[154] Clashes between the Chechens and Ingush and the Cossacks over the land question continued into 1918.[155]

On 11 May 1918, after the Bolsheviks had seized power in Russia, the North Caucasus state declared itself to be fully independent of the Russian Federation. Its independence was recognized by the Central Powers – Germany, Austria-Hungary, and Turkey – and Turkey also concluded a formal treaty with the new state in June 1918. The leading figures in the North Caucasus state were Tapa Chermoev, a Chechen entrepreneur and social activist, who became president, and Vassan-Giray Jabagi, who was chosen head of parliament.[156] With the establishment of this Mountain Republic (Gorskaya Respublika), as it became known, in 1918, an educational system was put in place under which Arabic and Turkish became the chief languages of instruction, though local languages, such as Chechen, were also employed. Turkish was recognized as one of the official languages of the republic.[157]

The Naqshbandiya revives

In addition to sparking the emergence of an independent Mountain Republic, headed by educated moderates, the political tumult of 1917 and 1918 also activated the Sufi Muslim leadership throughout the eastern North Caucasus. In August 1917, a congress of religious leaders meeting in the mountain *aul* of Andi in the Avar region of Dagestan decided to revive the tradition of the imamate which had been abandoned in 1859 following the capture of Shamil'. The Naqshbandi sheikh Najmuddin of Hotso (Gotsinskii) was chosen imam of Dagestan and Chechnya. The goals pursued by the revived *tariqat* were the restoration of a theocracy governed by the *sharia*; the expulsion of the Russians

---

[154] Pipes, *Formation*, p. 97.   [155] Muzaev, *Chechenskaya respublika*, p. 153.
[156] Avtorkhanov, "Chechens and Ingush," p. 152; Muzaev, *Chechenskaya respublika*, p. 153.
[157] Wixman, *Language Aspects*, pp. 119–20.

from the region; and the liquidation of Muslims who were supporting "infidel" rulers.[158]

Another key Naqshbandi leader to emerge at this time was Sheikh Uzun Haji, a gifted military leader, learned Arabist, and strict adherent of the *sharia*, who had spent fifteen years in a Siberian labor camp before February 1917. By 1918, Najmuddin and Uzun had at their command an army of 10,000 men, "the best fighting force in the North Caucasus."[159] The military prowess of this army proved to be a near-fatal surprise for General Denikin and his White Army.

In May and June 1919, the White regiments under Denikin had begun to move into the North Caucasus region occupying Dagestan and then the Terek. Denikin flatly refused to recognize the strong pro-independence sentiment among the mountaineers and held firmly to the slogan "Great Russia, One and Indivisible." At first, he placed the administration of the region in the hands of officers of native origin who served in his army, and made no attempt to interfere in local life. In August 1919, however, while making an all-out effort to capture Moscow, Denikin issued an order drafting the natives into military service. Traditionally exempt from the draft, the mountaineers refused to obey these orders, and Denikin then sent punitive detachments to teach them a lesson.

Having encountered and overcome serious resistance in Kabarda and North Ossetiya, Denikin then entered the territory of the Chechens and Ingush. With the aim of breaking down their opposition to the Whites, he burned down dozens of the largest cities of the region: Chechen-Aul, Alkhan-Yurt, Gudermes, Staryi-Yurt, and many others. This understandably elicited a strong desire for revenge on the part of the Chechens and Ingush. Denikin himself soon came to term the region a "seething volcano."[160]

By October–November 1919, "the White forces were engaged in a full-scale war with the natives of the Northern Caucasus . . . occurring at a decisive moment of the civil war when the fate of Moscow itself hung in the balance."[161] Led by Sheikh Uzun Haji, the combined forces of the mountaineers methodically liberated the mountains of Dagestan, Chechnya, Ossetiya, and Kabarda. Uzun then proclaimed the independence of the North Caucasus and announced the founding of a "North Caucasus Emirate."

By February 1920, Denikin had been forced to evacuate the territory of the Emirate, now a theocratic state modeled on Shamil"s earlier

---

[158] Bennigsen and Wimbush, *Mystics and Commissars*, p. 24.   [159] Ibid., p. 25.
[160] Avtorkhanov, "Chechens and Ingush," p. 153.   [161] Pipes, *Formation*, p. 215.

imamate. The Emirate was placed under the nominal rule of the Ottoman sultan. In March 1920, Uzun died at the age of ninety, and several months after this the Red Army – which had been offering limited support to the mountaineers in their struggle against the Whites – moved in to occupy the region.[162] While the Chechens' fate over the first six millennia of their existence had scarcely been a carefree one, their severest ordeal as a people had now arrived.

[162] Broxup, "The Last Ghazawat," pp. 114–15. Paul Henze has noted that, today, "The most celebrated holy place in Chechnya is the tomb of Uzun Haji in the *aul* of Dyshne in Vedeno district. It is visited by Muslims from all parts of the Caucasus, for he has become the 'patron saint' of all mountaineers after the manner of Sheikh Mansur nearly two centuries ago." (See Henze, *Islam in the North Caucasus*, p. 25, n. 37.)

2 Soviet genocide

In 1944 the Chechen–Ingush ASSR was liquidated.

From the *Large Soviet Encyclopedia*[1]

Stalin faithfully executed the orders of Nicholas I to exterminate the Mountaineers, albeit after a delay of more than a century.

Abdurakhman Avtorkhanov[2]

In the spring of 1920, the Eleventh Red Army – "a purely Russian army led by Russian commanders and Russian political cadres"[3] – moved in and occupied the lowlands of Dagestan. This army was feeling close to invincible, inasmuch as communist forces had just defeated the White Army in European Russia and had conquered Azerbaijan almost without firing a shot. Georgia and Armenia had also been subdued within a few short weeks. As a result of Denikin's intransigence and mistaken policies, the mountaineers looked with sympathy on the Red forces; in Dagestan, their arrival was even compared to a column of pilgrims on their way to Mecca.[4]

By August 1920, however, many mountaineers had formed a contrary view of the Reds. Ignorant of and indifferent to local conditions, the Reds, like the Whites before them, committed a series of mistakes which inflamed the peoples of the North Caucasus. Chauvinistic cadres from the Narkomnats (People's Commissariat of Nationalities) based in Rostov-on-Don applied the harsh methods of "War Communism" to the prickly mountaineers. Patriarchal traditions were attacked, as was the Islamic religion, and repeated indignities were visited upon the natives, such as punitive raids, police denunciations, and blackmail.[5]

In August, a rebellion broke out which had all the traditional

---

[1] In Robert Conquest, *The Nation Killers*, 2nd edn. (New York: Macmillan, 1970), p. 170.

[2] Abdurakhman Avtorkhanov, "The Chechens and Ingush During the Soviet Period and Its Antecedents," in Marie Bennigsen Broxup, ed., *The North Caucasus Barrier* (New York: St. Martin's Press, 1992), p. 184.

[3] Broxup, "The Last Ghazawat: The 1920–1921 Uprising," in Broxup, *North Caucasus Barrier*, p. 112.

[4] Ibid., p. 122.   [5] Ibid.

characteristics of a Muslim *gazavat*. The nominal leader of the revolt was Said-Bek, a great-grandson of Imam Shamil'. The political and spiritual leader of the revolt was an Avar, Najmuddin of Hotso (Got-sinskii), who, as we saw in chapter 1 (pp. 37–39), had been elected imam of Dagestan and Chechnya in August 1917. The military command of the uprising was divided between Naqshbandi sheikhs loyal to the late Uzun Haji's theocratic ideal and a group of former tsarist military officers led by Colonel Kaitmas Alikhanov, an Avar nobleman.[6]

The war between the Reds and the mountaineers lasted for about a year, but the rebellion was finally quelled only in 1925, when, as we shall see, the Bolsheviks succeeded in capturing Najmuddin and other surviving Naqshbandi sheikhs who had taken refuge in Chechnya. The revolt, which took place under the slogan "National Liberation and the *Shariat* State," began in the southern districts of Dagestan bordering on Georgia, but it soon spread throughout Dagestan and Chechnya.

Like Shamil"s forces in the period following the Crimean War, the rebels were massively outmanned and outgunned. The commander of the Eleventh Red Army, Todorskii, estimated in January 1921 that the rebels numbered slightly fewer than 10,000 fighters and were poorly armed, with antique rifles and swords along with some forty machine guns which they had captured in battle.[7] The mountaineer forces were *uzdens*, free men with loyalties to their clan and to their Sufi *tariqat*. They came from the same Chechen and Dagestani mountain settle-ments that had led the resistance to the tsarist advance over the previous century.

The Reds, as has been noted, massively outnumbered the lightly armed mountaineers. They had two full armies at their disposal: the Eleventh (the "Terek–Dagestan Army") and the Ninth (the "Kuban' Army"). The combined forces boasted twenty-seven rifle regiments, six cavalry regiments, six artillery groups, and two battalions of Inner Security, plus a number of special formations such as aviation, armored cars, technical units, and detachments of local and Moscow-based *cheka* (secret police). The total number of heavily armed Red fighters was 35,000–40,000.[8]

Of course, the mountaineers had no chance against such over-whelming numerical superiority and such advantages in firepower. Using military tactics modeled on the tsarist conquest of the region – but applied far more ruthlessly – the Reds moved from one valley to another, slaughtering and deporting the local population. The rebels

---

[6] Ibid., pp. 114–15.   [7] Ibid., p. 116.   [8] Ibid., pp. 116–17.

fought with their customary courage, and there were almost no survivors from among their 10,000-man force.[9] On occasion, they inflicted major casualties on the Reds; thus, for example, on 21 January 1921, they surrounded the elite Cavalry Regiment of the Moscow Cadet Brigade near Alleroy and killed ten officers and eighty-three cadets from the unit. The Red Army is reported to have lost 5,000 men in Dagestan alone.[10] The rebels also exhibited their usual tenacity: numerous uprisings broke out in supposedly pacified *auls*, and there were frequent assassinations of occupation Red forces.

In May 1921, following the storming of the Dido-Avar fortress of Gidatl in Dagestan, the struggle, which had commenced in August 1920, came to a bloody end. "[T]he backward Dagestani and Chechen masses," the victorious Bolsheviks trumpeted, "[have been] freed from the cabal of the White Guard officer class, and the lies and deceptions of parasitic sheikhs and mullahs." The Red Army, "the friend and mighty defender of the poor," was now in charge.[11] In 1923, approximately 10,000 mountaineers – the sources do not say how many of them were Chechens – were expelled from the mountains to the lowland regions.[12]

Stalin pledges his word

On 20 January 1921, at a time when the Said-Bek rebellion was still very much in progress, the Bolshevik people's commissar for nationalities, Iosif Stalin, met in Vladikavkaz with political moderates who had founded the Mountain Republic in 1917–18. The occasion was a periodic congress of that new republic. Stalin explained to the assembled delegates the policy of the All-Union Central Executive Committee (the Bolshevik government) regarding nationalities and proclaimed an amnesty for all those who had participated in the Said-Bek revolt, on condition that the uprising cease and the authority of the Soviet government be recognized. Stalin solemnly declared that the Soviet government acknowledged the internal sovereignty and independence of the mountaineers.[13]

In the name of the Bolshevik government, Stalin recommended the creation of a new "Soviet Mountain Republic," which would be granted a large degree of autonomy "so that the old dreams of the Mountain people might come true and their own independent government become a reality."[14] The assembled congress made its recognition of the Soviet government conditional upon the *sharia* being officially accepted as the basic constitutional law of the Mountain Republic. It also stipulated that

[9] Ibid., p. 117.   [10] Ibid., pp. 135–41.   [11] Ibid., pp. 139–40.
[12] Ibid., p. 143.   [13] Avtorkhanov, "Chechens and Ingush," p. 154.   [14] Ibid.

the central government should pledge not to intervene in the republic's internal affairs, and that the lands of the mountaineers – which had been taken away from them under the tsars – should be returned. Stalin formally accepted these conditions, and the congress then officially recognized the Soviet government.

Thus there came into (temporary) existence a Soviet Mountain Republic consisting of six administrative oblasts: Chechnya, Ingushetiya, Ossetiya, Kabarda, Balkariya, and Karachai. Dagestan was not included in this new entity; rather it was made an independent republic – the Soviet Socialist Republic of Dagestan. The new Mountain Republic bizarrely combined Bolshevik and Islamic symbols: there was a Soviet emblem on its banner but it had a *shariat* constitution. Portraits of Shamil' and his *naibs* replaced those of Lenin and other Politburo members in all administrative institutions, schools, and public places in the republic.

The Bolsheviks even took action on the key land question: several Cossack settlements were moved into the Russian interior on the orders of Stalin and Sergo Ordzhonikidze, and their lands were then returned to the Chechens and Ingush.[15] The leaders of the Mountain Republic were intellectuals who had supported the Bolsheviks from 1917 on and who had been attracted by the Bolshevik promise to give the nations of the North Caucasus the right to self-determination and secession. They naively believed that the Bolsheviks would respect the autonomy of their new republic.

The Bolsheviks renege

That the concessions made by the Bolsheviks had been purely tactical in nature began to become apparent a year and a half after Stalin's pledge of January 1921. The Bolsheviks had not forgotten the Said-Bek uprising of 1920–21 and were determined to "pacify" and disarm Chechnya, the site of some of the heaviest fighting. In the summer of 1922, the regime moved a large force into Chechnya, which seized several hundred rifles and three machine guns; several homes of "bandits" were burned down.[16] (This abusive term would be revived by Yeltsin and his entourage some seventy-two years later.)

By late 1922, following a self-evident strategy of "divide and rule," the Bolsheviks began to break up the Mountain Republic, which they had solemnly recognized the previous year. On 30 November 1922, they

[15] Ibid.
[16] V. A. Tishkov, E. L. Belyaeva, and G. V. Marchenko, *Chechenskii krizis* (Moscow: Tsentr kompleksnykh sotsial'nykh issledovanii i marketinga, 1995), p. 8.

created a Chechen Autonomous Oblast', thereby severing Chechnya from the remainder of the Mountain Republic. In July 1924, the remaining five oblasts of the republic were liquidated, and the former constituent parts of the republic became provinces of a capacious North Caucasian krai, an administrative entity with no religious or ethnic significance.[17]

Once Chechnya had been formally detached from the Mountain Republic in November 1922, the Bolsheviks initiated serious efforts to conduct a general disarming of the population. Not only did they confiscate existing personal weapons, but they also imposed an obligation on each household to surrender at least one firearm to the authorities. This forced disarmament was, of course, deeply resented by the Chechen populace, who saw it as preparation for forthcoming repressions and as an attempt to deprive them of rights guaranteed by the *shariat* constitution, to which Stalin and the Soviet government had just agreed.[18]

The Bolsheviks exact revenge

By the summer of 1925, the Bolsheviks felt themselves ready to make a serious attempt to "pacify" obstreperous Chechnya. Key archival documents relating to this sanguinary operation have recently been published in the journal *Istochnik*.[19] According to a communication from A. I. Mikoyan, secretary of the North Caucasus party *kraikom*, "Stalin gave his personal assent to the necessity of this operation."[20]

The operation itself was conducted from 23 August until 12 September. In a report to the Politburo, dated 5 September, I. S. Unshlikht, deputy chairman of the Revolutionary Military Council of the USSR, wrote with satisfaction: "An operation has been carried out in accord with the decision of the Politburo to disarm the Chechen Autonomous Oblast' and to remove the chiefs of counter-revolution and banditry." The operation, Unshlikht noted, had been conducted by combined forces of the North Caucasus Military District and the OGPU (secret police); the military contingent had numbered 6,857 troops, armed with 130 heavy-caliber machine guns, while the OGPU detachment had

[17] Ronald Wixman, *Language Aspects of Ethnic Patterns and Processes in the North Caucasus* (Chicago: University of Chicago Department of Geography Research Series, no. 191, 1980), pp. 136–37; Ol'ga Vasil'eva, "North Caucasus," in Klaus Segbers and Stephan de Spiegeleire, eds., *Post-Soviet Puzzles* (Baden Baden, Germany: Nomos, 1995), vol. II, p. 427.
[18] Avtorkhanov, "Chechens and Ingush," p. 156.
[19] "Stalin dal lichnoe soglasie," *Istochnik*, no. 5 (1995), 140–51.
[20] Ibid., 142. All the quotations in this section are taken from this article.

consisted of 341 persons. Eight bombers and artillery were also employed in the course of the operation.

Unshlikht's reports stress that the key to the success of the operation was a combination of deceit and blinding speed. "The concentration of troops on the territory of the oblast'," he wrote, "was conducted under the guise of participating in forthcoming maneuvers." These troops had been concentrated on the northern, eastern, and western borders of Chechnya, so that they could simultaneously thrust toward the center of the oblast' and "carry out the disarming of the populace and the removal of bandit elements." The southern border had been sealed off by special detachments of the Caucasus Red Banner Army.

In his report of 17 September, Unshlikht noted contentedly that the operation had given "a rather complete result." The "suddenness [vnezapnost']" of the assault, he underlined, was a major reason why the Chechens had not had time to take countermeasures. Nonetheless, Unshlikht was required to admit that the Red forces had encountered fierce resistance. The attempts to capture "especially important chiefs of banditry in Chechnya" such as Sheikh Najmuddin of Hotso (Gotsinskii) and Sheikh Amin of Ansalta (Ansalatinskii), Unshlikht reported on 8 September, had provoked fierce resistance.

When, for example, Najmuddin's surrender was demanded of the Chechen settlement where he had taken refuge, this demand was refused. The Bolsheviks then took "respected old men" of the community as hostages; this ploy also failed. Finally, they had to resort to "artillery fire and bombing from the air (twenty-two poods of bombs were dropped)"[21] to force his surrender on 5 September. Three days previously, Sheikh Amin had likewise given himself up after artillery shelling and bombing of the settlement where he had concealed himself.

In addition to being aimed at arresting (and later executing) important leaders of the 1920–21 rebellion, the operation also had the goal of seizing weapons. According to Unshlikht's report of 12 September, some 21,000 rifles and 3,000 revolvers were taken from the Chechens.

Simultaneously with the military operation, Unshlikht noted, a purge of "bandit elements" in the soviet apparatus was being carried out, and the revolutionary committees (revkomy) were being organized from representatives of the populace in sympathy with the Bolsheviks. There remained, however, he cautioned, a need to "sovietize the region, to strengthen the soviet and party apparatuses with reliable workers, and to provide economic assistance to the populace."

During the mass deportation of the Chechens in 1944, the regime,

[21] A pood is 16.38 kilograms.

one presumes, made use of the principal lessons of the 1925 operation: namely, the need for blinding speed and for deceit. These lessons had, however, apparently been forgotten at the time of the Russian military invasion of Chechnya in December 1994.

"Divide and rule" policy applied to Muslims

In addition to the use of overwhelming military and police force, the Bolsheviks were also politically successful in the North Caucasus region in the early to mid 1920s due to their astute "divide and rule" policies. This approach was successfully applied even in the religious sphere. Thus, between 1918 and 1926, in Dagestan, they succeeded in dividing the powerful Naqshbandiya *tariqat* by opposing the influential Sheikh Ali of Akusha to Najmuddin of Hotso. Similarly, in the Chechen–Ingush territory, they attracted Ali Mitaev, the head of the powerful Bammat Giray brotherhood, to their side; in 1920, Ali had been the head of the Chechen Revolutionary Committee. The Bolshevik regime's co-operation with these two men was temporary and tactical; in 1925, Ali Mitaev was executed, while Ali of Akusha was dispatched the following year.[22]

Russification

A key element in the Bolshevik strategy vis-à-vis the mountaineers was to create a small number of inclusive national groups through encouraging the assimilation of smaller peoples. The aim behind this approach was "to create ethnic groups large enough to maintain their individual identities, but too small to resist Russianization and Russification."[23] Toward this end, on 15 January 1934, the Chechen Autonomous Oblast' and the Ingush Autonomous Oblast' were combined into one autonomous oblast'. In December 1936, in accord with the new "Stalin Constitution," it was organized into a Chechen–Ingush ASSR situated within the larger Russian Federation. By fusing Chechens and Ingush together, the communists sought to create a combined "Vainakh" identity which would result in the assimilation of the Ingush and would leave both peoples vulnerable to Russianization and Russification.

Another way in which the regime carried out Russification was in the critical language sphere. When in January 1921, the Bolsheviks agreed to the formation of the Soviet Mountain Republic, they recognized Arabic as the official language of education in the new republic. In so

---

[22] Broxup, "Introduction," in Broxup, *North Caucasus Barrier*, p. 6.
[23] Wixman, *Language Aspects*, p. 152.

doing, they acceded to the wishes of the populace of the region; Arabic was to serve as a written *lingua franca* for the republic and, of course, to facilitate the instruction of religion in Muslim schools. The Koran was not supposed to be translated into the vernacular, and a knowledge of Arabic was thus a necessary conduit to the religion and its literature.

The regime soon undertook, through deceit and trickery, to detach the mountaineers from the Arabic language. During the years 1923–25, Latinized alphabets were constructed for all of the North Caucasian languages. An orthography in the Latin alphabet had been devised for Chechen as early as 1923.[24] In 1928–29, it was mandated that all languages previously written in Arabic script now had to be transcribed into the Latin alphabet.[25] The clear-cut aim behind this move was to remove Arabic as a *lingua franca* and an entree to Islam while avoiding the stigma of too obvious Russification, which would have resulted from a decision immediately to shift over from Arabic to Cyrillic.

That latter move was put off until 1938, when the Kremlin "advised" the peoples of the North Caucasus to give up the Latin for the Cyrillic alphabet.[26] The following year, 1939, the Soviet government also made the study of Russian as a second language obligatory in all schools of the USSR.[27]

Adjusting borders

Another means by which the Bolsheviks carried out Russification was the constant alteration of the borders of the autonomous regions. When a combined Chechen–Ingush Autonomous Republic was created in 1936, for example, it included territory and populace which had not previously been part of the Chechen oblast' or the Ingush oblast'. The reason for this action was clearly to dilute the ethnic "weight" of Chechens and Ingush in the new combined oblast'. In 1926, the Ingush Autonomous Oblast', with a total population of 75,133, had consisted of 93 percent Ingush and only 1 percent (900 persons) Russians. Similarly, in the same year, the Chechen Autonomous Oblast', with a total population of 309,860, had consisted of 94 percent Chechens and 2.9 percent Russians.[28]

In 1934, new Russian-dominated territories were added to the previous Chechen and Ingush Autonomous Oblasts. Groznyi Autono-

[24] See Johanna Nichols, "Chechen," in Rieks Smeets, ed., *The Indigenous Languages of the Caucasus* (Delmar, NY: Caravan Books, 1994), vol. IV, p. 3.

[25] Wixman, *Language Aspects*, p. 146.

[26] R. Karcha, "Genocide in the Northern Caucasus," *Caucasian Review*, 2 (1956), 77, Nichols, "Chechen," p. 3.

[27] Wixman, *Language Aspects*, p. 148.   [28] Ibid., p. 139.

mous City (whose population of 98,000 included 68,152 Russians and only 1,931 Chechens and 24 Ingush), Sunzha okrug (whose total population of 34,900 included 31,202 Russians and 2,522 Ukrainians but only 230 Chechens and 301 Ingush), and the southwestern part of Terskii okrug (also predominantly Russian) were combined with ancient Chechen and Ingush territories to create a more Slavic population mix.[29] By altering the administrative status of the Chechens and other Muslim peoples of the North Caucasus, the Soviets sought to break up a united sense of "mountaineer" identity. They also wanted to weaken the ethnic clout of each of these peoples by combining their lands with Russian-dominated territories. Russification was a common goal behind these practices.

In seeking to uproot a sense of united "mountaineer" identity, however, the regime unwittingly prepared the eventual emergence of a vigorous nationalism among the *ethnie* of the North Caucasus, peoples which, until the late 1930s, had not manifested a strong national self-awareness. As Jane Ormrod has observed: "Indifference on the part of the North Caucasian groups – both peasants and intelligentsia – to participate in the development of their 'national' cultures suggests that these cultures were not, at least in the 1920s and early 1930s, an important part of their identity. N. G. Volkova and L. I. Lavrov have characterized North Caucasian national consciousness in this period as a local, clan consciousness, together with a 'parallel consciousness' of a 'huge ethnic society' of North Caucasian *gortsy*. Initially, the North Caucasian peoples exhibited little consciousness of themselves as members of their officially recognized national groups. Only after twenty years of Soviet power did official national identity begin to emerge."[30] It was a strong separatist nationalism which was fifty years later to fuel the "Chechen Revolution" of 1991.

Anti-religious persecution

The major Bolshevik anti-Islamic drive coincided with the inception of forced collectivization in 1929, but, even before that time, the regime had moved to curtail the influence of Islam. Thus, in 1924, all medressehs were ordered shut down throughout the North Caucasus, except in Dagestan, where they remained open until 1926–27.[31] In

---

[29] Ibid.
[30] Jane Ormrod, "The North Caucasus: Confederation in Conflict," in Ian Bremmer and Ray Taras, eds., *New States, New Politics: Building the Post-Soviet Nations* (Cambridge, UK: Cambridge University Press, 1997), p. 98.
[31] Wixman, *Language Aspects*, pp. 142–44.

similar vein, all pilgrimages to the Muslim holy cities of Mecca and Medina were strictly prohibited.[32]

Collectivization

In the autumn of 1929, the Chechen party *obkom* received a telegram from Politburo member Andrei Andreev informing its members that the North Caucasus had been selected as the first territory in the USSR where "complete collectivization" would be introduced and where the rich peasantry (*kulachestvo*) would be liquidated as a class. Following this official announcement, representatives of the party Central Committee and other high-ranking party officials arrived in the *auls*, where they proceeded to confiscate real estate and personal property from some peasants, who were then arrested as *kulaks* and sent off with their families to Siberia. Other peasants had their possessions seized and turned over to the new kolkhozes (collective farms).[33]

As historian Alexander Nekrich has noted, this crude attempt to "collectivize" Chechnya represented a logical absurdity: "Chechnya did not have private ownership of land. Only in the mountain *khutory* did families own a certain amount of property individually. In the lowlands everything was held in common – the land, the water, and the forests. Therefore, the term 'kulak,' applied to the concrete conditions in Checheno-Ingushetiya, loses all meaning."[34]

Despite the illogicality of their program, the collectivizers aggressively pressed ahead with their plan. Between January and March 1930, the number of farms combined into kolkhozes increased six to seven times in Chechnya. While it was relatively easy to collectivize the lowland farming areas, where the population as a rule lived in compact communities, it was a different matter altogether to collectivize the highland districts, where distant pasture livestock farming remained the main occupation. Such migratory farming was viewed by the regime as "totally reactionary."[35]

Faced with a far-reaching and mindless assault on their economic livelihood and traditional way of life, the Chechens "rose as one." The most significant revolts occurred in Goiti, Shali, Benoi, Cheberloevskoe, Artury, and Nozhai-Yurtovskoe. The insurgents occupied all rural and regional institutions, burned official archives, and arrested the staff of

[32] Karcha, "Genocide," 76.
[33] Avtorkhanov, "Chechens and Ingush," p. 157.
[34] Alexander M. Nekrich, *The Punished Peoples* (New York: W. W. Norton, 1978), p. 44.
[35] Nikolai Fedorovich Bugai, "The Truth About the Deportation of the Chechen and Ingush Peoples," *Soviet Studies in History*, Fall (1991), 68–69. The original Russian version of this article was published in *Voprosy istorii*, 7 (1990), 32–44.

the *obkom* government, chiefs of the GPU included. In the town of Benoi, they seized the petroleum refineries.[36] According to Soviet archival documents, sixty-nine acts of "terrorism" were recorded in Chechnya in 1931–33, the victims being leading party and government workers, secret police agents, and so forth. The archives notably fail to explain the motivation behind these "terrorist" acts.[37]

What in fact did the rebels want? In the Chechen settlement of Benoi, the leaders of the uprising founded a provisional government and then presented the following demands to the Soviet authorities: "1. Illegal confiscation of peasant property, i.e., 'collectivization,' must be stopped; 2. Arbitrary arrests of peasants . . . must cease; 3. The GPU chiefs must be recalled from Chechnya and replaced by civil officers of Chechen origin . . . ; 4. The 'popular' courts imposed from above must be liquidated and the institution of *shariat* courts . . . reinstated; 5. The intervention of regional and central authorities in the internal affairs of the 'Chechen Autonomous [Oblast']' [must] be stopped and all the economic and political decisions taken by the [1917–18] Chechen Congress [enacted]."[38] As can be seen, the rebels wanted the Soviet government to honor the pledges made by Stalin to the new Mountain Republic in January 1921.

When confronted with firm and united opposition, the communists were prepared to take several strategic steps backwards. On this occasion, a government delegation, which included Central Committee member K. Nikolaev, arrived in Groznyi from Moscow to end the insurrection peacefully. A local "peace commission" was set up which included three Chechen religious leaders and the chairman and secretary of the oblast' party committee. This commission solemnly proclaimed: "Chechnya's internal matters will be settled in the future by the Chechen people."[39] The insurgents expressed satisfaction with the work of the commission and agreed to return to their homes.

As usual, the regime's concessions had been tactical and temporary. Four days after the commission's statement, at one o'clock in the morning, a GPU detachment surrounded the home of one of the chief insurgents, Shita Istamulov, who had led the revolt in Shali. Incredibly, the heavily armed Shita and his brother, Hassan, managed to hold off the GPU in a firefight lasting until dawn (Hassan was badly wounded). At daybreak, approximately a hundred Chechen horsemen arrived on the scene and cut the GPU unit to ribbons.

---

[36] Avtorkhanov, "Chechens and Ingush," pp. 157–58; Bugai, "The Truth," 69.
[37] Nekrich, *Punished Peoples*, p. 43.
[38] Avtorkhanov, "Chechens and Ingush," p. 158.   [39] Ibid.

Vexed at this act of betrayal on the part of the authorities, Shita appealed to all Chechens to join with him in a *gazavat* to reestablish Shamil''s imamate and to evict the Soviet "infidels" from the Caucasus. The towns of Shali, Goiti, and Benoi rose up, and the rebellion spread to Dagestan, North Ossetiya, Kabarda, Balkariya, and Karachai. This development, however, served to convince the communists that harsh punitive action had to be taken to pacify the region.

The Red Army moves in again

In the middle of December 1929, regular detachments of the Red Army began to arrive at the borders of Chechnya. Toward the end of that month, General Belov, commander of the North Caucasus Military District, sent a huge force against the insurgents: four infantry divisions; the 28th Combat Division from Vladikavkaz; the Vladikavkaz Infantry School; the Krasnodar Cavalry School; three artillery divisions; and two regiments of border guards. In addition, the attacking force included three GPU squadrons, commanded by Kurskii, vice chairman of the regional GPU.

This vast force soon began to overwhelm the rebels, and, by mid-January 1930, it had captured the insurgent centers of Shali and Benoi; in doing so, however, the Reds suffered heavy losses – practically the entire 82nd Infantry Regiment, for example, was wiped out in the battles for Goiti, and Belov lost an entire division near Shali. In April 1930, Belov triumphantly entered Benoi, only to find the town completely empty.[40]

Having taught the rebels an indelible lesson, the communists once again decided to change course. A special decree issued by the party Central Committee condemned "leftist deviationists" who had been responsible for collectivization. In Chechnya, collective farms were banned outright as having been premature. Leaders of the Chechen Communist Party were dismissed from their posts as "deviationists," and the Red Army was withdrawn from Chechen territory. A large quantity of commercial goods was made available to the populace at low prices, and an official government amnesty was proclaimed for the leaders and participants in the 1929–30 insurrection. The rebel leader, Shita Istamulov, returned to Shali and was appointed chairman of the Rural Consumers' Cooperative.

---

[40] Ibid., pp. 159–60.

GPU perfidy

This spasm of liberalization proved, however, to be of brief duration. In the autumn of 1931, Baklanov, chief of the Chechen oblast' GPU, invited Shita Istamulov to his office to receive an official amnesty document, which had been sent from Moscow. Foolishly, Istamulov agreed to come. At their meeting, Baklanov presented Istamulov with the document with one hand "while firing the entire charge of a Mauser pistol [into him] with the other."[41] The severely wounded Istamulov had time to stab the treacherous Baklanov to death before being finished off by the GPU guard stationed outside. Understandably envenomed, Istamulov's brother, Hassan, organized a partisan band which hunted down and killed GPU officers to avenge Shita's death; the band remained active until 1935.

The assassination of Istamulov marked the beginning of a broad-scale operation to eliminate "*kulak* counter-revolutionary elements and mullah–nationalist ideologists."[42] Arrest lists were drawn up by the GPU regional offices in Groznyi and Rostov-on-Don and then confirmed by the Soviet government. Some 35,000 persons were then arrested according to these lists and subsequently tried and convicted by an "Extraordinary Commission of Three" of the GPU, presided over by G. Kraft. Many of those who were arrested were also executed; few lived to regain their freedom.

In their campaign against the populace of Chechnya the *chekists* – virtually none of whom were ethnic Chechens – revived the tsarist system of taking *amanaty* (hostages) in order to induce Chechen "bandits" to surrender. The tsarist administration had been wont to free a hostage once a bandit gave himself up, "whereas there is not a single case in the history of Soviet Checheno-Ingushetiya of an *amanat* being freed after the surrender of the 'bandit.'" When a bandit would give himself up, "he was shot despite solemn promises to spare his life. As to the hostages they were all – men, women, and children – sent to Siberia."[43] Due to such behavior by the regime, the Chechens ceased believing the assurances of the Soviet government and coined a saying that can be translated as "lying like the Soviets."

Despite all obstacles, the collectivization campaign moved ahead, and by 1938, there were 490 collective farms on the territory of the Autonomous Republic of Checheno-Ingushetiya covering three-quarters of the arable land in the republic (308,800 hectares out of 401,200). Most of this arable land (246,900 hectares) was located in the

---

[41] Ibid., p. 160.   [42] Ibid.   [43] Ibid., pp. 165–66.

lowland areas. Fifteen machine-tractor stations were also established in the lowlands.[44]

Despite the apparent success of the collectivization effort, the Chechens and Ingush practiced a form of what might be called passive resistance to it. The number of collective farmers in the lowland areas who did not work a single day on a kolkhoz over a given year amounted to 17.4 percent, and 46.3 percent worked only fifty days a year. Some small kolkhozes, consisting of twenty to thirty households, were actually clans (*teipy*) which had merely changed labels. In the highland areas, despite the fact that 99.8 percent of households had nominally been collectivized, individual farming remained the de facto norm. Part of the reason for the regime's lack of control in the highlands was the poor level of education of the Communist Party cadres there. Out of 824 communists in the highlands, 50 were completely illiterate, 265 had no primary school education, and 275 had only a primary education; 153 had not completed secondary school.[45]

In addition to passive resistance, a number of Chechens continued to practice active physical resistance to the regime. According to documents in the archives of the Groznyi Regional Ministry of Internal Affairs (MVD), insurgent gangs over the course of just eleven months in 1938 "committed ninety-eight daring raids in which forty-nine Soviet officials were killed, livestock and horses were taken, and property worth a total of 617,000 rubles was stolen."[46]

The "beheading" of Checheno-Ingushetiya

As has been noted, elements among the educated strata of the mountaineers had originally supported the Bolsheviks in the period following the 1917 Revolution, believing that they would grant the peoples of the North Caucasus autonomy and also the right to self-determination and even secession. These so-called national communists composed an important segment of educated Chechens, but they soon fell into disfavor with the regime because they did not approve of its attitudes toward the Muslim clergy, the local bourgeoisie, or the old national intelligentsia. They also disagreed with the USSR's heavy-handed state language policy and its actions in the spheres of national culture and economic policy, especially forced collectivization and breakneck industrialization. Following the bloody crackdown of 1929–30, many

[44] Nekrich, *Punished Peoples*, p. 46. [45] Ibid., pp. 47–49.
[46] Bugai, "The Truth," 70.

national communists in the region came to the conclusion that Soviet communism was nothing more than a form of colonialism.[47]

Scholarly research institutes located in Checheno-Ingushetiya came under heavy fire. Members of these institutes were accused of having conducted sabotage in their work on national languages, in their compiling of dictionaries of terminology and other lexicographical research, and in their historical studies. The various North Caucasus unions of writers were accused of having engaged in anti-Soviet and anti-Russian activities. After being "exposed" in the press, some of these national communists were expelled from the party. One prominent Chechen intellectual, Khalit Oshaev, director of research for the Institute for Research on the Culture of the People of the North Caucasus, was removed from his post.

By the year 1937, the campaign against the North Caucasus intellectuals had reached a kind of crescendo: the Chechen–Ingush Party Committee vilified them for using in their writings bourgeois nationalist terms and concepts such as "Turkish" and "Arabic." Creative writers were accused of being concerned in their work only with "the past of their people," while ignoring the building of socialism.[48]

Following the assassination of Shita Istamulov by the GPU in 1931, the regime initiated a wide-ranging crackdown against educated Chechens. The secret police, led by G. Kraft, the head of its local section, conjured up a "counter-revolutionary center" of Chechens, allegedly headed by Tapa Chermoev and Vassan-Giray Jabagi (the original leaders of the 1917–18 Mountain Republic). Widespread surveillance of émigré Chechens – and especially of Chermoev – was initiated.

In 1932, the secret police sprang its trap and arrested the whole alleged "counter-revolutionary center." Mass arrests followed in the regions of Gudermes and Nozhai-Yurt, and 3,000 persons in all were detained. Those arrested were accused of having organized a "counter-revolutionary national center of Chechnya in preparation for an armed uprising."[49] In 1934, while assailing this mythical "center," a secretary of the Chechen–Ingush Party Committee, Evdokimov, quoted at length from the "letters of the millionaire Chermoev." But today it is known that Chermoev's letters – the principal material evidence in the trial of this "center" – were in fact directly fabricated by the NKVD. For

[47] R. Karcha, "The Struggle Against Nationalism in the Northern Caucasus," *Caucasian Review*, 9 (1959), 25–38.
[48] Ibid.
[49] Avtorkhanov, "Chechens and Ingush," pp. 166–68. On this 1937 purge, see also Aleksandr N. Yakovlev, *Po moshcham i elei* (Moscow: Evraziya, 1995), pp. 120–21.

discovering this non-existent "center," NKVD heads Kraft and Kurskii were given the prestigious Red Banner of Labor award.

The great purge strikes Chechnya

A "General Operation for the Removal of Anti-Soviet Elements" commenced in Checheno-Ingushetiya on the night of 31 July–1 August 1937. Individuals whose names appeared on NKVD arrest lists were seized and then transported in trucks to the republican capital of Groznyi. During that night and over the ensuing months, nearly 14,000 Chechens were arrested, representing 3 percent of the republic's total population. A single arrest order was signed for all the accused, and they were tried by an NKVD special *troika*. Some of those arrested were executed while others were sent to concentration camps. "[E]very night there were mass executions in the cellars of the NKVD to the accompaniment of the roar of motor-cars outside."[50] The bodies of those who had been shot were spirited off in trucks under cover of darkness and taken to mass graves in the forest.

Stalin's Great Terror continued to strike hard at Chechnya and Ingushetiya. At the beginning of October 1937, Shkiryatov, a candidate member of the Politburo, arrived in the republic accompanied by a large NKVD staff. A plenum of the republican party committee was summoned for 7 October. "In the course of this plenum Shkiryatov ordered the arrest of all Chechen and Ingush members of the regional party committee, and they were arrested immediately in the plenum hall itself. Shkiryatov's orders were then extended to all Chechen–Ingush official workers from the [chairman] of the Republic down to the [chairman] of the *selsoviets* (village councils)."[51]

The purge continued its mayhem. Throughout October and November 1937, all secretaries of the republican party committee were arrested, as were all chairmen of the twenty-eight executive committees of Checheno-Ingushetiya. Civil servants working for government, urban, regional, and rural institutions were seized, as were prominent Chechens and Ingush living outside the republic, such as the scholar Khalit Oshaev. "In Checheno-Ingushetiya in 1938 all the directors of district land departments, fourteen out of eighteen machine-tractor station directors, nineteen chairmen of district executive committees, and twenty-two secretaries of district party committees were removed. In 1939, twenty-one chairmen of district executive committees and

---

[50] Avtorkhanov, "Chechens and Ingush," pp. 174–75.   [51] Ibid., pp. 175–76.

twenty-three directors of district land departments were ousted. Most of them were arrested."[52]

In 1938, the case against 137 arrested leaders of the "bourgeois-nationalist center of Checheno-Ingushetiya" was ready. The accused were mostly young men – 82 of the 137 were under thirty years of age – who had risen to responsible positions in the republic; in a direct sense they represented the "future" of the region. The investigations of the accused were conducted under torture, and seventeen died before they were able to stand trial. Of the 120 survivors, only one pleaded guilty at the court-martial held at the North Caucasus Military District; the others declared that the crimes of which they were accused were a fabrication and that the confessions that had been extracted from them were false. "They displayed their scars, their broken teeth, and their injuries (one of them had been castrated during the interrogation)."[53] Nonetheless, all 120 were found guilty by the court-martial.

The overall effect of this sweeping purge of the republican leadership and intelligentsia was, as a leading Chechen émigré scholar, Abdurakhman Avtorkhanov, has concluded, that "the link that existed between the people and the authorities was broken when the intelligentsia was destroyed."[54] Specialist Timur Muzaev has expressed it similarly: "[T]he whole leadership . . . and the whole national intelligentsia were destroyed."[55] As the dark days of the Second World War approached, the republic found itself rudderless, deprived of an educated leadership.

As for the effect of the purge on the broader populace, the all-union census figures for 1937 and 1939 hint at a demographic tragedy. In 1937, the figure given for Chechens living in the USSR was 435,922; by 1939 – just two years later – that figure had diminished to 400,344.[56]

The insurrections of Izrailov and Sheripov

The Chechens, as was their custom, hit back at a regime perceived as seeking to destroy their livelihood and their very national existence. As a result of the communists' "General Operation for the Removal of Anti-Soviet Elements" of mid-1937, for example, thousands of Chechens (as well as many Ingush) joined guerrilla groups. In the areas of Galanchozh, Gudermes, and Kurchaloi, these groups assassinated the chiefs of local NKVD sections.[57]

---

[52] Nekrich, *Punished Peoples*, p. 50.
[53] Avtorkhanov, "Chechens and Ingush," p. 178.   [54] Ibid., p. 179.
[55] Timur Muzaev, *Chechenskaya respublika* (Moscow: Panorama, 1995), p. 154.
[56] Tishkov, et al., *Chechenskii krizis*, p. 10.
[57] Avtorkhanov, "Chechens and Ingush," p. 175.

In 1939, a new struggle against the communists broke out in the North Caucasus regions of Karachai and Balkariya, and soon it had spread to Checheno-Ingushetiya, where, in the winter and spring of 1940, it became particularly intense. It should be underlined that, at this juncture, Stalin and Hitler were officially still allies. The leader of the 1940 rebellion was Hassan Izrailov, who had born in Galanchozh in 1910. In 1929, Izrailov completed secondary school in Rostov-on-Don and, during the same year, joined the Communist Party – this was unusual background for a future leader of a Chechen insurrection. Izrailov became a permanent correspondent for the Moscow newspaper, *Krest'yanskaya gazeta*, in which he published articles highlighting one principal issue: "the plundering of Chechnya by the local soviet and party leadership."[58]

In the spring of 1931, Izrailov was arrested and sentenced to ten years' imprisonment for "counter-revolutionary slander" and "connections with a gang." Released from prison three years later, he, together with other Chechen and Ingush intellectuals, sent a declaration of warning to the Soviet authorities predicting a "general popular uprising" if the government persisted in its repressive policies. Once again, Izrailov was arrested and sentenced to prison.

In January 1940, following a second release from prison, Izrailov sent the new first secretary of the Chechen–Ingush party, Bykov, a letter in which he declared: "For twenty years now, the Soviet authorities have been fighting my people, aiming to destroy them group by group: first the *kulaks*, then the mullahs and the 'bandits,' then the bourgeois-nationalists. I am sure now that the real object of this war is the annihilation of our nation as a whole. That is why I have decided to assume the leadership of my people in their struggle for liberation."[59] The Chechen nationalist tone of this letter is noteworthy.

Izrailov's insurrection spread rapidly, and by early February 1940 he controlled Galanchozh, Sayasan, Cheberlo, and part of Shatoi region. Most of his unit's weapons had been captured from punitive detachments sent against them. A national congress was convened in Galanchozh which proclaimed the establishment of a "Provisional Popular Revolutionary Government of Chechnya–Ingushetiya" with Hassan Izrailov as its head. What is especially interesting about Izrailov is that he was an intellectual with a party background – indeed, the regime appeared to try to cultivate him at times – and he had no connection with a Sufi *tariqat*. His case, therefore, suggests the emergence during

[58] Ibid., p. 181.   [59] Ibid., p. 182.

this period of a potentially modern variant of Chechen (or perhaps "Vainakh") nationalism.

In February 1942, at a time when the German invaders were still 500 kilometers away from the territory of Checheno-Ingushetiya, Mairbek Sheripov, the brother of a well-known Chechen revolutionary, led an insurrection in Shatoi and Itumkala and soon joined together with Izrailov, uniting the general staffs of the two rebel groups. Both guerrilla groups conducted repeated raids on Soviet government offices and kolkhozes. In June 1942, Izrailov and Sheripov issued a joint "Appeal to the Chechen–Ingush People" in which they stated that the Germans would be welcomed in the Caucasus as guests only on condition that they officially recognized Caucasian independence.[60]

During 1941–42, at a time when Soviet military aircraft were generally inactive on the German front, the regime pulled out all the stops in an effort to suppress the Izrailov–Sheripov uprising, which it appears to have seen as a treasonous effort to ensure a Nazi victory in the Caucasus. In the spring of 1942, devastating Soviet air raids were twice directed against Chechen–Ingush *auls* in the mountains (for example, at Shatoi, Itumkala, and Galanchozh), and, after the saturation bombing had concluded, there remained more dead than alive in the charred villages. Large numbers of elderly and children were killed in the bombing.[61]

The Chechens and the war against Germany

The Stalin regime's justification for the subsequent mass deportation of the Chechens in 1944 was that, "as an entire people," they had supported the Nazi invaders against the Soviet government. Certainly, the Chechens and other mountaineers had reason enough to detest the Soviet regime, and the Germans cunningly targeted these resentments, promising the mountaineers, for example, full religious freedom and the opening of mosques, the abolition of collective farms, and the opening of schools conducted in the native languages of the mountain peoples. Despite such overtures, the Chechens remained generally cool to the Nazi advances. As Alexander Nekrich has written: "It is undoubtedly true that a section of the native population [of Checheno-Ingushetiya], especially in the upland areas, was hostile toward Soviet rule. This, however, is not the same as saying that they took a friendly attitude

[60] Ibid., p. 183.
[61] Ibid.; Muzaev, *Chechenskaya respublika*, p. 155; R. Karcha, "Soviet Propaganda Concerning the Rehabilitated People of the Northern Caucasus," *Caucasian Review*, 8 (1959), 7.

toward the Nazi army."[62] This was because, as Nekrich has noted, the race-based ideas of the Nazis generally proved "alien and unattractive to the Mountain Peoples of the Caucasus."[63]

It is important also to stress that the Germans were in fact stopped before they could establish political control over Checheno-Ingushetiya. The only part of the republic which they occupied was the western border town of Malgobek, "where the population was Russian."[64] Other than in that locale, the sole Germans to set foot in Chechnya were a handful of saboteurs parachuted into the republic. Making use of Soviet-era archives, historian Nikolai Bugai has written, for example, of "one group made up of nine men under the command of *Abwehr* [German intelligence] agent O. Gube [the pseudonym of an Avar from Dagestan], which landed in the vicinity of the village of Berezhki, Galashkinskii district, on the night of August 25, 1942."[65]

This group of saboteurs succeeded in recruiting thirteen Chechens for their cause. Three more parachute drops totaling forty men in all took place during August and September 1942. Among those parachuted into the republic were two Chechens, Sh. Gaziev and K. Ganizhev. (They were among the few dozen Chechens and Ingush who had been captured by the German army and who had then agreed to join the German-sponsored North Caucasus Legion.) After the arrest of O. Gube and other members of his group by the Soviets, the remaining saboteurs eventually linked up with the insurgents under Hassan Izrailov. Many Chechens and Ingush, it should be noted, volunteered to fight against the Izrailov–Sheripov partisans and the small number of German-trained spies who had joined up with them. The advance of the Germans into the Caucasus was halted in late 1942, and on 24 December the Red Army went on the offensive; the Chechen border town of Malgobek was liberated from German occupation on 3 January 1943.[66]

If perhaps less than a hundred Chechens chose actively to assist the Germans – the partisan groups of Izrailov and Sheripov had, as we have seen, been formed due to domestic concerns before the advent of the Germans into the Caucasus region and therefore should not be considered actively pro-Nazi – there were thousands of Chechens who sought to join the Red Army. Before the Bolshevik Revolution, there had been no obligatory military service for Chechens, but voluntary service in the imperial army had been welcomed, and seven Ingush and two Chechens had in fact risen to the rank of general. During the First World War, the

[62] Nekrich, *Punished Peoples*, p. 52.   [63] Ibid., p. 38.
[64] Avtorkhanov, "Chechens and Ingush," p. 147.
[65] Bugai, "The Truth," 70–71.   [66] Ibid., 71–72.

Chechens and Ingush had each supplied a regiment of volunteers to the so-called Wild Division (Dikaya diviziya) of the imperial army.

Following the German invasion of the USSR, the Soviet government did not permit the creation of such native formations. Instead, Chechens and Ingush were drafted and incorporated as individuals into Russian detachments of the Red Army. This caused much suffering for the mountaineers, since many of them could not speak Russian, and because their commanding officers forced them to eat pork, a staple of the army diet which, of course, violated the dietary laws of observant Muslims.

On the advice of General S. Mollaev, a Chechen, the Soviet military finally permitted the Chechen–Ingush Republic to incorporate volunteers into two military divisions, but these divisions were not accepted into the regular Red Army. The two divisions were poorly equipped, and many of the soldiers went about barefoot. In early August 1942, one of these divisions found itself – lacking tanks or artillery support – confronting the German army as it advanced toward Stalingrad. "On 4 August 1942 German tanks rolled over the bodies of many soldiers from this division."[67]

In October 1942, Chechens joined the thousands of volunteers who poured out to help erect defensive barriers around the city of Groznyi, which was directly threatened by the German advance. The defense effort was led by V. I. Ivanov, first secretary of the republican party committee.[68] Between early December 1942 and early March 1943, Chechens and Ingush contributed 12 million rubles to the Soviet war effort.[69]

Because they could not speak Russian and were forced to eat pork, as well as suffering other indignities, many Chechens chose to desert from the Red Army. In March 1942, the drafting of Chechens and Ingush into the military was discontinued. Five months later, however, in August 1942, a decision was made to mobilize them on a voluntary basis. A second mobilization was carried out in January–February 1943 and a third in March of that year.[70]

According to archival documents of the USSR NKVD, 17,413 men joined the Red Army as a result of these three voluntary mobilizations. They served with distinction until they were ordered withdrawn from their units in February 1944, and were then sent off as special deportees, mostly to Central Asia.[71] During the time that they were permitted to serve in the Red Army, a number of Chechens distinguished themselves

[67] Avtorkhanov, "Chechens and Ingush," pp. 179–80.
[68] Nekrich, *Punished Peoples*, p. 56.   [69] Conquest, *Nation Killers*, p. 46.
[70] Ibid., pp. 56–57.   [71] Bugai, "The Truth," 67, 77.

by their bravery: "By 5 October 1942, the Chechens had won forty-four decorations in the Red Army – more than several larger nations."[72]

The fourth deportation of the Chechens – genocide

Some two years and four months *after* the mass deportation of all Chechens from their native land in February 1944, the government of the Russian Federation finally got around to publishing a "Law Concerning the Abolition of the Chechen–Ingush Autonomous Soviet Socialist Republic," dated 25 June 1946; the law was signed by the chairman and the secretary of the RSFSR Supreme Soviet. "During the Great Patriotic War," the law read, "when the peoples of the USSR were heroically defending the honor and independence of the Fatherland . . . many Chechens . . . at the instigation of German agents, joined volunteer units organized by the Germans and, together with German troops, engaged in armed struggle against units of the Red Army."[73]

This statement by the Russian republican government was, of course, a flagrant misrepresentation of what had occurred. It passed over developments and factors which have been noted in the preceding section of this chapter (pp. 56–61). The RSFSR law then proceeded to indict all Chechens and Ingush in blanket fashion: "[T]he main mass of the population of the Chechen–Ingush . . . ASSR," the law declared, "took no counter-action against these betrayers of the Fatherland." And the law concluded: "In connection with this, the Chechens . . . were resettled in other regions of the USSR." As for the Chechen–Ingush ASSR, it had been "abolished."[74]

Deportation had been a staple element of Soviet domestic policy since the advent of forced collectivization. From the 1930s through the 1950s, some 3.2 million Soviet citizens (3.4 million according to other data) had become victims of this policy.[75] Among the reasons for the deportation policy cited in party and NKVD archives are: "the desire to defuse ethnic tensions"; the goal of "stabiliz[ing] the political situation"; the meting out of punishment for "acts against Soviet authorities, and to liquidate banditry"; and "punishment for collaboration with the fascists."[76]

---

[72] Conquest, *Nation Killers*, p. 46.
[73] Ibid., p. 47. On the forced deportation of Chechens and other "punished peoples" under Stalin, see Svetlana Alieva, ed., *Tak eto bylo*, 3 vols. (Moscow: Insan, 1993), and N. F. Bugai, ed., *L. Beriya–I. Stalinu: "Soglasno vashemu ukasaniyu . . ."* (Moscow: AIRO-XX, 1995).
[74] The law was published in both *Pravda* and *Izvestiya* on 26 June 1946.
[75] Bugai, "The Truth," 81; Nekrich, *Punished Peoples*, p. 98.
[76] Bugai, "The Truth," 67.

One suspects that it was "punishment for acts against Soviet authorities" extending throughout the communist period from 1917 to 1944, and especially the Izrailov and Sheripov insurrections, which motivated Stalin and his followers to deport the Chechens. As Nikita Khrushchev admitted in the course of his "secret speech" of 1956, there were no military considerations necessitating the deportation of the Chechens and other mountaineers in 1944, "because the enemy was being rolled back everywhere under the blows of the Red Army."[77]

The genesis of the deportation plan

On the basis of research conducted in the party and the NKVD archives, former Politburo member Aleksandr N. Yakovlev – a leading reformer in the Gorbachev leadership – has noted that the plan to deport the Chechens and Ingush from their historic homeland began to take shape during the autumn of 1943. This brutal operation was given the codename "Lentil" (*chechevitsa*, presumably a play on the word "Chechen") by the NKVD. In October 1943, a brigade of NKVD officials headed by deputy people's commissar B. Kobulov traveled to Checheno-Ingushetiya, where they compiled material on "anti-Soviet actions" which had occurred there from the first days of Soviet power in the North Caucasus to the time of their visit. A written report concerning the situation in the republic was then submitted to Lavrentii Beriya. On 13 November, Beriya wrote in his own hand: "To Comrade Kobulov. A very good report."[78]

In Kobulov's report, it was remarked that there were thirty-eight religious sects active in the republic and that the leaders of these sects were considered by the local populace to be saints. More than 20,000 persons were said to belong to these sects, which were alleged to engage in anti-Soviet activity. The sects were said to be aiding both local "bandits" and the Germans, and they were accused of summoning the populace to an armed struggle with Soviet power. As can be seen, the deportation operation was to be aimed in particular at the Sufi Muslim brotherhoods of Checheno-Ingushetiya. Four of Beriya's deputies – Serov, Appolonov, Kruglov, and Kobulov – were placed in charge of carrying out Operation Lentil, and, on 18 November, Beriya confirmed their plan.[79]

At first, the regime apparently intended to deport the Chechens, Ingush, Balkars, and Karachai – those peoples of the North Caucasus selected for severe retribution – to areas of western Siberia. In Nov-

[77] Nekrich, *Punished Peoples*, pp. 93–94.
[78] Yakovlev, *Po moshcham i elei*, pp. 121–22.   [79] Ibid., pp. 122–23.

ember 1943, an expanded meeting of the NKVD administrations of Altai and Krasnoyarsk territories and of Omsk and Novosibirsk oblasts was held, at which plans were made to deport approximately 235,000–240,000 persons to those regions. This plan was finalized in mid-December 1943, but by then it had been decided to deport the bulk of those arrested to Central Asia.[80]

At the end of 1943, NKVD and NKGB (another section of the secret police) forces entered the Karachai autonomous region and the Balkar part of the Kabarda–Balkariya Autonomous Republic and deported the population of these two areas.[81] Astonishingly, the Chechens appear not to have been informed of these operations and to have been caught off guard.[82] The breakdown of communications and the general chaos obtaining during the war were probably the reasons for this.

On 31 January 1944, the State Defense Committee approved a decree on the deportation of all Chechens and Ingush to the Kazakh and Kirgiz SSRs. The overall direction of the operation was put in the hands of Lavrentii Beriya, Politburo member and NKVD chieftain. His principal deputies were to be B. Kobulov and I. Serov. In his report to the State Defense Committee of 7 March 1944, Beriya noted that 19,000 operatives of the NKVD–NKGB and SMERSh (Death to Spies) and up to 100,000 officers and soldiers of the troops of the NKVD had participated in the deportation of the Chechens, Ingush, Kalmyks, and Karachai, 650,000 persons in all.[83] According to historian Alexander Nekrich, in addition to the huge number of NKVD troops, "three armies, one of them a tank army, were deployed in Checheno-Ingushetiya a few months before the deportations." Convoy guards and border guards also took part in the operation.[84]

As in the 1925 campaign to disarm Chechnya, the Soviet leadership chose to combine massive, overwhelming force with trickery and blinding speed. During the second half of January and the first half of February 1944, special detachments of the NKVD began to arrive in Checheno-Ingushetiya in American Studebaker trucks. The mountains were occupied de facto and each *aul* was supplied with its own garrison. Why were the troops there? Local newspapers explained that they had arrived to help repair roads and bridges and to carry out mountain maneuvers.[85] The populace was apparently fooled.

On 20 February, Lavrentii Beriya and his top NKVD lieutenants

[80] Bugai, "The Truth," 73.   [81] Karcha, "Genocide," 74.

[82] Conquest, *Nation Killers*, p. 102.

[83] *Iosif Stalin–Lavrentiyu Berii: "Ikh nado deportirovat!"* (Moscow: Druzhba narodov, 1992), p. 106; Bugai, "The Truth," 74.

[84] Nekrich, *Punished Peoples*, pp. 108–09.

[85] Avtorkhanov, "Chechens and Ingush," pp. 184–85.

arrived in Groznyi to take personal charge of the deportation. In his report of 22 February to the State Defense Committee, Beriya noted that the operation would begin at dawn on 23 February. "[I]t is proposed," he wrote, "to encircle the districts and to prevent the exit of populace to the territory of inhabited points. The populace will be invited to a gathering." Given the specific features of the mountain districts, Beriya thought that a total of eight days should be allotted for the deportation of all Chechens and Ingush. Over the first three days, he foresaw, "the operation will be completed in the plains and foothill districts and, partially, in certain settlements of the mountain districts containing more than 300,000 people." The next five days would be taken up with getting at and then deporting 150,000 persons living in the less accessible mountain regions.[86]

The "special operation" begins

February the 23rd dawned – "a fine, clear day"[87] – and in the city of Groznyi and throughout the republic the populace were summoned to help celebrate the twenty-sixth anniversary of the founding of the Workers' and Peasants' Army. In Groznyi, according to an eyewitness account: "[T]he deputy commander of the [Red Army] regiment appeared on the tribune. In a brief and dry speech he announced to the inhabitants the sentence of the Communist Party and the Soviet government." Since the populace of the republic had given aid to the Nazi armies, he said, the Communist Party and the Soviet government had decided to carry out a resettlement of all Chechens and Ingush. "[Y]our resistance," he warned, "is futile, as the regional center is surrounded by armed troops."[88]

The stunned and terrified crowd, headed by local officials, was then marched in fours to assembly points, where they were loaded onto trucks lacking seats or heating and taken to railroad stations. In some instances, women were allowed to go home to fetch a few small items for the journey. The local officials who had led the procession to the assembly points were themselves to be sent off with the others.[89]

In some settlements, the men had been invited to observe demonstrations of skill in horseback riding.[90] Instead, they were packed into trucks and taken off. Settlements in which the arrests were scheduled for the evening saw Red Army soldiers build blazing fires in the village squares, where singing and dancing then ensued. Once everyone had assembled in the squares, the men were immediately placed under arrest. "Some of

[86] In *Iosif Stalin*, pp. 101–02.   [87] Karcha, "Genocide," 80.   [88] Ibid.
[89] Ibid., 81–82; *Iosif Stalin*, pp. 105–06.   [90] Nekrich, *Punished Peoples*, p. 109.

the Chechens had weapons, and there was some shooting. But resistance was rapidly eliminated. The men were locked up in barns . . . The whole operation was effected in two or three hours. Women were not arrested but were told to pack their belongings and get ready to leave the next day with their children."[91]

In some regions, the populace was directly murdered. Thus the entire population of the village of Khaibakh – more than 700 persons – was burned alive on the orders of NKVD colonel Gveshiani. The correspondence between Beriya and Gveshiani has been preserved; the secret police chieftain warmly congratulated his subordinate for having committed the atrocity.[92] In other villages, people were drowned, shot, or killed with hand grenades.[93] The inhabitants of remote mountain villages were required to traipse for nearly two days along frozen mountain paths under NKVD escort. All the sick and the elderly were ordered left behind and were then put to death; those who lagged behind on the mountain paths were beaten with rifle butts, while persons too weak to continue were shot and their bodies left behind in the snow.[94]

All resistance by the Chechens was easily overcome. On the first day of the operation, 23 February, Beriya reported to the State Defense Committee that there had been "six attempts at resistance" and that 94,741 persons had been carted off by 11 a.m. On 1 March, he noted that 2,016 anti-Soviet elements had been arrested and that 20,072 firearms had been confiscated.[95]

A total of 6,000 motor vehicles were used in the vast North Caucasus deportation operation.[96] Trucks were filled with men who had been arrested the previous day and with women and children, and they were then transferred to freight cars at Groznyi and other rail centers. Only women were allowed to take some hand-luggage with them.[97]

The NKVD arrest order applied not only to all Chechens and Ingush living in the republic but also to all those dwelling within the borders of the USSR. About 30,000 Chechens living in northwestern Dagestan, for example, were rounded up and deported.[98] Similarly, Chechens and Ingush living in the city of Vladikavkaz in North Ossetiya were rounded up. Even those Chechens and Ingush incarcerated in NKVD-run

---

[91] Avtorkhanov, "Chechens and Ingush," pp. 184–85.
[92] For the Beriya–Gveshiani correspondence, see Zaindi Shakhbiev, *Sud'ba chechenoingushskogo naroda* (Moscow: Rossiya molodaya, 1996), p. 251.
[93] Muzaev, *Chechenskaya respublika*, p. 155.
[94] Yakovlev, *Po moshcham i elei*, pp. 128–29.   [95] *Iosif Stalin*, pp. 102–06.
[96] Bugai, "The Truth," 74.   [97] Avtorkhanov, "Chechens and Ingush," p. 185
[98] N. F. Bugai, "K voprosu o deportatsii narodov SSSR v 30–40kh godakh," *Istoriya SSSR*, 6 (1989), 140.

concentration camps were ordered to be deported.[99] Interestingly, Beriya decided to make use of the deportation operation to rid the region of some bothersome ethnic Russians as well: "village activists from among Russians in those districts which have a Russian population" were also to be sent away with the Chechens and Ingush.[100]

Exempted from deportation were Chechen and Ingush women married to representatives of non-punished peoples. Women of Russian nationality who were married to Chechens and Ingush were, on the other hand, ordered to be deported unless they agreed to divorce their husbands. In the latter case, they were permitted to remain behind in Checheno-Ingushetiya.[101]

The hunt for Chechens and the other peoples chosen for punishment proceeded relentlessly. In May 1944, Beriya issued a directive ordering the NKVD to scour the Caucasus region for representatives of these peoples, "not leaving out a single one." A total of 4,146 Chechens, Ingush, and others were unearthed in Dagestan, Azerbaijan, Georgia, Krasnodar krai, and Rostov and Astrakhan' oblasts. In April 1945, Beriya was informed that "2,741 Chechens had been deported from the Georgian SSR, 21 from the Azerbaijan SSR, and 121 from Krasnodar territory."[102] In Moscow, two Chechens managed to avoid deportation.[103]

All Chechens serving in the Red Army were ordered removed from their units, discharged from the military, and sent off to Central Asia. An order signed by I. Pavlov, NKVD troop commander for the Third Ukrainian Front, for example, commanded that all Chechens, Ingush, and so forth be turned over to the special settlement departments of the Kazakh SSR in Alma-Ata. Many Chechens and other deported peoples who had been serving in the military were first assembled in Murom and in Novosibirsk before being sent south. Some Chechen military personnel were kept in the Russian Federation to do forced labor, for example, to cut timber in Kostroma oblast'.[104]

The leaders of Operation Lentil – NKVD generals Appolonov, Kobulov, Kruglov, and Serov, plus People's Commissar of State Security Merkulov, and Abakumov, the head of SMERSh – were all awarded the order of Suvorov First Class for successfully carrying out the mass arrest of the Chechens and Ingush.[105]

[99] Bugai, "The Truth," 77.   [100] *Iosif Stalin*, pp. 101–02.
[101] Yakovlev, *Po moshcham i elei*, p. 123.   [102] Bugai, "The Truth," 77–78.
[103] Nekrich, *Punished Peoples*, p. 60.   [104] Bugai, "The Truth," 77.
[105] Yakovlev, *Po moshcham i elei*, p. 126.

Loading the freight cars

A vast number of freight cars were needed in order to deport the Chechens and Ingush to their various destinations in Central Asia. The Transportation Department of the USSR NKVD prepared the necessary special trains on schedule. From 23 January to 13 March, the USSR People's Commissariat of Railways was directed to deliver 350 freight cars a day; from 24 to 28 February, the figure was 400 cars a day. In all, 152 trains were formed, consisting of 100 cars each, for an overall total of 14,200 freight cars and 1,000 flat cars. Officially each deported family was permitted to take 500 kilograms of belongings with them, but in fact many seem to have been able just to grab a few small items.[106]

The belongings that the Chechens were unable to take with them "were appropriated by those who carried out the deportation – Beriya's [NKVD] agents and the soldiers assigned to the deportation operation."[107] In his report of 1 March to the State Defense Committee, Beriya noted that in Checheno-Ingushetiya 478,479 persons – almost half a million persons – had been loaded onto 180 special trains, of which 159 had already been sent off to their destinations.[108]

According to a report of People's Commissar Mil'shtein, commander of the NKVD Third Administration, about forty to forty-five persons were loaded into each freight car, with 40–50 percent of them being children. Due to the heavy percentage of small children, this degree of "compactness," Mil'shtein concluded smugly, was "fully expedient." In his report of 18 March, Mil'shtein noted that 194 special trains had departed, containing 521,247 Chechens, Ingush, and Balkars, and that a total of 12,525 freight cars had been used in the operation.[109]

A few Chechens elude the net

Some highland Chechens managed to elude the NKVD arrest net. An 8 July 1944 order from Lavrentii Beriya ordered the "liquidation of the remnants of Chechen bands" which had concealed themselves in Georgia. A large force was subsequently mobilized for this purpose.[110] Three years after the deportation, guerrilla fighting was still reported to be continuing in the higher mountains of Chechnya, Ingushetiya, and eastern Ossetiya. The movement's leader was Sheikh Qureish Belhorev, who was captured only in 1947. (Amazingly, he was not shot but merely

[106] Bugai, "The Truth," 73.
[107] Nekrich, *Punished Peoples*, p. 124. (These figures appear to differ somewhat from those cited in the previous paragraph.)
[108] *Iosif Stalin*, p. 103.   [109] Ibid., 115.   [110] Ibid., pp. 106–07.

given a ten-year prison sentence.) The regime sent in several NKVD divisions to suppress the rebel movement, but only by the middle of the 1950s did it succeed in coping with partisan detachments operating in the mountains.[111]

Riding the death trains

People's Commissar Mil'shtein, commander of the NKVD Third Administration, noted one annoying problem connected with sending hundreds of thousands of mountaineers off in packed freight cars, namely, "the impossibility of carrying out sanitation work" in the cars, as a result of which "there occurred cases of typhus."[112] An Ingush communist official, Kh. Arapiev, has recalled the agony of the journey to Central Asia: "Packed in overcrowded cattle cars, without light or water, we spent almost a month heading to an unknown destination . . . Typhus broke out. No treatment was available . . . The dead were buried in snow that was black from locomotive soot during brief stops at remote, uninhabited sidings next to the track."[113]

The local authorities tried to localize the typhus epidemic to the Chechens and Ingush "in order to get rid of them in a 'natural' way."[114] The local populace of settlements at which the special trains stopped were strictly forbidden to assist the dying by giving them water or medicine. In some cars, 50 percent of the imprisoned Chechens and Ingush were said to have perished.

Conditions upon arrival

According to historian Nikolai Bugai, in 1944, a total of 239,768 Chechens and 78,479 Ingush arrived in the Kazakh SSR, while 70,089 Chechens and 2,278 Ingush arrived in Kirgiz SSR. Much smaller numbers were sent to other Central Asian republics: 175 Chechens and 159 Ingush to the Uzbek SSR, and 62 Chechens and 14 Ingush to the Tajik SSR. Several thousand Chechens and Ingush who had been cashiered from the Red Army, together with their families, were later added to their number.[115] Relatively small numbers of Chechens were also scattered about Russian regions of the RSFSR: in Kostroma oblast', 1,183 Chechens, Ingush, and Karachai were required to work in the

[111] Alexandre Bennigsen and S. Enders Wimbush, *Mystics and Commissars* (Berkeley, CA: University of California Press, 1985), p. 29; Muzaev, *Chechenskaya respublika*, p. 155.
[112] *Iosif Stalin*, p. 115.   [113] In Bugai, "The Truth," 76.
[114] Avtorkhanov, "Chechens and Ingush," p. 186.   [115] Bugai, "K voprosu," 140.

timber industries of Galich and Bui;[116] at Krasnoyarsk in western
Siberia, about 4,000 Chechens were incarcerated in forced labor
concentration camps;[117] 585 Chechens and 79 Karachai were sent to
work in Ivanovo oblast'.[118]

The conditions awaiting the Chechens upon their arrival in Central
Asia were often inadequate to support life. According to one researcher:
"The most fearful and irremediable blow to the Chechen–Ingush people
was struck in the first two to three years, when starvation and the most
dreadful diseases obliged them to bury tens and hundreds of thousands
of their fellow tribespeople in the steppes of Central Asia."[119] Local and
government bodies failed to provide deportees newly arrived in the
Kirgiz SSR with the food allowances due them; the result was "the
increasing frequency of deaths from undernourishment and infectious
diseases among the resettled population."[120]

In the Kazakh SSR, even four years after the deportation operation,
there were 118,259 special settlers counted as being "in extreme need in
regard to food." It was reported that "thousands" of children had died
of undernourishment.[121] In a letter to the NKVD administration of
Kostroma oblast', M. Kuznetsov, a high-ranking NKVD official, com-
plained about "the bad state of living conditions" of Chechens and
other peoples who had been sent to logging organizations run by the
USSR People's Commissariat of the Timber Industry.[122]

In the sphere of housing, the situation was consistently abysmal. As of
1 September 1944, only 5,000 out of 31,000 special-settler families in
Kirgiziya had been provided with housing. In the Kameninskii district of
Kirgiziya, only eighteen apartments had been prepared for 900 families,
that is, a total of one apartment for every fifty families.[123] By September
1946, the situation in Kirgiziya remained appalling: only 4,973 out of
31,000 families had been provided with permanent housing.[124]

In the Akmolinsk oblast' of the Kazakh SSR, only 28 out of a planned
1,000 homes had been built for the special settlers by July 1946. By that
same date, in Taldy-Kurgan oblast', only 23 out of 1,400 had been
erected, and in Dzhambul' and Karaganda oblasts "no one even started
to work on housing construction for the special deportees."[125] Only
some fourteen years after the deportation, in 1958, had a reported 93.8
percent of all families deported to Kazakhstan and Kirgizstan (now

---

[116] Bugai, "The Truth," 77.
[117] Conquest, *Nation Killers*, pp. 103–04.   [118] Bugai, "The Truth," 77.
[119] A. Kh. Dudaev, dissertation (1964), Faculty of Law, Moscow University, cited in
    Nekrich, *Punished Peoples*, p. 118.
[120] Nekrich, *Punished Peoples*, p. 125.
[121] Ibid.   [122] Bugai, "The Truth," 79.   [123] Nekrich, *Punished Peoples*, p. 122.
[124] Bugai, "The Truth," 79.   [125] Ibid.

Kyrgyzstan) been supplied with permanent housing, "but by then it was time to leave again."[126]

How many died?

It is, of course, impossible to determine precisely how many Chechens died as a result of their forced deportation to the Kazakh and Kirgiz SSRs, but we can attempt an educated estimate. Citing figures from the NKVD's Department of Special Settlements, historian Nikolai Bugai writes that "a total of 144,704 (23.7 percent) of all the deported Chechens, Ingush, Balkars (1944), and Karachai (1943) died in the period from 1944 through 1948; that figure includes 101,036 Chechens, Ingush, and Balkars who died in the Kazakh SSR."[127] The Chechens, it should be noted, continued to undergo exceptionally harsh treatment until Stalin's death in 1953, and many more of them must have died in the period 1949–53, but, even if one were to stipulate a figure of 23.7 percent of the Chechen populace dead during the deportation years, it would represent more than a double decimation of their total population – raw genocide by anyone's definition.

Other specialists have sought to determine the death toll by examining Soviet census figures. The well-known ethnographer Valerii Tishkov and his coauthors (hereafter to be referred to as "the Tishkov group"), in their study *The Chechen Crisis*, have noted that the officially reported population of Chechens increased from 400,344 at the time of the all-union census of 1939 to a mere 419,000 at the time of the all-union census of 1959. Between 1926 and 1937 – an eleven-year period – the number of Chechens had, by contrast, increased from 318,373 to 435,922. Between 1959 and 1970 – also an eleven-year period – they increased from 419,000 to 612,674. And the Tishkov group concludes: "Indirect [kosvennye] losses of growth from the deportation constituted about 200,000 among the Chechens."[128]

In similar fashion, Robert Conquest, in his pioneering study *The Nation Killers*, observed that, in the period between 1939 and 1959, the Soviet population as whole grew by 22.3 percent, while that of the Chechens increased by a mere 2.5 percent. Between the censuses of 1926 and 1939, he noted, the Chechen population, by contrast, had grown by 28 percent.[129] Alexander Nekrich reached similar conclusions after examining the available Soviet census data. If the Chechen population had experienced "normal" growth between 1939 and 1959, he

---

[126] Nekrich, *Punished Peoples*, p. 122.   [127] Bugai, "The Truth," 67.
[128] Tishkov, et al., *Chechenskii krizis*, pp. 8–10.
[129] Conquest, *Nation Killers*, p. 160.

believed, it would have reached at least 590,000 by 1959 (instead, it numbered 419,000 – 171,000 less than it should have been). Nekrich stressed that his figures were "closer to minimal than maximal estimates."[130] It seems obvious from the Soviet census data that a demographic cataclysm struck the Chechens between 1939 and 1959.

Life in the "special settlements"

Conditions were exceedingly severe for the Chechens and other residents of the special settlements. They had to register their addresses once a month with the special registration office of the MVD. No deportees were allowed to leave their places of residence without permission from the MVD commandant. Chechens were not permitted to travel beyond a radius of three kilometers from their places of residence and, in 1948, the rules were made even harsher.[131]

In general, the special deportees – Chechens and non-Chechens alike – were assigned to do hard, exhausting physical labor. The 645,000 special settlers who had been sent to Kazakhstan and Kirgizstan were assigned to 4,036 kolkhozes, 254 sovkhozes, and 167 towns and workers' settlements, where they found work at 2,500 industrial enterprises.[132] The speaker of the Russian Supreme Soviet from 1991 to 1993, Ruslan Khasbulatov, an ethnic Chechen, has recalled that his mother and her four children were sent to a small village (Poludin) in the north of Kazakhstan, where they lived among other deportees – Volga Germans, Koreans, and Tatars – as well as among many Russians.

"Our exile," he remembers, "lasted for about ten years. I cannot recall a single incident of ethnic conflict . . . We were all in the same boat, living in equal poverty, with shortages of everything, particularly bread . . . Like other young boys, I did all I could to help mother and my family in their everyday chores. Mother worked as a milkmaid on the local collective farm. I can remember drawing buckets of water from a deep well, watering the cows, cleaning the cowsheds, looking after the calves, digging potatoes, and gathering loads of firewood . . . I stayed in the village attending to my peasant chores until I was thirteen . . . Following Stalin's death we moved to live closer to our relations, who lived not far from Alma-Ata . . . I had to quit school after the eighth grade."[133]

In addition to performing difficult agricultural work, the deportees

---

[130] Nekrich, *Punished Peoples*, p. 138.
[131] Ibid., pp. 118–19.   [132] Ibid., p. 122.
[133] Ruslan Khasbulatov, *The Struggle for Russia* (London and New York: Routledge, 1993), pp. 3–4.

"also formed a pool for labor on canals and railway construction. The railway from Frunze [now Bishkek, the capital of Kyrgyzstan] to Rìbach'e on Lake Issyk-kul, for instance, a difficult task involving cuttings through the gorges, was carried out almost entirely by Chechen, Ingush, and Tatar labor."[134] Detesting the work to which they were forcibly subjected, the Chechens, like other special settlers, attempted to avoid it whenever possible. In 1944, it was reported that 85,000 out of 219,665 able-bodied persons resettled in Kazakhstan were not in fact working.[135]

Alexander Nekrich has termed the process to which the Chechens and other deportees were subjected "pauperization." "[I]n 1943 and 1944," he concludes, "a million people were subjected not so much to expropriation as to pauperization. During the first years in the special settlements they were reduced to the status of disenfranchised and persecuted beggars."[136]

The deportation, as Ruslan Khasbulatov's above-cited memoir shows, was especially hard on children. Many children perished due to malnourishment and disease, but those who survived, in a number of cases, were deprived of schooling. In 1944, in the Kazakh SSR, only 16,000 out of 50,323 school-age children of special settlers attended school, while in the Kirgiz SSR the figure was 6,643 out of 21,015. Instruction, furthermore, was not conducted in the native language of the children, even though many – and especially the Chechens – did not know Russian.[137]

The Chechens incarcerated in Stalin's GULAG lived a particularly brutalizing existence. In Krasnoyarsk in October 1954 – during the year following Stalin's death – we find 4,000 Chechens escaping from one concentration camp into the taiga. In February 1955, it was reported that the Soviet police had tracked down and killed some 2,000 of them, but that the remainder had successfully hidden themselves in the taiga.[138] In the notorious Kolyma labor camps in the Russian Far East, there occurred a mass refusal of several hundred Chechens to go to work.[139]

One result of the deportation which was clearly unwanted by the regime was that the Sufi brotherhoods, actively spread by the Chechens and Ingush, expanded into areas of Muslim Central Asia, particularly into Kazakhstan and Uzbekistan.[140]

---

[134] Conquest, *Nation Killers*, p. 105.   [135] Nekrich, *Punished Peoples*, p. 124.
[136] Ibid.   [137] Ibid., p. 126.
[138] Karcha, "Genocide," 82–83; Nekrich, *Punished Peoples*, p. 120.
[139] Conquest, *Nation Killers*, pp. 103–04.
[140] Bennigsen and Wimbush, *Mystics and Commissars*, p. 30.

Chechnya officially wiped off the map

Once the Chechens and Ingush had been deported in 1944, the communist authorities began actively to redraw the map of the region. The Chechen–Ingush ASSR simply disappeared into a memory hole – as did the Chechens and Ingush themselves – to be replaced by a supra-ethnic territory called Groznyi (Groznenskaya) oblast'. In order to expunge all memory of the Chechens and Ingush, the party committee for the region decided on 19 June 1944 to rename most districts and district centers of the region.[141] Chechen-sounding names were supplanted by Russian ones: Achkoi-Martan district thus became Nove-sel'skii; Urus-Martan became Krasnoarmeiskii; Shalinskii became Mezhdurechenskii; and so on.[142]

The Soviet republic of Georgia – the home republic of Stalin and Beriya – was significantly enriched at the expense of the deported peoples. Thus the main Karachai and Balkar regions to the north and east of Mount Elbrus were annexed to Georgia, as was a part of the southern region of former Checheno-Ingushetiya. As a result of this "fattening" process, Georgia grew from 69,300 to 76,400 square kilometers. North Ossetiya was also rewarded, growing from 6,200 square kilometers to 9,200, while Dagestan increased from 35,000 to 38,200.[143]

Following the forced expulsion of all Chechens and Ingush in February 1944, the regime had to provide a replacement work force for those who had been abruptly removed. Since 35 percent of the population of predeportation Checheno-Ingushetiya had been ethnic Russians (while 50 percent had been Chechens), these Russians provided a demographic base for the newly created Groznyi oblast'. Russian students studying in the city of Groznyi were sent out to the collective farms to take care of livestock until new immigrants from Kursk and Orel regions could arrive.[144] After the livestock had been evacuated from Chechen mountain *auls*, the villages "were set on fire in order to deprive the 'bandits' [who had escaped the arrest net] of their means of

---

[141] Bugai, "The Truth," 79.   [142] Nekrich, *Punished Peoples*, pp. 59–60.
[143] Conquest, *Nation Killers*, pp. 68, 75. For a detailed listing of the affected areas, see "Protokol no. 67 zasedaniya Prezidiyuma Tsentral'nogo Komiteta KPSS ot 5–6 yanvarya 1957 goda," TSKhSD (Tsentr Khraneniya Sovremennoi Dokumentatsii [Center for the Preservation of Contemporary Documentation]), fond 89, perechen' 61, delo 7, Archives of the Soviet Communist Party and Soviet State, State Archival Service of Russia (Rosarkhiv) and the Hoover Institution on War, Revolution, and Peace, distributed by Chadwyck-Healey, Inc., 1101 King Street, Alexandria, VA 22314.
[144] Conquest, *Nation Killers*, p. 102; Avtorkhanov, "Chechens and Ingush," p. 185.

subsistence. For days one could see the *auls* burning in the moun-tains."[145]

After having been plundered by Beriya's NKVD troops, the homes of the Chechens situated in the lowlands were taken over by new settlers. On the orders of the authorities, tens of thousands of Russians, Ukrainians, Avars, Dargins, and Ossetians were resettled in Groznyi oblast'.[146] Staro-Yurtovskii district, for example, received 811 families from Kizlyar; Shatoi district got 81 Russian and 140 Dagestani families; Gudermes district received 2,800 new settlers; and so on.[147]

Despite this influx of new populace, the settlement of many of the villages and farm communities of the former republic proceeded with difficulty. "Houses and farm buildings abandoned by persons driven from their homes became dilapidated. Formerly there had been 28,375 farms in the territory of the Chechen–Ingush ASSR . . . [B]y May 1945, there were only 10,200 farms functioning there. The numbers of settlers . . . totaled only forty percent of the number of deportees. Twenty-two villages remained empty, and twenty villages were only partially re-settled." In late 1945, the first party secretary of Groznyi oblast', P. Cheplakov, proposed that an additional 5,000 households be transferred to the area from such places as Tambov, Penza, Saratov, and Yaro-slavl'.[148]

The livestock which had belonged to the Chechens and the Ingush was turned over to kolkhozes in other regions of the country, in particular, to farms in the Ukrainian SSR, Stavropol' krai, Voronezh, Kursk, and Orel oblasts. These operations were accompanied by enormous losses of livestock, which were reported to be "dying in large numbers, primarily due to exhaustion."[149] Many of the skills involved in highland livestock herding and in the cultivation of terraced land in the mountains which had been developed by the Chechens and Ingush over the centuries were lost forever.

The region's petroleum industry was also crippled by the expulsion of the Chechens and Ingush. Prior to 1944, about 4,000 representatives of these peoples – cadres who had been trained in the 1930s – had worked in engineering-technical jobs in the oil industry. Their abrupt removal led to a marked decline in the rate of petroleum extraction. The loss of experienced Chechen and Ingush drillers had a particularly negative consequence.[150]

---

[145] Avtorkhanov, "Chechens and Ingush," p. 185.
[146] Nekrich, *Punished Peoples*, p. 60.   [147] Bugai, "The Truth," 79.
[148] Ibid., 80.   [149] Ibid.   [150] Ibid.

The Chechens return home

Following the death of Stalin in 1953 and the subsequent removal and execution of Lavrentii Beriya, a year of uncertainty passed before the position of the special settlers began to be clarified. In July 1954, the USSR Council of Ministers issued a resolution "On the Lifting of Certain Restrictions on the Legal Status of Resettled Persons." Those deemed to be employed doing socially useful labor were henceforth permitted to live freely in the republic or region where they found themselves.

Registration with the MVD became an annual rather than a monthly requirement. All children under ten years of age were dropped from the registration list for special settlers. Young men and women over the age of sixteen were taken off the register if they were enrolled in educational institutions. These liberalizations were, however, accompanied by sporadic returns to a hard line. Thus, for example, a decree of the USSR Council of Ministers of 26 June 1955 ordered "the intensification of mass agitation and cultural-educational work among resettled persons."[151]

In May 1955, the newspaper *Kazakhstanskaya pravda* announced that it had become possible for residents of the Kazakh SSR to subscribe to a new republican weekly newspaper, to be published in the Chechen language. In November, it was reported that a Chechen–Ingush Art Theater had come into existence. In December 1956, Alma-Ata Radio announced that, in 1957, the Kazakh State Literary Publishing House would produce works in Chechen and Ingush.[152] While representing a step forward for the Chechens, these developments also seemed to be an attempt by the regime to keep the Chechens and Ingush firmly rooted in Kazakhstan.

As early as 1954, however, some Chechens and Ingush began to attempt illegally to "force their way" back onto the territory of their former republic. They would be discovered, removed, and arrested, but new Chechens and Ingush would then appear in their place.[153] Beginning in 1955, Chechens began to disappear from Central Asia in large numbers and then to reappear in Groznyi oblast', demanding that their former homes be returned. Throughout 1956 – and especially following the reformist Twentieth Party Congress under Khrushchev – "the unauthorized return of Chechens, Ingush, and Karachai increased in

---

[151] Nekrich, *Punished Peoples*, pp. 129–30.
[152] Conquest, *Nation Killers*, pp. 141, 143.
[153] Nekrich, *Punished Peoples*, p. 135.

frequency, and nothing could force the returnees to leave. In a number of cases incidents involving bloodshed and violence occurred."[154]

Thousands of Chechens gathered at railway stations to purchase tickets back to their homeland, but an official order was issued not to sell them tickets. In spite of all such warnings and numerous appeals, an estimated 25,000–30,000 Chechens and Ingush returned during 1956. When they would not be permitted to take possession of the homes in which they had formerly lived, they would make dugouts next to them and settle in, and, in an immensely symbolic move, they also brought back the remains of relatives who had died in Central Asia, so that they could find rest in the land of their ancestors.[155]

At first, the USSR Council of Ministers attempted to forbid this repatriation process. A bitter dispute broke out within the top Soviet leadership over whether or not the Chechens and Ingush should be permitted to return to their home territory. An attempt was made to organize the mass recruitment of Chechens and Ingush for work in other parts of the USSR, but the Chechens and Ingush spurned such proposals. The head of the Groznyi oblast' Communist Party, A. I. Yakovlev, vehemently opposed permitting the mountaineers to return, but Kovalenko, chairman of the oblast' executive committee and a reformer, favored both their return and the restoration of the Chechen–Ingush ASSR.

Struggling against the inevitable, the party leadership attempted to persuade the Chechens and Ingush to agree to the establishment of an autonomous republic for them, but located in Uzbekistan, with its capital being situated in the city of Chimkent. This proposal, too, found no takers; then the party leadership tried a new tack: the Chechens and Ingush, they said, would be permitted to return to the Caucasus, but the site of their republic would now be moved, and its capital would henceforth be not Groznyi, but Kizlyar near the Terek River in Dagestan.[156] This proposal, too, elicited no support. As in their earlier return from Ottoman Turkey following the uprising of 1877–78, the strong-willed Chechens were bent on returning to the land of their forefathers, and it appeared that nothing could stop them.

Faced with this tenacity, the regime was forced reluctantly to capitulate. A resolution of the party Central Committee of 24 November 1956 demonstrates the leadership's grudging acceptance of reality. "[I]t is impossible," the resolution noted, "not to take into consideration that fact that recently, especially after the Twentieth Congress of the CPSU and the removal of the Kalmyks, Karachai, Balkars, Chechens, and

---

[154] Ibid., p. 131.   [155] Ibid., p. 135.   [156] Ibid., pp. 134–35.

Ingush from the status of special settlers, strivings to return to their native places and to reestablish their national autonomies are growing stronger and stronger. Despite the existing interdiction, thousands of former special settlers are willfully returning to their former places of residence, which is creating great difficulties in providing them with housing and with employment."[157]

Confronted with this volatile situation, the Central Committee resolved to correct the "injustice" which had earlier been committed against the Chechen and Ingush peoples and to "reestablish their national autonomy." Despite this concession, however, the Central Committee also sought to induce as many Chechens and Ingush as possible not to return to their homeland: "The party and soviet organs of the republics and oblasts in which at the present time . . . Chechens and Ingush live should encourage the adhesion [zakreplenie] of a part of this populace to the place where they currently live, undertaking measures to improve their economic and work situations and to draw them into active social and political life."[158] Once again, the regime was moved by fatuous hopes.

The Central Committee resolution also insisted that those Chechens and Ingush who were to return to their homeland should do so in phased fashion, over the period 1957–60, "in an organized manner in small groups." This phased return would also create less havoc at the kolkhozes, sovkhozes, and enterprises in Kazakhstan and Kirgizstan where they were currently employed. This hope for a phased return also proved to be wishful thinking. Instead of the planned-for 100,000 repatriatees who were scheduled to have come back by the beginning of 1958, some 200,000 actually returned, double the desired number.[159] Trying to control the influx of Chechens and Ingush to their homeland was, it seemed, like trying to direct the ocean tides.

Once the Chechens and other deportees living in Kazakhstan and Kirgizstan had been officially "freed" in July 1956, the authorities sought to collect signatures from them to the effect "that they would not pretend to the return of property confiscated at the time of their deportation and that they would not return to those places from which they had been deported."[160] Tens of thousands of mountaineers refused to sign these documents. In October 1956, the Kazakh MVD reported to the USSR MVD that, of 195,911 Chechens, Ingush, and Karachai

---

[157] TSKhSD, fond 89, perechen' 61, delo 13, Archives of the Soviet Communist Party and Soviet State.
[158] Ibid.   [159] Conquest, *Nation Killers*, p. 155.
[160] V. N. Zemskov, "Massovoe osvobozhdenie spetsposelentsev i ssyl'nykh (1954–1960 gg.)," *Sotsiologicheskie issledovaniya*, 1 (1991), 17.

who had been removed from the republican special settlement list, a total of 55,177 had refused to sign the agreement. In the Kirgiz SSR, 20,735 Chechens, Ingush, and Karachai out of 47,889 also refused to sign. Those who refused to sign then "willfully" (*samovol'no*) returned to their place of former residence.[161]

Redrawing the map and promoting Russification

Once the regime had arrived at a painful decision to restore the Chechen–Ingush ASSR, there then arose the question of what its borders should be. The solution the regime came to, as Robert Conquest has noted, had the resurrected autonomous republic gaining "much territory north of the Terek," while losing "some [land] in the mountain valleys."[162] A decree of the Presidium of the Supreme Soviet of the RSFSR, contained in the party archives, spells out the territory of the new–old republic in detail.[163]

The basis of the revived Chechen–Ingush ASSR was to be the existing Groznyi oblast' – that is, the city of Groznyi itself and eight districts (*raiony*) which had previously belonged to that province – but added to it were to be: three districts which had earlier been part of Stavropol' krai; four districts and parts of two others which had since 1944 been part of the Dagestan ASSR; plus the city of Malgobek and one district and part of another from the North Ossetian ASSR. Some territory which had been part of Groznyi oblast' since 1944 was not to be given to the revived Chechen–Ingush ASSR: namely, the city of Kizlyar and four districts which were now to be part of Dagestan, and two other districts which were now to be attached to Stavropol' krai.

The clear-cut purpose behind this redrawing of the map was maximally to Russify the newly formed Chechen–Ingush ASSR, weakening and diluting the political clout of the mountaineers. The three districts which were added to the ASSR from Stavropol' krai – Shelkovskii, Kargalinskii, and Naurskii districts – consisted mainly of Terek Cossacks, as well as, in Shelkovskii district, of a number of Nogai, a Turkish people.[164] According to Alexander Nekrich, these three districts, which contained virtually no Chechens or Ingush and which were not part of their historic homelands, composed 27 percent of the total territory of the new ASSR (5,200 square kilometers out of 19,300). As a result of this illogical and artificial merging of territories and peoples, Chechens

---

[161] Ibid.   [162] Conquest, *Nation Killers*, p. 151.

[163] TSKhSD, fond 89, perechen' 61, delo 8, Archives of the Soviet Communist Party and Soviet State.

[164] Muzaev, *Chechenskaya respublika*, p. 156.

and Ingush came to make up only 41 percent of the population of their resurrected republic; in 1939, by contrast, they had composed 58.4 percent of Checheno-Ingushetiya's population.[165] In this way, the Khrushchev regime "made amends" to the Chechens for admitted wrongs of the past by aggressively Russifying and ethnically diluting the populace of the new ASSR. Given the exceptionally high birth rate characteristic among Chechens and Ingush, however, even this step would have only temporary effects.

A chilly welcome home

As has been noted, the regime had taken a decision to permit a phased return – over a four-year period – of those Chechens and Ingush who could not be persuaded to remain where they were. An organizing committee, headed by M. G. Gairbekov, later chairman of the Council of Ministers of the Chechen–Ingush ASSR, was established to oversee the repatriation process. The committee's careful plans soon went awry. The organizing committee had planned for 450 new families to arrive in Groznyi city during 1957, but, instead, 2,692 families came. In the republic as a whole, 48,000 families returned during 1957, while only 33,000 single-apartment dwellings had been readied for them.[166]

It was also difficult to normalize relations between the arriving Chechens and Ingush and those who had appropriated their land. "The return of the Chechens and Ingush was, to put it mildly, not greeted with special enthusiasm by the local population."[167] In the Mezhdurechenskii (soon to be returned to its former name of Shalinskii) district, to cite one example, of the 400 families (with 669 able-bodied members) who arrived, only ten people were given jobs in kolkhozes, while another twenty-one were offered employment at factories and offices.[168]

Mindful of the difficult lessons of the past, the regime did not permit the arriving Chechens and Ingush to settle in their former villages in the mountains (or, rather, in the former locations of those villages, since the mountain *auls* had uniformly been destroyed in 1944). Instead, working settlements were constructed for the new arrivals at sovkhozes, machine tractor stations, and other government enterprises scattered about the lowland regions of the republic. The regime's obvious aim was to keep the Chechens "away from the mountains, which had served as fortresses in their ancient struggles, in order to preserve a vigilant surveillance over

---

[165] Nekrich, *Punished Peoples*, pp. 137–38.
[166] Ibid., pp. 146–47.   [167] Ibid., pp. 147–48.   [168] Ibid., p. 148.

them."[169] The new sovkhozes constructed to house the Chechens were often situated in "thinly populated, dry, unhealthy areas."[170]

The Chechens were largely employed as workers in livestock-raising sovkhozes, much as they had been required to do during their period of exile in Central Asia. Other Chechens were used as a reserve of labor for industries based in Groznyi.[171]

For the first time since Stalin's 1921 pledge, however, the regime did undertake to relocate some Russians and Cossacks in order to accommodate the Chechens and Ingush. Thus, 2,574 families, most of them ethnic Russians, were moved to areas on the other side of the Terek. According to Soviet archival data, some 36,000 Russians also chose voluntarily to leave the new Chechen–Ingush ASSR. Many of those who abandoned the republic were communists. In Shalinskii district, for example, 300 party members left in 1957.[172]

At the time of their return, some Chechens were ordered to settle in the desert area to the north of the Terek, a region which had been made part of the republic for the first time.[173] During the 1960s and 1970s, a part of the Chechens were resettled in the Cossack districts in the north of the ASSR. "This was supposed to lead to the assimilation of the Chechens but instead resulted in their spreading and in the squeezing out of the Cossack populace from their *stanitsy* [villages]."[174]

The persistent adherence of many Chechens to Islam continued to concern the authorities. Articles in the local press singled out supporters of the *sharia* for particular invective and assailed Chechens who did not permit their children to join Soviet Youth Clubs and other institutions for communist indoctrination.[175]

An anti-Chechen pogrom

In August 1958, a fierce anti-Chechen pogrom erupted in the city of Groznyi, underscoring the simmering resentment felt by many Russians toward the newly returned mountaineers. A Russian sailor had asked a young woman to dance, and an Ingush who had had designs on her had intervened. A fight had broken out, and the sailor was killed. The next day, the sailor's funeral turned into a bloody mob action by the city's Russian populace, and the ensuing disturbances lasted for four days. An estimated 10,000 people assembled in the main square in Groznyi. A Russian woman who claimed to have formerly served in the regional

[169] Karcha, "Soviet Propaganda," 8.   [170] Ibid., 7–8.
[171] Conquest, *Nation Killers*, pp. 156–57.
[172] Nekrich, *Punished Peoples*, pp. 150–51.   [173] Conquest, *Nation Killers*, p. 157.
[174] Muzaev, *Chechenskaya respublika*, p. 156.   [175] Conquest, *Nation Killers*, p. 155.

party committee and in the Council of Ministers stood up and demanded the expulsion of all Chechens and Ingush from the republic; a mass search and disarming of all Chechens and Ingush – those found in possession of weapons were to be shot on the spot; and the establishment of "Russian power" in the region.

An elderly Chechen peddler from Urus-Martan wearing an astrakhan hat was seized and beaten to death by the mob while a group of soldiers looked on indifferently. Russians, including the local communists, "pinned on red ribbons so that the rampaging pogromists would not take them for Chechens or Ingush."[176] Fortunately, the local mountaineers exhibited exceptional self-restraint and, once looting broke out, the authorities were forced to restore order in the region. None of those who participated in the mass disorders was ever brought to justice, though the local party boss, A. I. Yakovlev, was transferred out of the republic in 1959.

As this incident demonstrated, the Chechens and Ingush were to be treated as second-class citizens in the republic named after them. Of 8,997 specialists with a higher education listed as living in Checheno-Ingushetiya in 1959, only 177 were Chechens and 124 Ingush. Similarly, of 8,000 teachers employed in the republic after its restoration, only 1,440 were Chechens and Ingush, and, of these, only 190 had educational degrees.[177]

Touting a colonial heritage

One of the aims of the party leadership of the restored republic was to emphasize the putative positive aspects of tsarist policies in the Caucasus. The exploits of General Yermolov were repeatedly extolled by party spokesmen. Anti-Russian movements of the nineteenth century in the North Caucasus, on the other hand, were criticized as having been perpetrated by "Turkish agents in the interests of Turkey and Iran."[178]

Beginning in the late 1950s, as part of Khrushchev's sweeping anti-religious campaign, there took place a systematic persecution of Sufi brotherhoods throughout the North Caucasus. Major trials of these brotherhoods were held in 1958, 1963, and 1964, and the accused were put to death, charged with "banditism" and "manslaughter."[179] According to a report issued in 1973 by a specialist in "scientific atheism," V. G. Pivovarov, 52.9 percent of Chechens continued to be religious believers (as opposed to 11.9 percent of ethnic Russians).[180] Pivovarov's

[176] Nekrich, *Punished Peoples*, pp. 152–53.
[177] Ibid., pp. 156–57.   [178] Ibid., pp. 163–64.
[179] Bennigsen and Wimbush, *Mystics and Commissars*, p. 31.   [180] Ibid., p. 51.

estimate for the Chechens, it should be added, was almost certainly too low.

Quiescent Chechens

The deportation of the Chechens in 1944 and the resulting genocide had (temporarily) served its purpose. Following their return from exile, the Chechens had become a subdued people. Under Brezhnev's lengthy rule (1964–82), their sense of humiliation and abasement grew. At the initiative of the powerful party secretary for ideology, Mikhail Suslov, campaigns were conducted in various autonomous republics to celebrate their "voluntary reunification" with Russia. In Groznyi, the "voluntary entrance of Checheno-Ingushetiya into Russia" was marked with elaborate fanfare under the leadership of the head of the republican party organization, Aleksandr Vlasov, a Russian. The fact that there had even occurred a nineteenth-century Caucasus War was consigned to oblivion, since that fact conflicted with the myth of a "voluntary unification" with Russia.

When a group of Chechen and Ingush historians – Magomed Muzaev, Abdula Vatsuev, and others – issued a sharp criticism of this falsified concept of a "voluntary union," the republican KGB organized their persecution; they were deprived of an opportunity to speak out publicly or to air their views in print; they were singled out for criticism at party meetings; and they were fired from their places of work.[181]

A striking example of the craven views being promulgated by the republican party leadership is an article entitled "To Form Internationalist Convictions," which appeared in the February 1988 issue of *Kommunist*, which was the party's leading USSR-wide theoretical journal.[182] The article, which appeared in the third year of Gorbachev's tenure as party general secretary, was written by Khazhbikar Bokov, chairman of the presidium of the Chechen–Ingush ASSR Supreme Soviet, i.e., the head of the republican parliament.

In this essay, the author repeatedly assailed what he called the "virus" of nationalism. It was incumbent upon Chechens and Ingush, he insisted, that they admit that they would be just another "underdeveloped country" had it not been for the "Russian people, who after the establishment of Soviet power deprived themselves of much in order to lead out onto the broad highway peoples who had previously been downtrodden and backward." During the Great Patriotic War, Bokov

---

[181] Muzaev, *Chechenskaya respublika*, p. 156.
[182] Kh. Bokov, "Formirovat' internatsionalistskie ubezhdeniya," *Kommunist*, 3 (February 1988), 87–95.

went on, "traitors, enemies of Soviet power" had been activated in the republic, and their crimes had been a factor behind the "tragedy" of deportation. There had in fact been "not a few traitors" among the Chechens and Ingush, though they had composed a small minority of the total populace.

Fortunately for the Chechens and Ingush, Bokov continued, the Russian people had remained a steadfast pillar of support: "[T]he Russian people, which itself endured so many harsh trials during the years of the cult of personality, always manifested such care for the peoples of Central Asia and the North Caucasus as can only be compared to what an elder brother demonstrates toward his siblings." The Russians were thus a wise and loyal "elder brother" for the wayward mountaineers.

The future of Chechens and Ingush, Bokov prophesied, would be bright if they managed to steer clear of "any manifestations of chauvinism and nationalism," and, especially, if they eschewed "religious fanaticism." "In the North Caucasus," he warned, "religion, unfortunately, holds a significant part of the populace in its tenacious grip, especially the village populace. In the Chechen–Ingush ASSR, for example, until now there are not a few weddings performed according to the *sharia*. Many funerals are organized according to Muslim customs." The populace had to be vigilant against the enticements of Muslim "servers of the cult." Forty percent of the students at one high school in Groznyi, Bokov noted with alarm, had termed themselves religious believers in a recent poll.

Bokov's article is a good example of the degree of humiliation to which the Chechens found themselves subjected just three years before the outbreak of what has come to be known as the "Chechen Revolution." By the year 1990, the muzzled and demoralized Chechens had had enough.

Summing up

The Chechens encountered new and fatal shocks with the coming to power of the communists in 1917. The Bolsheviks, who treated the Chechens with a savagery dwarfing even that exhibited by Yermolov, sought relentlessly to uproot them from their traditional religion and from their traditional economy, and maximally to achieve their Russification and Russianization. Unlike the Yeltsin leadership, Stalin and Beriya, both of them men from the Caucasus, did not suffer in the slightest from historical amnesia vis-à-vis the Chechens. On the contrary, they had a clear conception of who the Chechens were and the potential dangers that they represented for the young Soviet state.

When the Chechens dug in their heels against the headlong social, economic, and religious transformations being sponsored and implemented by the communists, the regime took a lethal decision to deport them as a people to Central Asia. As we have seen in this chapter (pp. 70–71), roughly a quarter of the Chechens, and perhaps more, perished in the course of this genocidal operation and its aftermath, which saw them deposited, often without a bare minimum of food and housing, in remote regions of Central Asia.

The Khrushchev leadership, which moderated many of the excesses of the Stalin period, did all that it could to weaken the Chechens, seeking to keep them penned in within Central Asia and, when that failed, combining traditional Chechen and Ingush territories with Russian and Cossack ones so that the Chechens and Ingush would compose a minority of the populace of the republic named after them. Under Leonid Brezhnev, the Chechens effectively remained a "punished people," with their forcible incorporation into the Russian Empire during the nineteenth century being triumphantly celebrated as a "voluntary union." Economically, the Chechens continued to suffer from acute "land hunger" and from severe poverty.

As had occurred in the tsarist period, these brutal and discriminatory policies and practices of the Soviet leadership produced results directly contrary to what had been intended. Thus the regime's evident desire to eradicate a sense of "mountaineer" consciousness among Chechens prompted a slow but steady growth in Chechen national awareness. By the late 1930s, the Chechens were already beginning to conceive of themselves as a discrete people, though a sense of ties to their Vainakh brethren, the Ingush, persisted, as did strong clan allegiances. All attempts to Russify and Russianize the Chechens failed utterly and served to produce an opposite result among this stiff-necked mountain people, who clung tenaciously to their ancient language and to their Sufi Muslim loyalties. They also manifested a fertility rate so high that it gradually overcame the regime's attempts administratively to drown them in a sea of Slavs.

At the beginning of the Gorbachev era, the Chechens were a people with a formidable list of grievances.

3   The eruption of the "Chechen Revolution"

[U]nlike in other [autonomous] republics, the idea of breaking away
from Russia was popular among most Chechens [in 1991].

North Caucasus area specialist Ol'ga Vasil'eva[1]

In order to understand the causes underlying the kaleidoscopic
"Chechen Revolution" of 1990–91 and the concomitant rise to power
of General Dzhokhar Dudaev, one needs to look closely at a number of
interlinked economic, social, and demographic processes occurring in
the Chechen–Ingush ASSR during the Brezhnev-to-Gorbachev years
(1964–91). As the Tishkov group has noted, within the republic of
Checheno-Ingushetiya during this period: "[T]here had taken place a
kind of division of the economy into two sectors: a 'Russian' one (the
oil-extracting industry, machine-building, systems of social mainte-
nance, and infrastructure) and a 'national' one (small village production, seasonal work, and the criminal sphere – and the ranks of this
second 'national' sector were continually increasing as new contingents
of young people came of working age)."[2]

Factors behind the "Chechen Revolution"

As a result of the formation of these two sectors – i.e., a "Russian" one
and a "national" one – industry and transport were experiencing a severe
labor shortage in Checheno-Ingushetiya at the same time that village
agriculture ceased being able to absorb the growth in labor resources
taking place among the core rural population of Chechens and Ingush.
Tens of thousands of unemployed villagers composed what came to be
known as "surplus rural populace." At the beginning of 1991, this labor
surplus in the villages was estimated to number between 100,000 and

[1] Ol'ga Vasil'eva, "North Caucasus," in Klaus Segbers and Stephan de Spiegeleire, eds.,
Post-Soviet Puzzles (Baden-Baden, Germany: Nomos, 1995), vol. II, p. 444.
[2] V. A. Tishkov, E. L. Belyaeva, and G. V. Marchenko, *Chechenskii krizis* (Moscow: Tsentr
kompleksnykh sotsial'nykh issledovanii i marketinga, 1995), p. 16.

200,000 people, or from 20 to 30 percent of the entire working populace of the republic.[3] At the time of the 1989 all-union census, it should be noted, Chechens still represented a largely rural populace, with 73.13 percent continuing to live in villages.[4] Wherever they dwelled, the Chechens also clung tenaciously to their native language: in 1989, at the time of the all-union census, 98.79 percent of them cited Chechen as their native language, while a mere 1.06 percent named Russian.[5]

A very high birth rate was noteworthy among Chechens (and Ingush) during both the Brezhnev and the post-Brezhnev periods. In 1980, the republic's natural growth per 1,000 inhabitants was 14.3; by 1985, it had increased to 16.8; in 1990, it was 16.1; and in 1992, it stood at 13.9. The comparable figures for the Russian Federation as a whole were much lower: 4.9, 5.3, 2.2, and −1.5.[6]

The Chechens and the Ingush became increasingly impoverished peoples during the years 1964–91, leading some of their youth to drift into criminality, and others to emigrate to other parts of Russia, as well as to the territory of the present-day CIS. By the mid-1980s, unemployment in the Chechen–Ingush Republic had become chronic, and, each summer, tens of thousands of villagers ventured beyond the borders of the republic to engage in seasonal work.

Following their return from exile in the mid- to late 1950s, many Chechens had found themselves gradually "pushed out" of the republic, forced to take temporary work in Siberia and in the Russian Far North. By 1979, the percentage of Chechens living in Checheno-Ingushetiya had fallen to 80.9 percent of their total numbers; by 1989, that percentage had declined further to 76.6 percent.

Of the 899,000 Chechens reported as living in the Russian Federation by the 1989 all-union census, 58,000 lived in neighboring Dagestan; while 15,000 lived in Stavropol' krai, 11,100 in Volgograd oblast', 8,300 in Kalmykiya, 7,900 in Astakhan' oblast', 6,000 in Saratov oblast', and so on.[7] A total of 59,310 Chechens lived outside the Russian Federation, with 49,500 of that number residing in Kazakhstan.

While rampant unemployment and rural overpopulation were serving to force many Chechens out of their home republic, ethnic Russians, too, were leaving Checheno-Ingushetiya, and in significant numbers. Over the period 1979–89, their numbers diminished by 42,273, from 336,044 to 293,771, a drop of 12.6 percent.[8] The much-discussed outmigration of ethnic Russians from Checheno-Ingushetiya, thus, began more than a decade before the coming to power of General Dudaev.

[3] Ibid.   [4] Ibid., p. 10.   [5] Ibid., p. 11.   [6] Ibid., p. 16.
[7] Ibid., pp. 9–10.   [8] Ibid.

It should be noted that propitious conditions had not been created for the recruitment of Chechens and Ingush into the oil industry in their own home republic (in fact, such recruitment was, in effect, being discouraged). When new specialists were needed in the oil industry, they were imported from central Russia.[9] Soon this issue became moot, as fewer and fewer new specialists were needed; by the second half of the 1980s, the petroleum resources of the Chechen–Ingush Republic had begun to dry up. During the years 1985–91, the extractable resources of oil in Chechnya decreased from 87 million to 58 million tons.[10]

The health and social services provided to the populace of the Chechen–Ingush ASSR were notoriously poor. The republic was characterized by a very high mortality rate from infectious and parasitical diseases (in 1987, 22.6 per 1,000, the mean figure for the Russian Federation as a whole being 13.9 per 1,000). The health care system in the republic was, not surprisingly, termed "one of the worst in Russia," as was its mortality rate for children.[11] In the three largely ethnic Russian regions located in the vicinity of Chechnya – Stavropol' krai, Krasnodar krai, and Rostov oblast' – the number of hospital beds per 10,000 persons in 1991 was 87.5, 94.1, and 94.8; in Checheno-Ingushetiya, by contrast, the figure was a low 76.0. The figures for number of doctors per 10,000 persons in the same three Russian regions during the year 1991 were: 112.6, 98.2, and 81.5; in the Chechen–Ingush ASSR, it stood at 58.9.[12] Environmentally, the republic suffered from the heavy pollution emitted by its numerous oil-processing plants.

In the housing sphere, Checheno-Ingushetiya ranked close to the bottom in the Russian Federation in terms of providing living space to its populace. In the three Russian regions of Stavropol' krai, Krasnodar krai, and Rostov oblast', the living space in square meters per person in 1991 stood at 96.3, 99.4, and 103.7 square meters, respectively. In Checheno-Ingushetiya, the figure, by contrast, was a low 78.0 square meters.[13]

Not surprisingly, incomes received for agricultural work in Checheno-Ingushetiya also lagged far behind the Russian Federation average. In 1985, the average monthly wage for a collective or state farm worker in the Chechen–Ingush ASSR was 82.5 percent of the Russian Federation average; by 1991, the average wage had fallen further to 74.8 percent of the Russian average. In nearby Stavropol' krai, Krasnodar krai, and Rostov oblast', by contrast, agricultural wages in 1991 were significantly

[9] Timur Muzaev, *Chechenskaya respublika* (Moscow: Panorama, 1995), p. 162.
[10] Tishkov, et al., *Chechenskii krizis*, p. 21.   [11] Ibid., p. 16.
[12] Vasil'eva, "North Caucasus," p. 448.   [13] Ibid.

higher, standing at 140.5 percent, 140.5 percent, and 118.6 percent of the Russian Federation average.[14]

Educational levels in the republic were likewise strikingly low. In 1989, of the total village population of Checheno-Ingushetiya – and it should be stressed again that three-quarters of Chechens continued to live in villages – 15.56 percent lacked any education whatsoever; 13.32 percent possessed only an elementary education; 23.25 percent had an incomplete secondary education; and only 34.14 percent had a complete secondary education. Among all Chechens living in the republic, a mere 4.67 percent could boast of a completed higher education.[15] With such information in mind, one can see that there were indeed powerful social, demographic, and economic factors underlying the 1991 "Chechen Revolution."

Preparing the revolution

In 1987 and 1988, the effects of Mikhail Gorbachev's campaigns of *glasnost'*, *perestroika*, and *demokratizatsiya* began to be felt even in the formerly rigidly controlled North Caucasus backwater of Checheno-Ingushetiya. As occurred in numerous other regions of the Soviet Union, so-called informal organizations (*neformaly*) made their appearance in the Chechen–Ingush Republic. In 1987, a scholarly society called "Caucasus" (Kavkaz) emerged, to be followed by the Union for the Assistance of *Perestroika* and The Popular Front of Checheno-Ingushetiya. The Chechen and Ingush *neformaly* were at this point heavily influenced by informal movements which had emerged in Russia, the Baltic republics, and in Transcaucasia.[16]

By the beginning of 1989, a spillover effect from the tumultuous processes occurring in Moscow and throughout the Soviet Union began to be felt more intensively in the Chechen–Ingush Republic. In January 1989, the republican Communist Party committee held a plenum at which it called upon local scholars henceforth to view the forced

---

[14] Ibid. For a discussion of the factors underlying the "Chechen Revolution," see Yusup Soslambekov, *"Chechnya (Nokhchicho') – vzglyad iznutri"* (Moscow: author publication, 1995), pp. 30–31.

[15] Tishkov, et al., *Chechenskii krizis*, p. 10.

[16] See the first book of memoirs by Dudaev's acting vice president Zelimkhan (Zelimkha) Yandarbiev, *V preddverii nezavisimosti* (Groznyi: author publication, 1994), pp. 7–8. The same work appeared in abridged form as a section of Yandarbiev's later book, *Checheniya – bitva za svobodu* (L'vov, Ukraine: Svoboda narodiv [sic] and Antibol'shevitskii blok narodov, 1996), pp. 9–76. On the role of informal organizations and "popular fronts" in the RSFSR during the Gorbachev period, see John B. Dunlop, *The Rise of Russia and the Fall of the Soviet Union*, 2nd edn. (Princeton, NJ: Princeton University Press, 1995), pp. 72–76.

deportation of 1944 "as our shared tragedy, which was based on political rather than national motives." The deportation, the party plenum declared, had been conducted by "those who had usurped the sacred Leninist covenants concerning internationalist socialist legality."[17]

The fact that it was the republic's Communist Party which raised the sensitive issue of the deportation (and, by implication, of the genocide of the Chechen and Ingush people under the communists) was an indicator that the republic would remain a quiet backwater no longer. In the spring of 1989, Vladimir Foteev, an ethnic Russian and a harsh political overseer of the republic, was abruptly removed from his post of first party secretary. A competition for his replacement ensued between republican second party secretary Doku Zavgaev, a Chechen, and Nikolai Semenov, a Russian and the first secretary of the Groznyi city party committee. In a sign that real change had arrived, Zavgaev, the Chechen, was selected.[18]

Zavgaev had been born in 1940 in the village of Beno-Yurt in the Nadterechnyi (i.e., Upper Terek) district of the republic located in the northwestern, Russianized region of Checheno-Ingushetiya, across the Terek River from Stavropol' krai. Zavgaev was thus a lowlander by origin. From the year 1958 on, he worked as a teacher, mechanic, chief engineer on a state farm, and the head of a group of state farms, and, lastly, was named minister of agriculture of the Chechen–Ingush Republic. Zavgaev graduated from the Mountain Agricultural Institute and from the Academy of Social Sciences at the party Central Committee in Moscow. He also held the candidate or lower doctoral degree in agricultural sciences. In 1983, he was named second secretary of the republican party committee, with responsibility for questions of agriculture, and, finally, as has been noted, in June 1989, he was elected first secretary of the Chechen–Ingush *reskom*, or republican Communist Party committee.[19]

While Zavgaev – who would be restored to power by Boris Yeltsin in 1995 – was decidedly not a reformer, he was expected to embrace the policies of *glasnost* and democratization emanating from the Soviet capital. It took little time for once-sleepy Checheno-Ingushetiya to be convulsed by the same revolutionary change sweeping the rest of the USSR, especially its non-Russian regions.

In July 1989, the first overtly political organization to emerge in the republic, Bart (Unity), was founded by a group of Chechen young

[17] Nikolai Fedorovich Bugai, "The Truth About the Deportation of the Chechen and Ingush Peoples," *Soviet Studies in History*, Fall (1991), 81.
[18] Muzaev, *Chechenskuya respublika*, pp. 158–59.   [19] Ibid., p. 71.

people, including General Dudaev's future acting vice president, Zelim-khan (Zelimkha) Yandarbiev (b. 1952). This organization, which was founded out of frustration and disillusionment with the activities of the Chechen–Ingush Popular Front, later (in February 1990) was transformed into the Vainakh Democratic Party. In August 1989, the leaders of Bart attended the first Congress of Mountain Peoples of the Caucasus, held in Sukhumi, Abkhaziya. At the congress, the *bartovtsy* advocated the idea of "a federal statehood of the peoples of the Caucasus."[20]

By early 1990, districts of the Chechen–Ingush Republic which had been considered pillars of stability and of conservatism had become politically charged. Public rallies and hunger strikes occurring during February and March helped force the removal of seven first secretaries of party district committees (*raikomy*) in the republic. In March 1990, there took place Russia-wide elections to the RSFSR Congress of People's Deputies, and a majority of the deputies who were elected to the congress from Checheno-Ingushetiya supported radical democrats in Moscow and throughout the Russian Federation adhering to the organization "Democratic Russia."[21]

The republican first party secretary, Doku Zavgaev, tried as best he could to ride the waves of change unleashed by the Gorbachev reforms. In March 1990, he had himself elected chairman of the Chechen–Ingush republican Supreme Soviet, which meant that he combined the powerful posts of republican and Communist Party leader. Zavgaev was also elected a deputy to the RSFSR Congress and was elevated to membership in the USSR-wide Communist Party Central Committee. It appeared at the time that virtually nothing could dislodge him from his numerous powerful posts.

The emergence of the "national radicals"

During the spring of 1990, a new and potentially destabilizing force emerged when the young Chechen "national radicals" (the term was coined by anti-Dudaev Chechen author Timur Muzaev) united within the Vainakh Democratic Party and began to speak out actively on key republican issues. The new organization's leaders saw their chief goal as the creation of a "sovereign Vainakh republic." Their program advocated a program of affirmative action for Chechens and Ingush; it insisted that those two peoples should henceforth be accorded a major "piece of the pie" in the distribution of real power in the republic. The radicals' program also demanded the "separation of atheism from the

[20] Yandarbiev, *V preddverii*, pp. 9–13.
[21] Muzaev, *Chechenskaya respublika*, p. 159.

state," i.e., a cessation of anti-Muslim religious persecution, and argued for the reestablishment of traditional national institutions in the republic such as the Mekhk khel or "Council of Elders." It also advocated putting an end to artificial migration into and out of the republic.[22]

By the summer of 1990, a number of leading representatives of the Chechen intelligentsia had begun to argue in favor of holding a Chechen National Congress. It should be noted that, at this point, the concept of a "Vainakh" identity conjoining Chechens and Ingush was in process of being dropped by many Chechens (and by many Ingush as well). Henceforth, Chechens increasingly saw themselves as a discrete, separate people. In November 1990, the Chechen National Congress assembled and "in the name of the Chechen people declared the sovereignty of the Chechen Republic Nokhchi-cho."[23] The Chechen–Ingush Republic was declared by the congress to be a sovereign state which intended to sign the union and federal treaties of the USSR on equal terms with the union republics (i.e., Ukraine, Estonia, and so on) of the Soviet Union.

As background, it should be noted here that, in the course of the tense struggle for power occurring in 1990 between Gorbachev and Yeltsin, the former had sought to weaken the latter and his power base, the Russian Federation, by encouraging autonomous republics within the RSFSR to declare their own sovereignty. A Soviet law, announced on 26 April 1990, laid bare this tactic when it made all autonomous republics "subjects of the USSR," thereby effectively weakening the territorial integrity of the RSFSR.[24] After being narrowly elected chairman of the Russian Supreme Soviet in May 1990, Yeltsin countered Gorbachev's divide-and-rule approach by obtaining an official "declaration of sovereignty" by the Russian Federation on 12 June 1990. Following this declaration by Russia, however, some autonomous republics within Russia began to assert their own sovereignty; thus the North Caucasus autonomous republic of North Ossetiya proceeded to declare itself "a union republic, albeit as part of Russia."[25]

---

[22] Ibid., pp. 159–60.   [23] Ibid., p. 160.

[24] For the text of the law of 26 April 1990 (No. 1457-I), see "O razgranichenii polnomochii mezhdu Soyuzom SSR i sub"ektami federatsii," in *Vedomosti s'ezda narodnykh deputatov SSSR i Verkhovnogo Soveta SSSR*, 19, 9 May 1990. In Article 1 of this law, it is stated that "Autonomous republics . . . possess the full plenitude of state power on their territory beyond those powers which they delegate to the Union and to union republics" (p. 430).

[25] Richard Sakwa, *Russian Politics and Society* (London and New York: Routledge, 1993), pp. 115–16, and Radio Free Europe–Radio Liberty's *RFE–RL Daily Report*, 13 March 1991. For Zelimkhan Yandarbiev's comments on the struggle between the USSR and the RSFSR and its implications for the Chechen Republic, see his second volume of memoirs, *Checheniya*, p. 89.

Commenting on the results of this harsh struggle between Gorbachev's Soviet Union and Yeltsin's Russian Federation, Emil' Pain and Arkadii Popov have observed: "Gorbachev's team wanted to exploit the issue of republican separatism within Russia as a weapon to be wielded against the Russian leadership headed by Yeltsin. In November 1990, the draft version of the Union Treaty that was developed by the leadership of the USSR and the CPSU was first published. The draft conferred rights upon 'republics that are parts of other republics' (i.e., republics that are a part of Russia), to participate in the Union Treaty on an equal footing with respective Soviet republics."

And Pain and Popov continue: "These plans, which directly contradicted the standing USSR and RSFSR constitutions and were clearly designed to put political pressure on Yeltsin, exacerbated the separatist tendencies in Russia's autonomous [regions], including the Chechen–Ingush ASSR. In other words, the tug-of-war between the Russian and Soviet governments, and their intense competition for votes and the political support of the Russian provinces, decisively precluded any possibility of military intervention in the Chechen–Ingush Republic."[26]

Returning to developments in Chechnya, the organizational committee of the Chechen National Congress included political moderates such as the writers Abuzar Aidamirov and Musa Akhmadov, the poet Apti Bisultanov, and historians Yavus Akhmadov and Abdula Vatsuev, along with other respected public figures. Lechi Umkhaev, a well-known people's deputy at the republican level, became chairman of the congress's organizational committee. The young "national radicals" at the congress, however, disapproved of the organizational committee's penchant for what they called "*apparat* games" and tried to insinuate their own members onto the committee.[27] There ensued a sharp power struggle between moderates and radicals for control of the committee.

The Communist Party boss of Checheno-Ingushetiya, Doku Zavgaev, vainly attempted to get out in front of the unfolding "Chechen Revolution." The November 1990 Chechen National Congress, which had declared the republic's sovereignty, had been held with the active support of both the republican Communist Party apparatus and the leadership of the republican Supreme Soviet, both of them, of course, chaired by Zavgaev. There existed at this time, as Ruslan Khasbulatov, a well-known Chechen politician active on the RSFSR level, has noted in

[26] Emil A. Payin and Arkady A. Popov, "Chechnya," in Jeremy R. Azrael and Emil A. Payin, eds., *US and Russian Policymaking with Respect to the Use of Force* (Santa Monica, CA: RAND, 1996), posted on Discussion List about Chechnya, 6 November 1996. The text of the draft Union Treaty appeared in *Pravda*, 24 November 1990.

[27] Muzaev, *Chechenskaya respublika*, p. 160.

his short book on the crisis, three distinct factions which were represented at the November 1990 Congress: the official party leadership,
which looked to Zavgaev for direction; a "centrist" faction headed by
former USSR minister for the petrochemical industry, Salambek
Khadzhiev, which at the time wanted a fully independent republic; and
a radical faction including Yandarbiev, Bislan Gantamirov (Gante-
mirov), and Yaragi Mamodaev, which advanced the slogans of a fully
independent republic and an Islamic state.[28]

It is important to underline that all three of these factions – including
Zavgaev's Communist Party group – were advocating, at a minimum,
the granting of full "sovereignty" to Checheno-Ingushetiya. On 26
November 1990, as has been noted, the Supreme Soviet of the
Chechen–Ingush Republic, responding to a proposal made by the
Chechen National Congress, had officially adopted a "Declaration on
the State Sovereignty of the Chechen–Ingush Republic."[29]

As early as the 23–26 November Chechen National Congress,
however, the radicals began to prevail in their struggle against the two
rival factions. In response to a proposal made by one of the young
radical leaders, Yaragi Mamodaev, a Soviet air force major general and
ethnic Chechen serving in Estonia, but physically present as a guest at
the congress, Dzhokhar Dudaev, was elevated to membership on the
executive committee of the National Congress. Dudaev had spoken to
the congress and impressed its delegates with his strength of character
and decisiveness.

In his first volume of memoirs, Zelimkhan Yandarbiev recalls that few
at the congress had been acquainted with General Dudaev before he
delivered his "short but brilliant" remarks. At the suggestion of a fellow
activist of the Vainakh Democratic Party, Salaudi Yakh"yaev, the two
went to see Dudaev, and both came away "convinced that Dudaev was a
man capable of giving a new impulse to the [Chechen] national-
liberation movement." After taking a night to mull things over, Dudaev
agreed to permit his nomination for the position of chairman of the
executive committee (*ispolkom*) of the National Congress.[30]

On 1 December 1990, Dudaev, still serving as commander of the
Soviet military garrison in Tartu, was elected chairman of the *ispolkom* of
the congress. The *ispolkom* had been created by the November 1990
congress in order to carry out that body's decisions on: the implementation of political sovereignty; achieving the rebirth of the Chechen

---

[28] Ruslan Khasbulatov, *Chechnya: mne ne dali ostanovit' voinu* (Moscow: Paleya, 1995),
p. 8.
[29] Muzaev, *Chechenskaya respublika*, p. 101.　　[30] Yandarbiev, *V preddverii*, p. 25.

language; and restoring the cultural and historic memory of the Chechen people.[31]

In late 1990 and early 1991, the work of the *ispolkom* was in fact headed by Lechi Umkhaev, a political moderate, who backed cooperation with, as well as the exertion of careful pressure upon, the party leadership under Doku Zavgaev. This situation changed radically in March 1991, however, once General Dudaev had retired from the Soviet air force and moved to Groznyi to head up the work of the *ispolkom*.

On the 17th of that same month of March 1991, voters in Checheno-Ingushetiya cast ballots in Gorbachev's "All-Union Referendum on the Preservation of the [Soviet] Union." The turnout of eligible voters was 58.8 percent, the lowest among all of the autonomous republics of the RSFSR (the Republic of Komi in the north of Russia came in second lowest with a turnout of 68 percent). This lackluster turnout in the Chechen–Ingush Republic suggested that its citizens were not particularly enthusiastic about preserving the USSR. Of those who did cast votes in the republic, 75.9 percent – or 44.6 percent of eligible voters – cast ballots in favor of preserving the Soviet Union.[32]

It should also be noted that the Chechen–Ingush Supreme Soviet, chaired by Communist Party boss Doku Zavgaev, took a decision on 11 March not to hold an RSFSR-wide referendum (promoted by Yeltsin and his allies) on the question of the introduction of the post of Russian president. The rationale for Zavgaev's action was apparently that "several issues between the autonomous republic and the RSFSR central authorities were not solved."[33]

Dudaev's arrival in Chechnya in March 1991 coincided with another key development in the Russian Federation. In April 1991, the RSFSR Supreme Soviet proceeded to pass a "Law on the Rehabilitation of Repressed Peoples." This law immediately became a banner for all aggrieved groups within the Russian Federation; in Chechnya, it was seen by many as affirming a right to restore a lost independence and to create their own statehood. The law also served to inflame Russian Cossacks, who began to make demands for the return of traditional

---

[31] Muzaev, *Chechenskaya respublika*, p. 101.

[32] See Ann Sheehy, "The All-Union and RSFSR Referendums of March 17," RFE–RL, *Report on the USSR*, 29 March 1991, p. 22, and her essay, "Power Struggle in Checheno-Ingushetiya," RFE–RL, *Report on the USSR*, 15 November 1991, p. 21. Concerning the second Sheehy essay, Paul B. Henze has written that he "was able to confirm most of her detailed analysis of events in (and relating to) Chechnya in 1991 during my own visits to Chechnya and Georgia in 1992." See Paul Henze, *Islam in the North Caucasus: The Example of Chechnya*, P-7935 (Santa Monica, CA: RAND, 1995), p. 32, n. 48.

[33] *RFE–RL Daily Report*, 13 March 1991.

Cossack lands which had been included in the Chechen–Ingush Republic by Khrushchev. Since 1990, Cossack groups had been agitating for the return to Stavropol' krai of the Kargalinskii, Naurskii, and Shelkovskii districts located in the northern region of Checheno-Ingushetiya. These Cossack demands, in turn, agitated many Chechens, always sensitive where the volatile "land question" was concerned.[34]

In May 1991, General Dudaev, now ensconced in Groznyi, declared that the Supreme Soviet of the republic was henceforth deprived of any legitimacy, in connection with the November 1990 proclamation of sovereignty. He affirmed that the *ispolkom*, chaired by himself, planned to assume all power in the republic during the transitional period leading up to new elections. Dudaev was supported in these statements by parties and movements of a national-radical orientation (the Vainakh Democratic Party, the Islamic Path, the Green Movement, and others). On the other hand, he was sharply opposed by Lechi Umkhaev, first deputy chairman of the *ispolkom*, and by Umkhaev's supporters.[35] Oddly, the Supreme Soviet of the republic, headed by Doku Zavgaev, allowed Dudaev's sharp challenge to pass without comment.[36]

On 8–9 June, Dudaev and his supporters among the delegates to the Chechen National Congress held a meeting at which they declared themselves henceforth to be the "Common National Congress of the Chechen People" (Russian initials: OKChN). Dudaev was named chairman of the newly formed OKChN and Yusup Soslambekov (b. 1956), one of the leaders of the Vainakh Democratic Party, was named first deputy chairman. Zelimkhan Yandarbiev and Khusein Akhmadov (b. 1950) became deputy chairmen of the new organization. Activists from the Vainakh Democratic Party and from other national radical parties joined together to compose the ranks of the *ispolkom* of OKChN.[37]

During the spring of 1991, General Dudaev also took steps to alleviate the perceived geopolitical isolation of Chechnya. Aslan Abashidze, president of the Adzharian Autonomous Republic within Georgia, arranged a meeting between Dudaev and Georgian president Zviad

---

[34] Fiona Hill, *"Russia's Tinderbox": Conflict in the North Caucasus and Its Implications for the Future of the Russian Federation* (Cambridge, MA: John F. Kennedy School of Government, Harvard University, Strengthening Democratic Institutions Project, September 1995), pp. 46–47, 69–71.
[35] Muzaev, *Chechenskaya respublika*, p. 101.   [36] Ibid., p. 162.
[37] Ibid., p. 102. Muzaev's book contains useful short biographies of leading figures – both Chechen and Russian – during the period of the conflict. See also "Key Actors in the Chechen Conflict," in Diane Curran, Fiona Hill, and Elena Kostritsyna, *The Search for Peace in Chechnya: A Sourcebook, 1994–1996* (Cambridge, MA: John F. Kennedy School of Government, Harvard University, Strengthening Democratic Institutions Project, March 1997), pp. 66–80.

Gamsakhurdia in the town of Kazbegi. Gamsakhurdia wanted Dudaev's support against the South Ossetians, who were seeking to separate from Georgia and then to join North Ossetiya as part of the Russian Federation. The Georgians, Gamsakhurdia informed Dudaev, "had no difficulty in supporting the Chechens on the basis of mutual hostility to Russia and to communism." At Kazbegi, the two leaders also discussed future mutual cooperation in establishing a Caucasian commonwealth of free and independent states.[38]

As long as Gamsakhurdia remained in power in Georgia, Dudaev enjoyed the possibility of having a geopolitical and trade "back door" leading through Georgia to Turkey and to the Black Sea; once Gamsakhurdia had been ousted, in January 1992 (he was offered asylum by Dudaev), this back door slammed shut.

The month of June 1991 witnessed the elections for the Russian presidency. Eighty percent of those who cast ballots in Checheno-Ingushetiya voted for Boris Yeltsin, a considerably higher percentage than the RSFSR average.[39]

Commenting on the strong support shown for Yeltsin in the Chechen–Ingush Republic in this election, Emil' Pain and Arkadii Popov have written: "One has to keep in mind that it [i.e., the period of mid-1991] was a time of inflammatory, revolutionary slogans of an impassioned anti-imperial and anti-communist character. These slogans, to a large degree, served as a basis for Boris Yeltsin's campaign for office as the first Russian president. In an attempt to garner votes from the non-Russian population in the provinces, Yeltsin's team promised to maximize the autonomy of Russia's constituent republics, and was willing to ignore the anti-constitutional games played by republican authorities and nationalist movements that advocated different versions of ethnic sovereignty. This tactic brought about the expected short-term [election] results in Chechnya."[40]

During the period extending from June 1991 to the August 19–21 putsch in Moscow, the *ispolkom* served as a center of radical opposition to the republican communist leadership under Zavgaev. While possessing relatively small numbers of followers, the national radicals pressed ahead energetically with the formation of filials of the *ispolkom* within all Chechen-dominated districts in the republic; these filials would

---

[38] In Henze, *Islam in the North Caucasus*, p. 32.

[39] On the elections, see the excerpts from the Govorukhin Commission report in *Pravda*, 27 February 1996, p. 2. For the membership of this commission, see Muzaev, *Chechenskaya respublika*, p. 40. For the full text of the commission's report, see *Komissiya Govorukhina* (Moscow: Laventa, 1995).

[40] Payin and Popov, "Chechnya."

subsequently provide structures for the "Chechen Revolution" which was to erupt in August. The members of the *ispolkom*, it should be noted, were persistently harassed by the authorities and had to have their newspapers and leaflets published outside the republic, in the Baltic republics and in Georgia.[41]

Excursus on Dzhokhar Dudaev

Dudaev was born in January 1944 – just one month before the forced deportation of all Chechens – in the village of Yalkhori, Chechen–Ingush ASSR, the seventh child of a family which eventually numbered ten children. His family spent the harsh deportation years in the Pavlograd and South Kazakhstan oblasts of the Kazakh SSR. In 1957, they, like many other Chechens, were permitted to return to the newly revived Chechen–Ingush ASSR.

Becoming enamored of a career in the Soviet military, Dudaev enrolled first at the Syzransk Helicopter School and then, in 1962, at the Tambov Higher Military School for Long-Range Aviation Pilots. In 1966, he graduated from that school with the specialty "pilot-engineer." In 1966, he was also given membership in the Communist Party. After serving in the Moscow and the Trans-Baikal Military Districts, he enrolled in the military command program of the Yurii Gagarin Air Force Academy, whence he graduated in 1974.

Dudaev married a Russian woman whom he had met in Kaluga oblast', Alla Fedorovna, the daughter of a military officer and by profession an artist and a poet. At the time of their marriage, Dudaev held the rank of air force senior lieutenant. Neither family seems to have been enthusiastic about the match, but the couple's intentions remained firm, and, after Alla had completed her education, she was able to marry Dudaev. The couple subsequently had two sons (born in 1971 and 1984) and a daughter (born in 1974).

Dudaev subsequently received appointments in Ukraine and in Estonia and eventually rose to the rank of major general in the air force. In addition to speaking Chechen and Russian, Dudaev was said to be able to speak Kazakh, Uzbek, and Ukrainian, as well as some Estonian.

In 1986–87, Dudaev was assigned to the town of Mary, Turkmenistan, where he reportedly participated in bombing raids carried out on positions of the mujahedin located in the western regions of Afghanistan.[42] This fact was later made much of by his enemies in the Russian leadership. Secret police (Russian Federal Counter-Intelligence Service,

[41] Sheehy, "Power Struggle," p. 22.   [42] See *Ogonek*, 12 (March 1995), 21.

or FSK) chairman Sergei Stepashin, for example, asserted in early 1995: "Dudaev did not create any Islamic state. In general, if one can so put it, he is an anti-Islamicist. He carpet-bombed his fellow Muslims in Afghanistan."[43] Stepashin's statement seems to be motivated by spite, but it is apparently true that Dudaev was the recipient of the "Award for Afghanistan," a decoration given to Soviet military personnel who distinguished themselves in combat operations during the Soviet–Afghan war.

A leading Chechen opponent of Dudaev's, Yusup Soslambekov, has asserted that the general was in fact an "atheist" and was ignorant of the most fundamental Muslim beliefs and practices, for example of the number of times a day one should bow down in the direction of Mecca.[44] (One should note that, while this may have been true of Dudaev before he assumed the Chechen presidency, once he had become Chechen head of state, he was careful to project himself as an observant and respectful Muslim.)

From 1987 through March 1991, Dudaev commanded a division of nuclear-armed, long-range bombers from a base located in the Estonian city of Tartu, and also served as chief of that city's military garrison. His tenure there coincided with a sharp upsurge in Estonian nationalism ("the Estonian revolution") which eventually prepared the way for that republic's full political independence. It seems clear that Dudaev's experience in Tartu influenced his own emerging nationalist and separatist views; if a small people numbering fewer than one million like the Estonians could achieve independence, he must have thought, then why not the more than 900,000 Chechens? Dudaev reportedly refused to take part in the Soviet regime's harsh repressive actions conducted against Estonia in early 1991.[45] (Future historians will want to examine this episode carefully.)

In their useful study entitled "Russian Politics in Chechnya," Emil' Pain, a leading specialist on ethnic affairs and an adviser to President Yeltsin, and his coauthor, Arkadii Popov, have noted that Dudaev's political rise in Checheno-Ingushetiya was due, in large part, to the fact that he had been absent for many years from the republic and that he therefore lacked connections to any of the leading political clans which

---

[43] "Kontrarazvedka v Chechne," *Argumenty i fakty*, 5 (1995), 1, 3.
[44] Soslambekov, *Chechnya*, p. 39.
[45] For Dudaev's biography, see Muzaev, *Chechenskaya respublika*, pp. 68–69; *Moscow Times*, 18 December 1994, p. 21; *New York Times*, 15 December 1994, p. A8; *Ogonek*, 12 (March 1995), 21; and *Chechenskaya tragediya: kto vinovat* (Moscow: Novosti, 1995), p. 14. For interviews with Dudaev's wife, Alla, following his death, see *Izvestiya*, 8 June 1996, and 30 January 1997, and *Komsomol'skaya pravda*, 9 January 1997.

were competing for power. He was brought back to Chechnya as "a person without ties."[46]

Stanislav Govorukhin, an outspoken Russian nationalist filmmaker who served as chairman of the Russian State Duma's commission which looked into the causes of the Russian–Chechen war, has observed that Dudaev was at first intended to be a "marionette" in the hands of Chechen nationalist "puppeteers." "It was intended," Govorukhin stated, "to use Dudaev as a bulldozer to sweep aside the communist authorities [in Checheno-Ingushetiya]. He did indeed sweep them aside like a bulldozer. But he turned out to be smarter and more cunning than his puppeteers. He began to lead them about by the nose and then simply dictated to them his conditions . . . Then when they saw that . . . he was an intelligent and cunning politician, they offered various positions to him, up to that of deputy minister of defense. But he had already developed ambitions, and he understood that he would be president of Chechnya."[47]

Sergei Stankevich issues a firm warning

In his first volume of memoirs, Zelimkhan Yandarbiev writes that, on 22 June 1991, he received a note from Sergei Stankevich, deputy chairman of the Moscow City Council, requesting a meeting in Groznyi. Though Yandarbiev does not say it, it was well known at the time that Stankevich was close to the just-elected president of the Russian Federation, Boris Yeltsin. (It was announced the following month that Stankevich had been appointed to the influential post of Russian state councilor.)[48]

At the June 1991 meeting of Stankevich and Yandarbiev in Groznyi, the former took strong exception to the intention of Chechen national radicals to construct their own independent state. "Stankevich," Yandarbiev recalls, "essentially denied the real right of the Chechen people to self-determination. He even accused the Chechen people of entertaining a desire to resolve the problem of their rebirth at the expense of Russia. He openly threatened the use of any and all force and measures in order to cut off the attempts of Chechnya to separate, 'up to a return to the situation of the middle of the previous century [i.e., the Caucasus War],' as he put it."[49] From Stankevich's comments – assuming that they have been correctly reported by Yandarbiev – we can

---

[46] Emil' Pain and Arkadii Popov, "Rossiiskaya politika v Chechne," *Izvestiya*, 7 February 1995, pp. 1, 4.

[47] From a commentary by Govorukhin accompanying extracts from a report issued by the Govorukhin Commission, in *Pravda*, 27 February 1996, p. 2. The excerpts appeared in the 27 February through 6 March issues of *Pravda*.

[48] *RFE–RL Daily Report*, 31 July 1991.   [49] Yandarbiev, *V preddverii*, p. 37.

see that influential Russian leaders were pondering the option of an armed invasion of Chechnya less than a fortnight after Yeltsin's election as Russian president in 1991.

The "Chechen Revolution" triggered by the August coup

By the month of August 1991, Chechnya was already in what might aptly be termed a pre-revolutionary condition. When, on 19 August, the State Committee for the State of Emergency (Russian initials: GKChP) announced in Moscow that it had assumed power throughout the USSR, this presented a marvelous opening to Dudaev and to the nationalists around him, especially since Doku Zavgaev and the communist leadership of the republic seemed unable to adopt a principled position with regard to the putsch. As Marie Bennigsen Broxup has noted: "All telephone links with Checheno-Ingushetiya were cut for some time. The leadership of the Republic was overtaken by 'mental paralysis.' The republican radio and television went silent, Doku Zavgaev was in Moscow, and the acting chairman of the Supreme Soviet, Petrenko, went into hiding. Only the National Chechen Congress and the Vainakh Democratic Party led by Zelimkhan Yandarbiev reacted without panicking. They immediately set up operation headquarters in the former building of the *gorkom* [city Communist Party committee]."[50]

Dudaev has stated his view that, had the GKChP succeeded in taking power in August, then it "was preparing an especially refined genocide for the Chechen people."[51] He was presumably thinking of the GKChP's announced "war on crime," which could have been directed against the Chechens as an alleged "criminal people."[52]

The absence from the republic of party leader Zavgaev and the pronounced wavering of the entire republican Communist Party leadership played into the hands of Dudaev and the national radicals. The latter reestablished contact with Moscow through such leading Chechens in the Soviet capital as Ruslan Khasbulatov, then first deputy chairman of the RSFSR Supreme Soviet, and people's deputy and retired MVD major general Aslambek Aslakhanov. A meeting to protest the Moscow putsch was held at 9:30 a.m. on 19 August in Groznyi, next

[50] Marie Bennigsen Broxup, "After the Putsch, 1991," in Marie Bennigsen Broxup, ed., *The North Caucasus Barrier* (New York: St. Martin's Press, 1992), p. 221. Broxup takes much of her information from the 30 August 1991 issue of the Groznyi newspaper, *Svoboda*.

[51] In *Megapolis-ekspress*, 25, 27 July 1994, p. 18.

[52] On this, see the chapter concerning the putsch in Dunlop, *Rise of Russia*, pp. 196–99.

to the building of the republican Council of Ministers; this meeting eventually turned into a ten-week-long continuous demonstration. Addressing the crowd, Zelimkhan Yandarbiev and other nationalists exhorted their fellow Chechens: "It is necessary to create underground organizations and armed formations. We have to raise the people to repulse the GKChP."[53]

In the late morning or early afternoon of 19 August, Zelimkhan Yandarbiev was arrested by the secret police, and the protest meeting was forcibly dispersed by the militia. "The militia and KGB in the square," Yandarbiev has recalled, "now outnumbered the protesters . . . Forming a long column, the militia advanced upon the meeting. At that moment, I was seized by several men in civilian clothing and in the uniform of the militia who had crept up from behind me."[54] Yandarbiev was taken first to Groznyi KGB headquarters, where he was given a stern warning by a deputy procurator; later that same day, however, he and fellow Vainakh Democratic Party activist Salaudi Yakh"yaev, who had also been seized, were released after acting party leader Petrenko had been warned by Dudaev that he would be held personally responsible for Yandarbiev's arrest.[55]

Also on 19 August, OKChN issued a fiery appeal to the working people of the republic calling for "an indefinite general political strike," to begin on 21 August, and for civil disobedience to be shown until such time as the "criminal junta" in Moscow was defeated. According to Yandarbiev, the *ispolkom* of OKChN, also on the 19th, "began to create battle detachments and strike groups which took under control all [Soviet] military bases and vital communication centers, not only in Groznyi but throughout the republic."[56]

The republican Communist Party leadership, it appeared, continued to entertain hopes that the putsch would succeed. At 4 a.m. on 20 August, the republican militia, acting on orders from Communist Party *gorkom* boss Kutsenko, attempted unsuccessfully to raid the headquarters of OKChN. On the evening of the same day, a joint KGB–MVD force sought to liberate the building of the *gorkom* but was driven off by national guards loyal to OKChN. Later that same night, the Groznyi city soviet military garrison was put on alert, and fresh troops and military hardware were introduced into the republic from both the east and west. Some rural areas of Checheno-Ingushetiya were occupied by the army under pretext of helping out with the harvest. In response, OKChN warned all Soviet military bases in the republic that, "if they

[53] Yandarbiev, *V preddverii*, p. 41.   [54] Ibid., p. 42.
[55] Broxup, "After the Putsch," p. 220.   [56] Yandarbiev, *V preddverii*, p. 46.

[were] suspected of aggressive intentions, then force [would] be used against them."[57]

When it became clear on 21 August that the Moscow putsch had irrevocably failed, Doku Zavgaev immediately returned to Groznyi and then convoked a session of the republican Supreme Soviet at which he declared that all was quiet in the republic.[58] The Govorukhin Commission, which considered Zavgaev to be a "good Chechen," has sought to clear him of charges that he actively collaborated with the coup, but even it has felt required to note that, during the two days he was in Moscow, Zavgaev "did not make clear his position" and engaged in fence-straddling.[59]

On 22 August, the day on which the coup suffered a final defeat in Moscow, the leadership of Dudaev's *ispolkom* demanded during a huge mass meeting held in Groznyi that the members of the Supreme Soviet of the republic resign, since it had been unable to adopt a principled position vis-à-vis the attempted Moscow putsch. The *ispolkom* also insisted that the republican Council of Ministers, Procurator's Office, KGB, MVD, and, in general, all official bodies of executive power in Checheno-Ingushetiya resign. That evening, demonstrators surrounded the republican television center and, after a short clash with the militia, seized the building. Dudaev then spoke on television and explained the political goals of the national radicals.[60]

The "Chechen Revolution" was now moving ahead with blinding speed. From all regions in the republic, impoverished Chechens – "rural surplus population" – flowed into the capital of Groznyi, seeking to overthrow the detested Communist Party *nomenklatura*, headed by Doku Zavgaev. There was quite clearly an element of "social revolution" in this influx of populace into the capital. Also involved in the movement were representatives of the republic's "shadow economy," especially those seeking to obtain large profits from the oil industry. One of Dudaev's most influential supporters and financial backers at this time was the afore-mentioned "major entrepreneur" Yaragi Mamodaev.[61] Finally, a number of Muslim fundamentalists also supported the revolution, believing that Dudaev would eventually be induced to create an Islamic republic. Religious and clan leaders in the villages helped to swing the rural populace over to the side of Dudaev and OKChN.

[57] Ibid., p. 47.
[58] Broxup, "After the Putsch," p. 222.   [59] In *Pravda*, 27 February 1996, p. 2.
[60] Muzaev, *Chechenskaya respublika*, pp. 163–64; Broxup, "After the Putsch," pp. 220–21.
[61] For Mamodaev's biography, see Muzaev, *Chechenskaya respublika*, pp. 76–77. On Mamodaev's role in Dudaev's coming to power, see *Komsomol'skaya pravda*, 1 September 1993, p. 3.

Dvoevlastie

On 25 August, an emergency session of the Zavgaev-controlled Supreme Soviet opened in Groznyi. The assembled deputies rejected the demands of Dudaev's *ispolkom* and instead affirmed their support for their chairman, Zavgaev. What Russians term *dvoevlastie* (dyarchy or dual power) had now become an ominous reality. (The Russian Federation would later experience its own excruciating *dvoevlastie* during the period from December 1992 to October 1993.)

At this pivotal juncture, Doku Zavgaev might well have been contemplating the use of force against the national radicals. If such were the case, he might have prevailed. According to ethnic affairs specialists Emil' Pain and Arkadii Popov, the possibility of a successful use of force by Zavgaev to suppress the emerging revolution existed until early October 1991: "[I]t would indeed have been possible," they write, "to carry out a police operation to 'disarm the illegal armed formations [of Dudaev].'" And they continue: "[I]n Chechnya, there still functioned the organs of the procuracy, the militia, and state security, all of them subordinated to central power, and in Groznyi there were quartered [heavily armed] military units, while the army of Dudaev's fighters was basically limited to firearms." Pain and Popov note that the Chechen Revolution was not being supported by the overwhelming majority of the Ingush populace (14 percent of the republic's population), nor by the so-called Russian-language populace (26 percent of the total). Even more significantly, they maintain, it was also not being supported by 40 percent of the Chechens themselves, especially by those living in Groznyi and in the northern regions of the republic.[62]

The leadership of the Russian Federation, however, proceeded effectively to pull the rug out from under Zavgaev and to empower Dudaev. On 26 August, there arrived in Groznyi a member of the Presidium of the Supreme Soviet of the RSFSR, General Aslambek Aslakhanov, an ethnic Chechen with close ties to Khasbulatov, and Inga Grebesheva, a deputy chairwoman of the RSFSR Council of Ministers. Both sternly warned Zavgaev against using force to resolve the political crisis. Their actions objectively served to support the Dudaev-led opposition.[63]

That the leadership of the Russian Federation intended to jettison Zavgaev as head of Checheno-Ingushetiya seems clear. According to then acting RSFSR Supreme Soviet chairman Khasbulatov, Yeltsin called him shortly after the collapse of the August putsch and informed

[62] Pain and Popov, "Rossiiskaya politika v Chechne," *Izvestiya*, 1 February 1995, pp. 1, 4.
[63] Muzaev, *Chechenskaya respublika*, p. 164.

him that his plan was "to replace Zavgaev with Khadzhiev." Salambek Khadzhiev (b. 1941), a specialist in the Soviet oil industry and a corresponding member of the USSR Academy of Sciences, had briefly served as USSR minister for the petrochemical industry under Gorbachev. As Khasbulatov tells it, Yeltsin's plan to replace Zavgaev with Khadzhiev failed "because Khadzhiev's authority was not high enough" in Chechnya.[64] Indeed, according to Khasbulatov, there were rumors circulating in Chechnya that Khadzhiev had himself cooperated with the GKChP in the launching of the August putsch.

Also in late August, according to Khasbulatov, he was able to convince General Petr Deinekin, commander of the Soviet air force, to fly to Groznyi in an attempt to convince Dudaev to return to a career in the military. Deinekin did as he was asked, but, though warmly received by Dudaev, he failed in his task. Later, Generals Boris Gromov and Ruslan Aushev (subsequently elected the president of Ingushetiya) failed on a similar mission.[65]

Under heavy pressure from the Moscow authorities, the members of the Presidium of the Chechen–Ingush Supreme Soviet agreed to resign their posts, but Zavgaev and his deputy chairman defiantly refused to do so. An attempt to negotiate a settlement with the Dudaev-led opposition failed, and the full parliament once again rejected ultimatums presented by the *ispolkom* of OKChN, declaring the actions of the national radicals to be unconstitutional.

By the beginning of September, the *ispolkom* under Dudaev increasingly controlled the situation on the ground in Groznyi. A national guard, largely armed with rifles and pistols, had been formed by the radicals, and, by the end of August, they had succeeded in seizing the main television and radio stations in the city. The building of the republican Council of Ministers was taken over on 1 September, with the green flag of Islam being raised over it. On 1–2 September, the third National Congress of the Chechen People was held, and it declared the Supreme Soviet of Checheno-Ingushetiya deposed, and granted full power on the territory of the republic to the *ispolkom*.

On 3 September, the newly formed presidium of the Chechen–Ingush Supreme Soviet, once again chaired by Zavgaev, belatedly decided to enforce a hard-line policy and declared the introduction of emergency rule in the city of Groznyi; it also announced that presidential elections would be held in the republic on 29 September. By this time, however, a majority of the districts of Checheno-Ingushetiya had gone over to the Dudaev-led *ispolkom*. The attempted crackdown by Zavgaev and his

---

[64] Khasbulatov, *Chechnya*, pp. 11–12.   [65] Ibid., p. 12.

followers thus had the counterproductive result of inducing the national radicals to take decisive action.[66]

Dudaev stages a coup

On the evening of 6 September, as Doku Zavgaev was chairing a session of the elected deputies of Checheno-Ingushetiya at all levels, Dudaev's national guard stormed the parliament building. Several deputies were wounded in the assault, while the first secretary of the Groznyi Communist Party *gorkom*, Vitalii Kutsenko, died from injuries received when he threw himself out of a third-floor window, apparently in a panicked attempt to avoid being seized. Such is the version put forth by most careful students of the revolution, including by Emil' Pain and Arkadii Popov, who write: "[T]rying to save himself from the bandits, he [Kutsenko] threw himself out a window."[67] Less scrupulous opponents of Dudaev assert that Kutsenko was directly murdered by Dudaev's guard, who allegedly hurled him out the window to his death. Stanislav Govorukhin, chairman of the Govorukhin Commission, is one who holds this view.[68]

According to Yusup Soslambekov, at the time an ally of the Dudaev forces, Doku Zavgaev resigned his post under extreme pressure from leading Khasbulatov supporter and member of the presidium of the RSFSR Supreme Soviet, General Aslambek Aslakhanov. Once Aslakhanov had made his appearance in Groznyi, Soslambekov recalls, Zavgaev was physically prevented from carrying out the decree which he had issued "On the Introduction of Emergency Rule into the Chechen–Ingush Republic." The local MVD refrained from obeying Zavgaev, heeding instead the wishes of the powerful Chechen visitor from Moscow, who also happened to be chairman of the Committee on Questions of Legality, Law and Order, and the Struggle with Crime of the RSFSR Supreme Soviet, thus exercising "concrete authority over the power structures in all of Russia." On 6 September, Soslambekov writes, General Aslakhanov "personally accepted the resignation of Zavgaev."[69]

In his 1994 book on the Chechen crisis, Aslakhanov limits himself to recalling that he visited Zavgaev in his office, after which the communist leader soon went out to address the assembled crowd, affirming that "he

---

[66] Muzaev, *Chechenskaya respublika*, 164–65; Broxup, "After the Putsch," p. 225.

[67] Pain and Popov, "Rossiiskaya politika v Chechne," *Izvestiya*, 7 February 1995, pp. 1, 4.

[68] In *Pravda*, 27 February 1996, p. 2. A similar claim is made in *Chechenskaya tragediya*, p. 16.

[69] Soslambekov, *Chechnya*, pp. 10–11.

was giving up his powers, as he did not want bloodshed."[70] Aslakhanov's intimation is that Zavgaev publicly resigned under pressure from him. In his first volume of memoirs, Zelimkhan Yandarbiev recalls: "Zavgaev abdicated his 'throne' publicly before the people, and all sins were forgiven him. The leadership of the *ispolkom* of OKChN even made a gentleman's gesture and did not demand a written declaration of resignation." This, he remarks, turned out to be a mistake, as the following day Zavgaev changed his mind and "tried to abdicate his abdication."[71]

Moscow's hesitant reaction

How did Moscow react to these stormy and portentous events taking place in Groznyi? On 7 September, Ruslan Khasbulatov, speaking on the Russian television news program "Vesti," openly welcomed the fall of his adversary, Zavgaev.[72] Four days later, on 11 September, a delegation headed by RSFSR state secretary Gennadii Burbulis and minister of information and the press Mikhail Poltoranin – both at the time close advisers of Yeltsin – flew to Groznyi in an attempt to promote an agreement between the radicals and the remnants of the former republican government.[73] Also serving as members of the delegation were outspoken "democrat" Fedor Shelov-Kovedyaev (later briefly named Russian first deputy minister of foreign affairs), and an elected RSFSR people's deputy, Isa Aliroev, an ethnic Chechen. The Burbulis delegation was able, on 15 September, to persuade the republican Supreme Soviet to dissolve itself and to transfer its power to a Provisional Supreme Council, which was entrusted with organizing new elections.[74]

Interpretations of this key visit to Chechnya by Burbulis, Poltoranin, and their party have differed greatly. One well-known political scientist and journalist, Fedor Burlatskii, has commented acidly: "[T]wo democrats, Mikhail Poltoranin and Gennadii Burbulis, brought Dzhokhar Dudaev to Chechnya, as, in his time, Babrak Karmal was brought to power in Afghanistan."[75] This scathing assessment strikes one as wide of the mark. The two "democrats" obviously did not bring Dudaev to

[70] Aslambek Aslakhanov, *Demokratiya prestupnoi ne byvaet* (Moscow: author publication, 1994), p. 73.
[71] Yandarbiev, *V preddverii*, p. 56.   [72] Broxup, "After the Putsch," p. 226.
[73] Muzaev, *Chechenskaya respublika*, p. 165. Soslambekov writes that the delegation arrived on 10 September. See Soslambekov, *Chechnya*, pp. 11–12.
[74] Sheehy, "Power Struggle," p. 23.
[75] Fedor Burlatskii, "Uroki kavkazskoi kampanii," *Nezavisimaya gazeta*, 31 January 1995, p. 2.

power, but they did, apparently, counsel against a use of force to oust him. Retired military officer and elected people's deputy Sergei Yushenkov has, in contrast to Burlatskii, praised Burbulis and Poltoranin precisely for their approach: "[T]hey were able to move the issue from a coercive solution of the problem to the plane of a negotiation process."[76] On the other hand, the anti-Dudaev Chechen member of the Burbulis delegation, Isa Aliroev, has criticized its actions, recalling that he "tried to convince his colleagues that there was not broad support for Dudaev but that the commission firmly stood on the side of 'democracy' and set only one condition: that of legitimacy. From Moscow there arrived a group of high-class jurists to work out a scenario for the coming to power of Dudaev."[77]

On the same day that the Burbulis delegation flew to Groznyi, 11 September, the leadership of the Russian Federation decided to respond less irenically to disturbances involving thousands of Chechens and Dagestanis in the town of Lenin-Aul, located in the Kazbek district of the Dagestan ASSR, not far from the border with Chechnya. The demonstrators were demanding an immediate reallocation of lands which had been confiscated by the regime following the deportation of the Chechens in 1944. Once again, the key "land question" had come front and center. When word spread among the Chechens that a military column was advancing from North Ossetiya to Lenin-Aul to crush the disturbances, hundreds of peaceful protesters, including many women and the elderly, closed down the Rostov-to-Baku highway and forced the column to turn back.[78] This episode shows graphically that elements in the Russian leadership (apparently led by Vice President Rutskoi) were, in the first days after the August putsch, prepared, if necessary, to employ military force to pacify the North Caucasus region. As they would in the future, however, the Russian "hawks" seem to have miscalculated badly.

On 14 September, Ruslan Khasbulatov arrived in Checheno-Ingushetiya, and, on the following day, he personally chaired the final session of the Chechen–Ingush Supreme Soviet. The parliament building had been ringed in advance by Dudaev's national guard to put maximum pressure on the deputies. Under heavy pressure from Khasbulatov and from the leaders of the Dudaev-led OKChN, the assembled deputies adopted a resolution to retire their chairman, Doku

---

[76] S. N. Yushenkov, *Voina v Chechne i problemy rossiiskoi gosudarstvennosti i demokratii* (Moscow: author publication, 1995), p. 11.

[77] In *Komsomol'skaya pravda*, 1 September 1993, p. 3.

[78] Broxup, "After the Putsch," p. 227.

Zavgaev, and to dissolve the parliament of which they were members. New parliamentary elections were set for 17 November. During the transitional period leading up to the election, power, as has been noted, was to be in the hands of a Provisional Supreme Council of OKChN, consisting of thirty-two deputies. Khusein Akhmadov, a deputy with close ties to the radicals, was selected head of the provisional council, which was tasked with preparing the upcoming elections. It also initiated such actions as handing over the House of Political Education in Groznyi to the republic's recently opened Islamic Institute.[79]

On 15 September, Khasbulatov returned to Moscow. He would not return again to his native Chechnya until February 1994, following his release from a Moscow prison. One is inclined to agree with Pain and Popov who claim that, at this point, Khasbulatov "indubitably sought to support Dudaev as his viceregent in Chechnya." But, as they also correctly note, "The general had other plans."[80]

Also on 15 September, meeting in the city of Nazran', the Ingush, who, like the Chechens, had been radicalized by recent events, announced during an emergency congress of Ingush deputies of all levels the establishment of an "Ingush Autonomous Republic within the RSFSR." The Ingush were thus intentionally setting a more moderate course than their Vainakh brethren, the Chechens.[81]

By this time, it had become clear that the Provisional Supreme Council of OKChN was planning to hold *presidential* as well as parliamentary elections in October. This development prompted a strong negative reaction among anti-Dudaev circles both in Chechnya and in Moscow itself. On 25 September, five members of the Provisional Council, headed by one of its deputy chairman, Yurii Chernyi, who was close to Khasbulatov, condemned the attempts by OKChN to assume the plenitude of power in the republic. On the following day, 26 September, Ruslan Khasbulatov sent a telegram to the Provisional Council, to the Council of Ministers of the republic, and to OKChN warning them that, in the event of a usurpation of power by "an informal organization," the results of any elections conducted by the usurpers would be deemed invalid. On 6 October, however, the *ispolkom* of OKChN dissolved the Provisional Council for "undermining and

[79] Ibid., pp. 226–27. See also Yandarbiev, *V preddverii*, p. 57.
[80] Pain and Popov, "Rossiiskaya politika v Chechne," *Izvestiya*, 7 February 1995, pp. 1, 4.
[81] Muzaev, *Chechenskaya respublika*, p. 166; *Rossiiskie vooruzhennye sily v chechenskom konflikte: analiz, itogy, vyvody (analiticheskii obzor)* (Moscow: Holveg, 1995), p. 8. A second expanded edition of this book, bearing the same title, was also published in 1995. The title page of the second edition contains the names of the volume's coauthors: N. N. Novichkov, V. Ya. Snegovskii, A. G. Sokolov, and V. Yu. Shvarev. All references are to the first edition.

provocative activity" and declared itself to be "the revolutionary committee for the transition period with full powers."[82]

Rutskoi's gambits

Threatening noises were increasingly emanating from Moscow, and Dudaev's supporters in the Chechen–Ingush Republic felt required to take strong defensive action. On 5 October, barricades were erected on Freedom Square in front of the Council of Ministers' building in Groznyi after thirteen members of the Provisional Supreme Council, allegedly supported by the local KGB, decided to oust that body's chairman, Khuscin Akhmadov, a supporter of Dudaev. Viewing this as an attempt by the KGB to usurp power, OKChN then announced the dismissal of the Provisional Council, arrested the procurator of the Chechen–Ingush Republic, Aleksandr Pushkin (not, of course, the great nineteenth-century poet), and occupied the buildings of the KGB and Council of Ministers in Groznyi, but failed to take the headquarters of the MVD.[83]

The following day, 6 October, saw the Russian vice president, General Aleksandr Rutskoi, arrive in Groznyi as head of a self-described peacemaking delegation, which included such unlikely peacemakers as Andrei Dunaev and Viktor Ivanenko, heads, respectively, of the RSFSR MVD and RSFSR KGB. While in Groznyi, Rutskoi met with both the members of OKChN and the Provisional Supreme Council, but these meetings produced no concrete results. Upon his return to Moscow, Rutskoi angrily compared the situation in Chechnya with that of Nagorno-Karabakh, and he alleged that the unrest in the republic had been fomented by Georgian ultra-nationalist president Zviad Gamsakhurdia, a ploy designed to discredit the Chechen radicals. Rutskoi described Dudaev's supporters as a "gang terrorizing the population" and said that the gang numbered only some 250 men.[84]

In his memoirs, Zelimkhan Yandarbiev writes that, during the visit of Rutskoi's delegation, Andrei Dunaev, chairman of the RSFSR MVD, directly threatened that Russia might have to resort to force to deal with the Chechen problem. In response, he was told, according to Yandarbiev, that "if Russia resorts to coercive methods . . . it will then have to deal not only with Chechnya but with the entire Caucasus." Yandarbiev also indicts General Rutskoi for involving himself, during his visit to Groznyi, in a shadowy plot by the Groznyi KGB and MVD to remove

---

[82] Muzaev, *Chechenskaya respublika*, p. 166.
[83] Broxup, "After the Putsch," p. 228, and Sheehy, "Power Struggle," p. 23.
[84] Muzaev, *Chechenskaya respublika*, p. 166; Broxup, "After the Putsch," pp. 228–29.

the chairman of the Provisional Council, Khusein Akhmadov, from his position.[85]

Having returned to Moscow, Rutskoi, on 8 October, proceeded to the RSFSR Supreme Soviet, where, with Khasbulatov's support, he easily persuaded that body's members to vote a resolution "on the political situation in the Chechen–Ingush Republic," which effectively returned the republic to a pre-putsch *status quo ante*. After declaring that within the republic "state institutions are being seized and so are officials," and that "the life, rights and property of citizens in the Chechen–Ingush Republic are being subjected to growing danger," the RSFSR parliament adopted a series of resolutions which, *inter alia*, proclaimed: that the Provisional Supreme Council should henceforth be regarded as "the only legitimate body of state power" in the republic; that Bandi Bakhmadov, a procurator, had replaced Khusain Akhmadov as Provisional Council chairman; that all illegal armed formations within the republic must turn in their weapons by 2400 hours on 10 October; and that the Provisional Council under Procurator Bakhmadov's chairmanship "should adopt all the necessary measures to stabilize the situation in the Chechen–Ingush Republic and to ensure law and order."[86]

On 9 October, Rutskoi ratcheted up his charges. He gave a lengthy interview to Russian Television during which he accused the Dudaev-led OKChN "of having killed Kutsenko, the Groznyi CPSU chairman," and labeled the members of the OKChN *ispolkom* criminals and brigands. The Russian vice president recommended that Yeltsin take "specific measures to detain these criminals," acting under Article 218 of the RSFSR Criminal Code (which treated the illegal possession of weapons), and Articles 67 and 68 of the code (which concerned terrorism directed against lawful authorities).[87]

Rutskoi's inflammatory words and the harsh resolutions adopted by the RSFSR Supreme Soviet were denounced by General Dudaev as "virtually a declaration of war on the Chechen–Ingush Republic." On 8 October, the Chechen national guard was put on heightened alert, and a general mobilization was announced of all Chechen males between the ages of fifteen and fifty-five; all Chechens serving in the USSR armed forces were ordered home; and the autumn Soviet military draft in the republic was canceled; all activities of the Russian Procuracy in the republic were also effectively halted.[88] A crowd of 50,000 Dudaev supporters demonstrated in front of the Council of Ministers building in Groznyi and then seized it. The presidium of the *ispolkom* of OKChN

[85] Yandarbiev, *V preddverii*, p. 58.
[86] Broxup, "After the Putsch," p. 229 and n. 16.   [87] Ibid., p. 230.
[88] From the Govorukhin Commission report in *Pravda*, 29 February 1996, p. 2.

assailed the position of the Russian Federation as "coarse, provocative interference in the internal affairs of the Chechen Republic." Zelimkhan Yandarbiev, chairman of the Vainakh Democratic Party, called upon his supporters to arm themselves and declare holy war against the Russian state. The assembled Chechen masses, many of them unemployed, responded enthusiastically to Yandarbiev's message.[89]

Incensed at this intransigent response to his threats, Rutskoi repeated his invective against the "criminal" OKChN and announced that he had been empowered by the presidium of the RSFSR Supreme Soviet to declare a state of emergency in Checheno-Ingushetiya. Pronouncing himself opposed to bringing in the Soviet military at this point, he maintained that the Chechen–Ingush MVD was prepared to take "appropriate action" to stop the actions of the Chechen "political clique." Openly playing the Russian nationalist card, Rutskoi warned that the 300,000 Russians living in the Chechen–Ingush Republic were very much at risk. Khasbulatov supported Rutskoi's call for "very tough measures" and stated his opinion that OKChN consisted of no more than 200 to 300 desperate terrorists. On 10 October, the RSFSR Supreme Soviet adopted a resolution outlining measures for the restoration of order and legality in the republic.[90]

In his memoirs, Zelimkhan Yandarbiev writes that, "the closer we came to the elections of 27 October, the harsher became the opposition of the pro-Russian forces [in Checheno-Ingushetiya]." He recalls that Valentin Stepankov, procurator general of the RSFSR, arrived in Groznyi as part of a delegation from Moscow. While in Groznyi, that delegation "held a joint meeting with the so-called Supreme Provisional Council, headed by [Procurator] Bakhmadov."[91] Yusup Soslambekov, at the time a close Dudaev ally, recalls that: "Moscow named General Ibragimov minister of internal affairs of the Chechen–Ingush Republic. He, together with the Provisional Supreme Council headed by B. Bakhmadov, was to recruit loyal people into the organs of internal affairs and unite his adherents around the MVD. Then it was planned to arrest the leaders of the *ispolkom*, for which the Procuracy General and the MVD had prepared written orders."[92] Those named in these arrest orders, Soslambekov writes, included Dudaev, Yandarbiev, Soslambekov himself, and Movladi Udugov.

On 18 October, General Dudaev warned the republic's populace to prepare for a war which he deemed inevitable, "since hostile forces were massed in North Ossetiya and Dagestan preparing to attack the

[89] Muzaev, *Chechenskaya respublika*, p. 167.
[90] Broxup, "After the Putsch," pp. 230–31, Sheehy, "Power Struggle," p. 23.
[91] Yandarbiev, *V preddverii*, p. 59.   [92] Soslambekov, *Chechnya*, p. 12.

Republic and strangle the revolution." He declared that "a continuation of the genocide against the Chechen people" was once again a distinct possibility, and he reported that 62,000 men had already signed up for the republican national guard and the people's militia. Preparations for elections to the Chechen presidency and to a new parliament – set for 27 October – proceeded apace.[93]

The following day, 19 October, Yeltsin inserted himself into the fray. The Russian president ordered the Chechen opposition under Dudaev to submit unconditionally, within three days, to the resolution of the RSFSR Supreme Soviet. He declared that, if the Chechen opposition failed to comply, then "all measures provided for in the laws of the Russian Federation would be employed to normalize the situation and ensure the protection of the constitutional order."[94]

On 23 October, the RSFSR Procuracy in Moscow issued a decree underlining that "citizens are subject to criminal liability for the over-throw or forcible change of the state and public system, for violating the integrity of the RSFSR, [and for] whipping up national or religious hatreds." National guards and other armed formations in Chechnya, the decree noted, were not regulated by legislation and were therefore "unlawful."[95]

Despite these harsh threats issued by Yeltsin, Rutskoi, the RSFSR Supreme Soviet, and the Russian Procuracy, Dudaev and the Chechen national radicals proceeded without hesitation toward the holding of presidential and parliamentary elections on 27 October.

The seizure of KGB headquarters in Groznyi

Before we discuss the elections, it is necessary briefly to backtrack and discuss one key event which occurred during early October: namely, the takeover by the Dudaev forces of KGB headquarters in Groznyi. As has been noted, one of the officials accompanying Vice President Rutskoi on his visit to Groznyi on 6 October was RSFSR KGB chairman Viktor Ivanenko. According to the anti-Yeltsin opposition newspaper *Den'*, one of Ivanenko's top assistants had made an earlier secret visit to the republic in September.

"[In September] there secretly arrived in Groznyi," the *Den'* account maintains, "one of the deputies of Ivanenko (at that time the chairman of the KGB of Russia). For two days, in the former hotel of the party *obkom* [*reskom*], he conducted long, secret negotiations with Dudaev. After he flew out, Dzhokhar Dudaev declared loudly that a high-ranking

---

[93] Broxup, "After the Putsch," p. 231.   [94] Ibid., p. 234.   [95] Ibid.

representative of the KGB had come to Chechnya to organize a state coup but had not been able to seize him [i.e., Dudaev]. Following this, he, Dudaev, had given an order to seize the KGB building. In the carrying out of this order, it turned out that there were only three persons in the building."[96]

Accounts carried by *Den'* and by its successor publication, *Zavtra*, must be treated with caution, since they are often inaccurate and misleading. However, in this instance, the *Den'* account is supported by information provided in an interview with General Aslambek Aslakhanov, at the time a committee chairman of the Russian Supreme Soviet. "[T]he building of the KGB in Groznyi," Aslakhanov recalled in August 1993, "was capable of withstanding a two- or three-month-long siege which employed artillery. Its communications and technical equipment were designed to control the whole of the North Caucasus. During the time that the building was stormed, only four employees were present, and only one of them was armed. The attackers took the building in several minutes' time. Scores of boxes containing secret documents magically disappeared. I am certain that it was a deal [sdelka]."[97]

If these two accounts are basically accurate, it would appear that the Yeltsin leadership quietly agreed to turn over the KGB headquarters in Groznyi, with its advanced communications equipment and its technology and valuable archives, to the militants some time in early October 1991. (The handing over of vast quantities of military hardware and ammunition to General Dudaev will be treated in chapter 5, pp. 164–68.)

Dudaev is "elected" president

On 27 October, elections for the republican parliament and the Chechen presidency took place, and, not surprisingly, a spate of irregularities occurred. Seven candidates for the Chechen presidency had earlier withdrawn from the race, citing the clearly unjust conditions of the elections. Members of the republican Central Election Commission were named by the *ispolkom* of OKChN; local election commissions

---

[96] "Chechenskaya situatsiya: vzglyad iznutri," *Den'*, 26, 4–10 July 1993, p. 3.
[97] "Ruka Moskvy v Chechne ili ruka Chechni v Moskve?," *Rossiya*, 34, 18–24 August 1993, p. 4. In his 1994 book, *Demokratiya prestupnoi*, General Aslakhanov states that the lists of KGB agents were destroyed before Dudaev's coming to power (p. 88). But Soslambekov, in his book *Chechnya*, writes that Dudaev did obtain the names of the agents (p. 11). Yandarbiev maintains in his second volume of memoirs, *Checheniya*, that "the property and archives [of the Groznyi KGB] were stolen by those who had been posted there as guards . . . i.e., basically by the band of Bislan Gantamirov" (p. 90).

were formed from among Dudaev supporters; and the legislation according to which the elections were conducted was not confirmed by any legal body, not even by a special committee on elections which had been created by the Third Congress of OKChN. "In essence," anti-Dudaev author Timur Muzaev has concluded, "the elections were conducted by the social organization whose leader was running for the position of head of state."[98]

"During the course of the entire election campaign, for which less than two weeks were given," Emil' Pain and Arkadii Popov have written, "the republic lived under conditions of de facto military rule." And they continue: "[I]n some districts, the number of ballots cast exceeded the number of registered voters, and in the ballot boxes which were placed out in the town squares packets of ballots allegedly filled out by representatives of the Chechen diaspora were put into the voting urns."[99]

When the election results were announced on 30 October, it emerged that Dudaev had easily bested his two remaining rivals. According to a report issued by Major General I. Sokolov, commander of the North Caucasus Military District, who cited published Chechen election results, a total of 490,000 persons took part in the election, representing 77 percent of eligible voters in the republic. Of this number, 416,181, or 85 percent, voted for General Dudaev. Sokolov went on to note that neither the Ingush nor a part of the Russian-language populace in the republic had participated in the election.[100]

What is one to make of the announced official election results? Nationalities specialist Sergei Arutyunov, a corresponding member of the Russian Academy of Sciences, noted in testimony before the Russian Constitutional Court on 13 July 1995: "Of course, Dudaev was rather proclaimed than elected president," and "the elections would not have been deemed lawful by independent international observers." But Arutyunov went on to observe that, according to public opinion surveys, interviews conducted by specialists, and a wealth of other data, "one may say without doubt that, in 1991, not less than 60 percent, and probably up to 70 percent of the population of Chechnya, of the voters of Chechnya, did indeed genuinely support Dudaev."[101] In a certain

[98] Muzaev, *Chechenskaya respublika*, pp. 167–68.
[99] In "Rossiiskaya politika v Chechne," *Izvestiya*, 7 February 1995, pp. 1, 4.
[100] In *Belaya kniga. Chechnya, 1991–1995: fakty, dokumenty, svidetel'stva*, 2 vols. (Moscow: Tsentr obshchestvennykh svyazei FSK Rossii, 1995), vol. I, pp. 11–12. Somewhat different figures were reported by the Chechen Electoral Commission. See Curran, et al., *Search for Peace*, pp. 95–96. On the election results, see also Hill, *"Russia's Tinderbox"*, p. 82, and Sheehy, "Power Struggle," p. 24.
[101] See "Istoricheskaya pamyat' Chechni," *Novoe vremya*, 29 (1995), 12–15.

sense, therefore, if Arutyunov is right, this flawed election can none-theless be regarded as an expression of the Chechen popular will.

Russia decides to invade Chechnya . . . sort of

The formal announcement of the Chechen election results on 30 October ushered in an exceptionally tense period in Russian–Chechen relations. The anti-Dudaev Provisional Supreme Council of the Chechen–Ingush Republic immediately declared the election results to be fabricated and unconstitutional. The following day, 2 November, the Fifth Congress of RSFSR Deputies, meeting in Moscow under Khas-bulatov's chairmanship, decreed that the elections in Chechnya had been unlawful and that they directly contradicted the Constitution of the RSFSR.[102] (While Boris Yeltsin was later to dissolve this Khas-bulatov-led congress, he always upheld its November 1991 decree on the Chechen presidential elections as having been lawful; Dudaev's acting vice president, Zelimkhan Yandarbiev, for his part, considers this 2 November decree to have essentially constituted the beginning of a new Russian–Chechen war.)[103]

Reacting to the threatening noises emanating from Moscow, General Dudaev, on 1 November 1991, issued a decree declaring the Chechen Republic to be a fully independent state. The following day, the just-elected Chechen parliament passed a resolution (*postanovlenie*) ratifying Dudaev's decree.[104]

In response to these moves, the Russian leadership decided to initiate a military-police takeover of Chechnya. On 7 November, Yeltsin issued a presidential decree "On the Introduction of Emergency Rule into the Chechen–Ingush Republic."[105] This represented the beginning of the long-expected crackdown against the rebellious republic.

Unfortunately for Yeltsin and his associates, the November crack-down occurred too late. As Emil' Pain and Arkadii Popov have noted, in order to have been successful, the suppression of Dudaev should have been accomplished by early October at the latest. Why, then, the critical delay? Because, as Pain and Popov explain, "there was taking place a tense struggle with the remnants of the union structures."[106] The sharp power struggle between Yeltsin and the RSFSR, on the one hand, and Mikhail Gorbachev and the USSR, on the other, was entering its final,

---

[102] See *Rossiiskie vooruzhennye sily*, p. 8.   [103] Yandarbiev, *Checheniya*, p. 370.
[104] Yandarbiev, *V preddverii*, p. 66. See also Soslambekov, *Chechnya*, p. 17. For the text of the Chechen parliament's resolution, see Curran, et al., *Search for Peace*, pp. 97–98.
[105] In *Rossiiskie vooruzhennye sily*, pp. 8–9.
[106] In "Rossiiskaya politika v Chechne," *Izvestiya*, 7 February 1995, pp. 1, 4.

climactic phase.[107] The leadership of the Russian Federation was too distracted by this brutal contest to be able sufficiently to focus on rebellious Chechnya.

By November 1991, Pain and Popov underline, "[A]ll organs of federal authority in Chechnya had already been disbanded, and all military garrisons had been blockaded." In addition, the building of the republican KGB had now been seized "together with lists of its agents." This last-named development meant that "the Russian special services were unable to create in Chechnya a full-fledged network of agents."[108]

On the evening of 8 November, Russian Television communicated the text of Yeltsin's decree of the previous day which introduced emergency rule into Checheno-Ingushetiya. The newly elected Chechen parliament gathered in emergency session and swiftly granted Dudaev emergency powers for the defense of the republic's independence. On the same day, Dudaev countered Yeltsin's decree by introducing military rule into the republic. He also renewed the enlistment of volunteers into the Chechen national guard and proposed to Yeltsin's official representatives in the republic that they relinquish their powers. According to the commander of the North Caucasus Military District, Major General I. Sokolov, Dudaev's forces, as of 1 November, consisted of 62,000 men in the national guard and another 30,000 in the popular militia. The actual fighting detachments (*boevye otryadi*) of the national guard, however, he reported, consisted of a mere 2,000 men.[109]

The Chechens, it should be noted, also enjoyed at this time strong support from the other Muslim peoples of the Caucasus region. On 27 October, an Abkhaz deputy announced in Groznyi that, if force were used against the Chechens, it would be tantamount to a use of force against all the peoples of the Caucasus. In mid-October, congresses of the Avars and the Muslims of Dagestan declared that, if the RSFSR were to invade the Chechen–Ingush Republic, they would fight along with the Chechens and Ingush.[110]

Commenting on Yeltsin's decision to declare a state of emergency in Checheno-Ingushetiya, Emil' Pain and Arkadii Popov have written: "[W]e know a few things about President Yeltsin's sensational decree of 7 November that . . . removed Dudaev from power and placed the republic under the control of Akhmet Arsanov, who had been one of the

---

[107] On this struggle, see Andrei Grachev, *Final Days: The Inside Story of the Collapse of the Soviet Union* (Boulder, CO: Westview Press, 1995); Jack F. Matlock, *Autopsy of an Empire* (New York: Random House, 1995), pp. 605–77; and Dunlop, *Rise of Russia*, pp. 256–84.

[108] In "Rossiiskaya politika v Chechne," *Izvestiya*, 7 February 1995, pp. 1, 4.

[109] See *Belaya kniga*, vol. I, p. 12. See also Yandarbiev, *V preddverii*, pp. 66–67.

[110] Sheehy, "Power Struggle," p. 25.

Chechen–Ingush republic's deputies to the federal parliament. It is now known that Arsanov, who had been previously appointed as the representative of the Russian president in Checheno-Ingushetiya on 27 October [1991], was the formal sponsor of the decree. On 6 November (i.e., only several hours before Yeltsin's decree was announced) Arsanov sent the Russian president a desperate telegram from Groznyi in which he insisted on an immediate declaration of a 'state of emergency.'"

And Pain and Popov continue: "Arsanov's involvement was implicitly confirmed by President Yeltsin, who, two days after his decree was rejected by the Russian parliament, issued another decree. This new decree removed Arsanov as presidential representative." The two authors, it should be noted, avoid the trap of seeking to make Arsanov a lone scapegoat for the failed Russian crackdown: "[I]t is difficult," they write, "to imagine that such an important document [i.e., on emergency rule] could have been prepared that night. Most likely, the outline, and perhaps even the full text of the decree, had already been prepared in anticipation of an opportune moment to issue it. Arsanov's telegram proved to be just such an occasion."[111]

Lightly armed Russian troops are flown in

On the night of 8–9 November, planes from the Soviet air force carrying RSFSR MVD troops touched down at Khankala Airport on the outskirts of Groznyi. By dawn on the 9th, Dudaev's national guards had blockaded the airport and had also placed the main railroad station in Groznyi under guard. Throughout the day on 9 November, a mass meeting numbering tens of thousands took place in Freedom Square in Groznyi supporting the Chechen declaration of independence and defending the Dudaev-led government. The threat of a Russian invasion served palpably to unite the people of Chechnya around their new president. In the middle of the day, the newly elected Chechen parliament administered the oath of office to President Dudaev.

Toward evening on the 9th, as a result of negotiations conducted between a deputy minister of internal affairs of the RSFSR MVD, General Komissarov, and the Dudaev forces, an agreement was reached to release the troops blockaded at Khankala Airport. They were then taken out in buses.[112]

Why did the Russian forces decide so ignominiously to withdraw from

[111] Payin and Popov, "Chechnya." For a short biography of Arsanov, see Muzaev, *Chechenskaya respublika*, p. 57. On Arsanov, see also Yandarbiev, *V preddverii,* pp 62–63.

[112] Muzaev, *Chechenskaya respublika*, p. 168.

Checheno-Ingushetiya? Concerning the arrival of MVD forces at Khan-kala Airport on 9 November, Ruslan Khasbulatov has observed: "It turns out that the planes bearing paratroopers – 300 men – had landed in Groznyi. But without any personal weapons. They had brought the weapons to Mozdok [in North Ossetiya]. So the lads – the paratroopers – got out of the planes and found themselves encircled."[113] Pavel Fel'gengauer (Felgenhauer), military correspondent for the newspaper *Segodnya*, has reported a more plausible version, namely that the MVD forces were in fact lightly armed: "A regiment of lightly armed Interior Ministry troops that had been airlifted into Groznyi surrendered its arms to the Chechen rebels without a fight when it became clear that the army would not support them."[114] If Fel'gengauer is correct, the Russian invasion plan provided for Soviet military forces based in Checheno-Ingushetiya to come decisively to the support of the Russian MVD.

Khasbulatov recalls that he was stunned to hear the news of the debacle taking place at Khankala Airport: "I telephone Rutskoi. He said that he understands nothing. Everything had been agreed with everyone, and now no one wants to help. They cite Gorbachev." Khasbulatov relates that the decree on emergency rule had been prepared by Rutskoi and then agreed in advance with USSR defense minister Evgenii Shaposhnikov and USSR MVD minister Viktor Barannikov, as well as with "a close aide to Gorbachev." "And of course," he notes, "it had been prepared at Yeltsin's instructions and with his full approval." Khasbulatov reports that he telephoned Shaposhnikov and Barannikov and that both of them emotionally defended their inaction by pointing out that, as USSR ministers, they had to obey the wishes of Soviet president Gorbachev.

According to Khasbulatov, Yeltsin at this critical juncture simply disappeared from view (as he was to do, again, at the time of the December 1994 military invasion of Chechnya). "They kept looking for Yeltsin," he recalls, "but could not find him." Soviet president Gorba-chev, however, was more than prepared to talk to Khasbulatov. "You are going too fast," Gorbachev cautioned him. "No MVD troops are needed there . . . Why, in general, did Yeltsin issue such a decree?" On the subject of the Russian president, Gorbachev confided to Khas-

[113] Khasbulatov, *Chechnya*, p. 19.
[114] Dr. Pavel Felgenhauer, "The Chechen Campaign," Conference on the War in Chechnya: Implications for Russian Security Policy, 7–8 November 1995, sponsored by the Department of National Security Affairs, Naval Postgraduate School, Monterey, California, unpublished manuscript. An essay of similar content by Felgenhauer, entitled "A War Moscow Cannot Afford to Lose," appeared in *Transition*, 31 May 1996, 28–31.

bulatov: "I myself am looking for him [Yeltsin], but they can't find him."
Khasbulatov's conclusion concerning this entire bizarre episode:
"Yeltsin's decree [on emergency rule] was consciously sabotaged [by
Gorbachev]."[115] (Another conclusion which could be drawn, it seems,
is that Yeltsin's disappearance from view was, in part, motivated by a
desire to have Rutskoi and Khasbulatov left holding the bag if something
went wrong with the invasion.)

Retired MVD major general Aslambek Aslakhanov has recalled that
Dudaev's representative in Moscow, Sherip Yusupov, called him at 3
a.m. on 9 November and informed him that emergency rule was in
process of being introduced into the Chechen Republic. "I immediately
flew to Moscow," Aslakhanov remembers, "and went to see the USSR
minister of internal affairs, V. Barannikov. I expressed to him my
indignation at this action. I said that this was precisely what Dudaev
needed. 'Emergency rule' would provoke a war in the North Caucasus. I
asked him to halt the introduction of forces, which he did after speaking
with M. Gorbachev."[116] If Aslakhanov is telling the truth here, then his
views and actions concerning the invasion differed significantly from
those of his mentor, Ruslan Khasbulatov.

Gorbachev's press secretary, Andrei Grachev, has provided a USSR
government perspective on events surrounding the aborted invasion:
"On November 7, 1991," he writes, "the ever-unpredictable leadership
of the Russian Federation, steering the country left and right with an
unsteady hand on the tiller, declared a state of emergency in the
Chechen republic . . . which was demanding independence from the
Russian Federation. Yeltsin sent an ultimatum to Chechen leader
Dzhokhar Dudaev, and then promptly made himself completely inac-
cessible, as he had often done in the past."

And Grachev continues: "Naturally, no good came of this high-
handed approach except that it provided some free publicity for Dudaev
. . . But the issue was taking on alarming proportions, threatening to
turn into another bloody and unresolvable Afghan war. In fact, a
division of the Russian Ministry of Interior had already started its
movement toward Groznyi when Gorbachev on his own initiative
ordered the troops to stop and immediately approached Russian parliament speaker Ruslan Khasbulatov, urging him in the absence of Yeltsin
to cancel the president's decree. The decree was rescinded, the fuse put
out, and Russia's image preserved."[117]

While he has compressed and somewhat distorted events and under-

[115] Khasbulatov, *Chechnya*, pp. 19–20.
[116] Aslakhanov, *Demokratiya prestupnoi*, p. 107.
[117] Grachev, *Final Days*, p. 99.

standably slanted his account in a pro-Gorbachev direction, Grachev essentially tells the same story as do the other commentators cited here. (Gorbachev, curiously, does not mention the episode in his 1995 memoirs.)[118] It should be noted that Gorbachev's role in the crisis was less passive than Andrei Grachev suggests. As the military journalist Pavel Fel'gengauer has written: "Boris Yeltsin proclaimed martial law in Chechnya . . . But Mikhail Gorbachev . . . ordered the army to remain strictly neutral and take no part whatsoever in enforcing martial law. This order . . . was willingly passed to the troops in and around Groznyi by then Chief of Staff General Vladimir Lobov . . . The Russian Supreme Soviet promptly overruled Yeltsin's martial-law decree and the Chechen secessionist movement was allowed to develop."[119]

Though Khasbulatov had been a strong backer of the introduction of emergency rule, he quickly understood that Yeltsin's disappearance from the scene, plus Gorbachev's fierce opposition to a military operation that would have resulted in large-scale bloodshed, had effectively scuttled the entire operation. Several days after the failed "invasion," on 11 November, an emergency session of the RSFSR Supreme Soviet therefore took a decision *not* to confirm Yeltsin's decree on the introduction of emergency rule into Checheno-Ingushetiya. Yeltsin's decree was revoked on the grounds that it had been "technically insufficiently prepared."[120]

Yandarbiev's account of the attempted invasion

In his second volume of memoirs, Zelimkhan Yandarbiev provides detailed information concerning the reaction of the Dudaev forces to the attempted Russian invasion.[121] According to Yandarbiev, a crowd of Dudaev supporters gathered in Groznyi on the morning of 9 November and then "besieged the main bastion of the threat to independence," MVD headquarters. The crowd was led by Said-Akhmad Adizov of the Chechen Council of Elders. As for Yandarbiev, he managed to get into the MVD building, where he spoke with both General Vakha Ibragimov, head of the local MVD, and General Komissarov, deputy chairman of the RSFSR MVD. These two generals, plus a third general, Yandarbiev recalls, "were in constant contact with Moscow" by telephone.

The Chechen nationalists, Yandarbiev recounts, took decisive action

---

[118] Mikhail Gorbachev, *Zhizn' i reformy*, 2 vols. (Moscow: Novosti, 1995).
[119] In Felgenhauer, "Chechen Campaign."
[120] Yandarbiev, *V preddverii*, p. 67. See also Yandarbiev, *Checheniya*, p. 99.
[121] Yandarbiev, *Checheniya*, pp. 91–97. All quotations in this section are taken from these pages.

to thwart the threatened invasion. Isa Arsamikov and other fighters blockaded the Russian MVD *spetsnaz* forces who had been flown into Khankala Airport. Several military transport planes were directly prevented from landing at the airport when Khamzat Khankarov and others set up obstacles on the runways. The Russian military bases in Groznyi and Shali were blockaded by nationalists, while "all railroad stations, bridges, highways, and other places of possible [troop] movement were taken under control." Yusup Soslambekov was named acting Chechen minister of defense. A women's battalion, led by Marzhan Dombaeva and Lyudmila Lobanova, was active in the defense of the city. The "position of the Union," i.e., of Gorbachev, Yandarbiev concludes his account, was the key factor making it possible to find a peaceful way out of the crisis.

A bold terrorist act

Following the publication of Yeltsin's decree introducing emergency rule into Checheno-Ingushetiya, General Dudaev had stated to Agence France Presse that "terroristic acts" against Russia were a possible option for the Chechens. On 9 November, three Chechen fighters unexpectedly hijacked a Russian TU-154 plane, carrying 171 passengers, scheduled to fly from Mineral'nye Vody (in adjacent Stavropol' krai) to the city of Ekaterinburg in the Urals. The hijackers threatened to blow the plane up. Instead of flying to Ekaterinburg, the plane was ordered flown to Ankara, Turkey, where the hijackers attempted to hold a press conference during which they intended to condemn the Russian crackdown in Chechnya. The Turkish authorities, apparently concerned about a Russian reaction, refused to permit the press conference to be held, and had the plane sent back to Russia on 10 November, but they, significantly, did not send the hijackers back to Russia for trial. When the three hijackers eventually made their way back to Chechnya, they were greeted there as "national heroes." One of the hijackers subsequently would acquire Russian and world fame for leading a daring and bloody raid on the Russian city of Budennovsk in 1995: Shamil' Basaev.[122]

In its November 1991 standoff with the Russian Federation, Chechnya gained the support of the revived Confederation of Mountain Peoples, consisting of representatives of fourteen nationalities from the

---

[122] On this episode, see TASS Report, 11 November 1991, in RFE-RL, *USSR Today*, 11 November 1991, p. 1028/02–03; *Chechenskaya tragediya*, p. 61; and Elizabeth Fuller, "Shamil Basaev: Rebel with a Cause?," *Transition*, 28 July 1995, p. 47. See also Yandarbiev, *Checheniya*, pp. 96–97.

North Caucasus region. On 10 November, the Confederation took a decision to declare a general mobilization of volunteers from the region in order to defend the "Chechen Revolution."[123] (The Confederation will be discussed in detail in chapter 4, pp. 140–47.)

Events in Checheno-Ingushetiya over the remainder of calendar year 1991 can be fairly briefly summarized. On 21 November, Dudaev, seemingly convinced that a Russian invasion was no longer a realistic threat, lifted martial law in the republic.[124] On 30 November and on 1 December, a referendum "on the creation of an Ingush Republic within the RSFSR" was conducted in the three Ingush districts of the Chechen–Ingush ASSR. Seventy-five percent of the eligible Ingush populace cast votes, and 90 percent of them voted "yes"; Ingushetiya had now formally separated itself from Chechnya.[125] The Chechens seem at the time to have accepted this expression of the popular will of their Vainakh brethren without serious complaint. Henceforth the Chechen struggle for secession from Russia would be a lonely one, without the support of the Ingush.

Concerning the decision of Ingushetiya to separate from Chechnya, ethnographer Galina Soldatova has observed: "The 1991 declaration by Chechnya of its independence within the framework of the 1934 boundaries [i.e., within a combined Chechen–Ingush oblast'] placed the Ingush face to face with the necessity of having to address immediately a whole range of problems: territorial, economic, cultural, social . . . The aspiration of Ingushetiya to remain within Russia was primarily dictated by the following reasons: (1) the Ingush counted on Russia's assistance in resolving their territorial disputes with the Ossetians and Chechens; and (2) the Ingush wished to avoid ethnic assimilation [with the Chechens], which would have been a real possibility . . . According to the 1989 census, the Chechen population of the former Checheno-Ingushetiya was more than four times greater than that of the Ingush."[126]

In December 1991, Umar Avturkhanov (b. 1946), a former MVD official who was to emerge as one of the chief political opponents of Dudaev, was elected chairman of the Provisional Council of the Administration of Nadterechnyi district, located in the northwest region of the republic. Avturkhanov then declared that he did not recognize Dudaev's authority.[127] Serious internal opposition to General Dudaev, covertly

---

[123] In RFE–RL, *USSR Today*, 11 November 1991, p. 03.

[124] Hill, *"Russia's Tinderbox"*, p. 83.   [125] In *Rossiiskie vooruzhennye sily*, p. 9.

[126] Galina U. Soldatova, "The Former Checheno-Ingushetiya," in Leokadia Drobizheva, Rose Gottemoeller, Catherine McArdle Kelleher, and Lee Walker, eds., *Ethnic Conflict in the Post-Soviet World* (Armonk, NY: M. E. Sharpe, 1996), p. 211.

[127] Muzaev, *Chechenskaya respublika*, p. 54.

backed by Russia, had therefore already begun to rear its head in Chechnya.

In the same month of December, according to Zelimkhan Yandarbiev, Moscow successfully organized a putsch in Georgia, which led to the removal of President Zviad Gamsakhurdia from power. This development seriously threatened newly independent Chechnya, since it "deprived them [the Chechens] of support (both purely political and economic) from Georgia; Chechnya was now de facto fully blockaded."[128]

The abortive November 1991 invasion and the threatening developments taking place in Georgia served to convince the Chechen leadership that it needed maximally to arm Chechnya, and swiftly. By late November and early December 1991, it became clear that General Dudaev intended to appropriate all USSR and RSFSR military weaponry, ammunition, and hardware located on Chechen soil. By his decree of 26 November, Dudaev ruled that all such armaments must remain within the republic and could not be taken out of it. At the beginning of December, then deputy USSR defense minister Pavel Grachev arrived in Groznyi for talks with Dudaev. The Chechen president on that occasion agreed to assist the Russian troops to withdraw from the republic "if a part of their arms and military hardware were handed over to him."[129] But Dudaev, it soon emerged, had his eye on more than "a part" of these armaments.

As the year 1991 came to an end, it appeared that the "Chechen Revolution" had fully triumphed. The Soviet Union, by contrast, had come to an inglorious end, while the future of the Russian Federation looked charged and problematic.

[128] Yandarbiev, *Checheniya*, p. 116.
[129] In the Govorukhin Commission report, in *Pravda*, 29 February 1996, p. 2.

4   Dudaev in power, 1992–1994

JOURNALIST: But in Chechnya there is anarchy.
GENERAL DUDAEV: No more so than in Russia.[1]

The three years which separate the triumph of the Chechen Revolution in late 1991 from the Russian military invasion of Chechnya in December 1994 represented a fast-paced period of convulsive political and social change. Groups in opposition to the Dudaev government began to emerge within Chechnya, especially in its northern lowland regions, and they were aided and abetted, to a growing extent, by the Russian government. Dudaev and his aides showed themselves incapable of running a government, and the Chechen economy, not surprisingly, collapsed. But Russia itself entered a period of intense political turmoil, as the presidency under Yeltsin and the parliament under Ruslan Khasbulatov (who became closely allied with Vice President Rutskoi) moved toward the exceptionally dangerous condition of *dvoevlastie* (dyarchy), culminating in the bloody events of October 1993.

After Yeltsin succeeded in dissolving the Khasbulatov-led Russian Congress and Supreme Soviet in late 1993, he and his entourage finally became free to direct more concerted attention to separatist tendencies within the Russian Federation. The signing of a power-sharing treaty with previously rejectionist Tatarstan in February 1994 left Chechnya as the sole secessionist holdout in Russia. The Yeltsin leadership began in earnest to seek to destabilize Chechnya and, by one means or another, to remove Dudaev from power.

The economy under Dudaev

As we saw in chapter 3 (pp. 85–88), the economy of Checheno-Ingushetiya had been in decline even before General Dudaev took power in September–October 1991, but it seems clear that Dudaev's policies – or, rather, his lack of policies – served to accelerate that down-

---

[1] In *Moskovskie novosti*, 31 (1994), p. 10.

ward movement. As Fiona Hill has commented: "The new Chechen elite . . . was composed of radical nationalists from the political fringes with no prior administrative experience; leaders of the so-called 'Chechen mafia' who specialized in extra-legal activities; members of the Chechen diaspora from outside the borders of the USSR . . . and a handful of educated young idealists whose proposals for reform were thwarted at every turn. They were all woefully ill-equipped to deal with the multiple challenges of creating a new Chechen nation state and creating a functioning market economy." As for Dudaev himself, Hill notes, his "political naivete and bad judgment compounded the economic difficulties."[2]

The economic plans of Dudaev and his supporters did indeed suffer from a pronounced utopianism. Their grandiose scheme of turning independent Chechnya into a "second Kuwait," for example, had little basis in reality. One idea advanced by the Chechen leadership was to construct "a gigantic water pipeline for water in the North Caucasus to the Middle East – to sell Chechen drinking water to Arab countries!"[3] There is evidence that Dudaev himself was aware of a lack of competence of his economic advisers. Thus he is reported to have made several unsuccessful attempts to attract Russian economists of the first rank – Grigorii Yavlinskii, Mikhail Bocharov, and Evgenii Saburov – to come to the republic to serve as its prime minister.[4] According to one former minister of the Soviet petrochemical industry, Salambek Khadzhiev – who later emerged as a leading opponent of Dudaev – the Chechen president offered him the post of prime minister in January 1992.[5] Since no competent candidate could be found who would take the post, Dudaev himself had to assume the premiership on an acting basis, and he, of course, understood almost nothing about economics.[6]

[2] Fiona Hill, *"Russia's Tinderbox"*: *Conflict in the North Caucasus and Its Implications for the Future of the Russian Federation* (Cambridge, MA: John F. Kennedy School of Government, Harvard University, Strengthening Democratic Institutions Project, September 1995), pp. 76–78.

[3] In Emil' Pain and Arkadii Popov, "Rossiiskaya politika v Chechne," *Izvestiya*, 8 February 1995, p. 4.

[4] V. A. Tishkov, E. L. Belyaeva, and G. V. Marchenko, *Chechenskii krizis* (Moscow: Tsentr kompleksnykh sotsial'nykh issledovanii i marketinga, 1995), p. 22.

[5] In *Moskovskii komsomolets*, 23 March 1995, p. 2.

[6] For examples of Dudaev's views on economic questions, see the interviews with him in *Izvestiya*, 21 August 1993, pp. 1, 4; *Megapolis-ekspress*, 10–11 (1994), 19; *Segodnya*, 31 May 1994, p. 10; and *Moskovskaya pravda*, 15 July 1994, p. 7. For Dudaev's ideas on Chechen state-building, see his essay, *K voprosu o gosudarstvenno-politicheskom ustroistve Chechenskoi Respubliki* (Groznyi: author publication, 1993). For interviews with Dudaev on political questions, see *Moskovskie novosti*, 35 (1993), p. 12A; *Segodnya*, 11 January 1994, p. 10; *Nezavisimaya gazeta*, 7 July 1994, p. 1; *Literaturnaya Rossiya*, 28, 15 July 1994, p. 5; *Megapolis-ekspress*, 23, 27 July 1994, p. 18; *Pravda*, 30 July 1994, pp. 1, 2; and *Moskovskie novosti*, 31 (1994), p. 10.

Beginning in 1992, Chechnya ceased altogether to pay taxes into the Russian federal budget, and it was incapable of generating lawful sources of revenue. The key industries in the republic were the oil-extraction and, especially, the oil-processing industry. Oil extraction, however, went into a sharp decline, from a total of 2.6 million tons in 1992 to 1.2 million tons in 1993. By the beginning of December 1994, no more than 100 of Chechnya's 1,500 oil wells were still producing.[7] The volume of oil processing in Groznyi's outmoded plants also had to be cut back significantly. Oil passing through the republic's pipelines was increasingly being tapped off and otherwise stolen. In 1993, more than 47,000 tons of petroleum product, with a worth estimated at 4 billion rubles, was directly stolen.[8]

Specialists Emil' Pain and Arkadii Popov have noted that the nearly 60 percent decline in oil extraction which occurred in 1992 was directly connected with the mass outflow of Russian-language populace who had previously been employed chiefly in that industry (60,000 such persons left in 1992). "Precisely at that time (i.e., the end of 1991 and the beginning of 1992)," they observe, "the polling organization VTsIOM carried out a survey of the migration plans of [ethnic] Russians residing in a number of union republics and autonomous republics of the Russian Federation, and it turned out that the percentage of those wishing to leave independent Chechnya was higher than in any other part of the former Soviet Union. Thirty-seven percent of the Russian population, i.e., more than in Tajikistan, which was in the grip of a civil war, planned to leave."[9]

During 1992–94, there took place a sharp decline across the board in Chechnya's industrial and agricultural production. According to Goskomstat of Russia (the official bureau of statistics), industrial production in the Chechen and Ingush Republics declined by 30 percent in 1992 (the Russia-wide average being 18.8 percent) and in 1993 by 61.4 percent (the Russia-wide average being 16.2 percent). The production of food products per person declined by 46 percent in the republic (as opposed to a Russia-wide figure of 18 percent). Finally, unemployment rose sharply, by 16 percent in 1993.[10] These were catastrophic developments. There commenced an outflow of populace from Chechnya's dying cities, and those who were able to went to stay with relatives in villages, while others simply left the confines of the republic.

[7] Robert E. Ebel, "The History and Politics of Chechen Oil," *Post-Soviet Prospects*, Center for Strategic and International Studies (CSIS), Washington, DC (January 1995), p. 3.

[8] In Tishkov, et al., *Chechenskii krizis*, p. 21.

[9] Pain and Popov, "Rossiiskaya politika v Chechne," *Izvestiya*, 8 February 1995, p. 4.

[10] In Tishkov, et al., *Chechenskii krizis*, p. 23.

In the countryside, too, the situation became increasingly grim. "The collapse of the kolkhozes and sovkhozes was accompanied by a plundering of property, by a curtailment of agricultural production, and by attempts at spontaneously divvying up land or allotting it on the basis of clan and communal law. The previously existing forms of agriculture were preserved only in the northern regions (i.e., near the Terek) and even there only in part."[11]

This headlong economic collapse forced Dudaev and his circle increasingly to turn to questionable sources of support. It became a matter of simple survival. As Emil' Pain and Arkadii Popov have noted: "When legal sources of existence disappear, then criminal ones are developed." Chechnya was transformed into the largest center of counterfeit money and of false financial documents on the territory of the former USSR. "In 1993 alone," Pain and Popov report, "9.4 billion rubles of counterfeit bonds were seized on the territory of Russia, of which 3.7 billion were of demonstrable Chechen production."[12] The republic also became a major transit point for various contraband, including weapons and narcotics. The gun market in Groznyi emerged as the largest black-market clearing house for weapons in the CIS. "The local commander of Russian forces," Stephen Handelman has written, "estimated that more than 150,000 firearms were at large in the Chechen capital, a city with 400,000 inhabitants."[13] Automatic weapons and hand grenades could be purchased at the open air market like apples or cabbage.

The Groznyi Airport represented yet another problem. "Each month from Groznyi Airport," Pain and Popov note, "planes of various Russian air companies made 100–150 unsanctioned flights abroad."[14] Criminals from any point in Russia and from the entire CIS were able to fly in and out of this airport unhindered. "Entire airplanes, filled to the brim with narcotics, could come here."[15]

A large number of Chechens would not have had the means to subsist had it not been for the inflow of oil from other regions of Russia to Chechnya to be processed. The volume of such incoming oil exceeded by more than two times the volume extracted from the wells of

[11] Vadim Korotkov, "Chechenskaya model' etnopoliticheskikh protsessov," *Obshchestvennye nauki i sovremennost'*, 3, May–June (1994), 104–12.
[12] Pain and Popov, "Rossiiskaya politika v Chechne," *Izvestiya*, 8 February 1995, p. 4.
[13] Stephen Handelman, *Comrade Criminal: The Theft of the Second Russian Revolution* (London: Michael Joseph, 1994), pp. 204–05.
[14] Pain and Popov, "Rossiiskaya politika v Chechne," *Izvestiya*, 8 February 1995, p. 4.
[15] Ibid. For comments by Dudaev's acting vice president Zelimkhan Yandarbiev on the situation at Groznyi Airport, see his second book of memoirs, *Checheniya – bitva za svobodu* (L'vov, Ukraine: Svoboda narodiv [sic] and Antibol'shevitskii blok narodov, 1996), p. 154.

Checheno-Ingushetiya. The pipelines passing through Chechnya became a lucrative target for thieves. "On the territory of Chechnya in 1993, more than 47,000 tons of petroleum products were plundered . . . assessed at 4 billion rubles."[16] If Salambek Khadzhiev, the specialist on the Chechen oil industry, is to be believed, the figure was much higher – he has claimed that between 10 and 15 million tons of oil "went astray" in Chechnya during the period 1991–94. In addition to "pirating" oil which was moving through the pipeline, Chechen "businessmen" siphoned off high-grade oil from trunk lines, replacing it with lower grades, and they sold oil purchased at domestic prices (or simply stolen outright) for hard currency export. (Domestic prices were less than 45 percent of world prices, so selling even small amounts of oil was highly profitable.)[17]

Train robberies and truck hijackings also proliferated. As Russian government spokesman Sergei Shakhrai stated before the Constitutional Court on 10 July 1995: "During the period 1992–94, on the territory of Chechnya, there were performed 1,354 attacks on rolling-stock with the goal of seizing the cargo. About seventy attacks on passenger trains have been documented."[18]

Yandarbiev's admissions

In his second volume of memoirs, Zelimkhan Yandarbiev, who served as acting vice president under Dudaev, has admitted that a number of high-ranking Chechen officials were corrupt and sought to profit from their positions. In Yandarbiev's view, General Dudaev, while incontestably a great man and a Chechen national hero, was often a poor judge of character; a number of Dudaev's personnel appointments – even to such key agencies as the MVD, DGB (secret police), and procuracy – were, Yandarbiev believes, poorly considered. Thus Mogomed Vakhaev, who headed up Dudaev's Commission on External Trade Relations, "was able to steal from the republic 8 million dollars," while Minister of

---

[16] Tishkov, et al., *Chechenskii krizis*, p. 21.
[17] In Elaine Holoboff, "Oil and the Burning of Grozny," *Jane's Intelligence Review*, 7, 6 (1995), 254. For a discussion of the "Eldorado" of illegal oil commerce in Chechnya, see the comments of a former ally and then leading opponent of Dudaev, Yusup Soslambekov, in his book, *"Chechnya (Nokhchicho') – vzglyad iznutri"* (Moscow: author publication, 1995), p. 33. See also the comments of retired MVD major general Aslambek Aslakhanov in his book, *Demokratiya prestupnoi ne byvaet* (Moscow: author publication, 1994), p. 77. It should be underscored that in the case of Chechnya all statistics are questionable and must be taken with a grain of salt.
[18] In *Rossiiskie vesti*, 12–13 July 1995. For Yandarbiev's views on the train robberies, see Yandarbiev, *Checheniya*, pp. 156, 289.

Agriculture Ruzbek Bisultanov appropriated oil products which he said had been sent off to Lithuania.[19]

The bad reputation acquired by the city of Groznyi, Yandarbiev underlines, was in large part due to its mayor, Bislan Gantamirov, another ill-considered Dudaev appointment, who plundered the city for a year and a half until he was finally replaced during a period in which he was ill. Gantamirov, who, together with the head of the Groznyi city administration, "privatized" and then sold off much of the capital's property, later became one of the foremost leaders of the anti-Dudaev opposition supported by Russia.[20]

Finally, Yandarbiev notes with regret that "all of the power [organs in Chechnya] – the MVD, the DGB, the *spetsnaz*, the OMON and DON, and the Shali tank regiment – participated in the plundering of petro-products, under the guise of guarding them."[21] On the other hand, Yandarbiev contends that many of the crimes ascribed to the Chechens – such as the train robberies – were actually provocations organized by the Russian special services, which actively sought to destabilize Dudaev's government.[22]

"The pot calling the kettle black"

In light of the sharp upsurge in criminal activity in Chechnya, some Russian nationalist critics have sought to depict what happened in the republic as a "criminal revolution" and to describe the Chechen leadership as a "criminal regime." To take one prominent example of this tendency, Stanislav Govorukhin, a well-known Russian parliamentarian and committee chairman, has declared: "As the author of this term [i.e., 'criminal revolution'], I can assure you that the greatest success of this revolution was achieved precisely in this subject of the Federation, in Chechnya. Precisely there did there indeed emerge a 100 percent criminal regime."[23] This defamatory view of Chechens was actively promulgated by the public affairs administrations of the Russian Federal Counter-Intelligence Service (FSK), MVD, and Defense Ministry.[24] The following is a fairly typical passage from a volume issued by the FSK, entitled *White Book. Chechnya, 1991–1995*: "The Dudaev

[19] Yandarbiev, *Checheniya*, pp. 173, 207.   [20] Ibid., p. 251.
[21] Ibid., p. 289.   [22] Ibid., pp. 289–90.
[23] In *Pravda*, 29 February 1996, p. 2.
[24] See, for example, the collections *Kriminal'nyi rezhim. Chechnya, 1991–1995* (Moscow: Kodeks and MVD RF, 1995), and *Belaya kniga. Chechnya, 1991–1995: fakty, dokumenty, svidetel'stva*, 2 vols. (Moscow: Tsentr obshchestvennykh svyazei FSK Rossii, 1995). The volume *Chechenskaya tragediya: kto vinovat* (Moscow: Novosti, 1995) also appears to reflect the views of the Russian intelligence services.

regime," the book asserts, "creating a social base for itself, released from the penal colonies more than 250 condemned murderers, a mass of rapists, and other criminals. And it not only let them out but it armed them."[25]

More judicious and even-handed commentators have seen the Chechens as in reality being junior partners in a wave of corruption and criminality emanating from the Russian capital of Moscow. Referring to criminal activities conducted in Chechnya, Emil' Pain and Arkadii Popov stipulate: "Of course, all of these operations could be carried out only with the cooperation of mafia groups and venal bureaucrats throughout all of Russia, and, in the first place, in Moscow." Thus, for example, they note: "The robbery of trains, it turned out, did not take place without preparation from Moscow: the dispatchers knew in advance what was contained in which train."[26]

While Dudaev had "nationalized" the republic's oil companies and refineries, this did not, it turned out, in practice adversely affect relations between Chechnya and many Russian companies and oil officials. The Dudaev government had little difficulty in exporting oil (whether illegally siphoned off or locally produced) despite the regime's poor relations with official Moscow. Sergei Stepashin, at the time the head of the Russian FSK, confirmed that "corruption originating from Dudaev's regime reached ministerial level in Moscow and that manipulation of oil export quotas was one mechanism used for profiteering." Through such adroit manipulation, Dudaev was able to receive quota allocations and export oil from Chechnya via Russian pipelines and through its terminals. Stepashin asserts further that "Chechnya's export quotas were not approved by the Fuel and Energy Ministry (as would be normal procedure) but received from a federal corporation called Roskontrakt [formerly the State Committee for Supplies] between 1992 and 1993."[27]

According to *Jane's Intelligence Review*, whatever the mechanism for the transportation of oil into Groznyi, it was transported out of Chechnya through the western pipeline which went from Groznyi to Novorossiisk, a city on the Black Sea coast, via Tikhoretsk. This pipeline had the capacity to transport 17 million tons of oil a year. "[B]y the autumn of 1994," *Jane's* reports, "the Groznyi–Baku line may have been reversed so as to flow in a northerly direction. Western companies were offered a deal by the Chechen authorities whereby oil shipped across the

[25] *Belaya kniga*, vol. I, p. 4.
[26] Pain and Popov, "Rossiiskaya politika v Chechne," *Izvestiya*, 8 February 1995, p. 4.
[27] In Holoboff, "Oil and the Burning," 254.

Caspian by tanker could be put into the Baku–Groznyi line for trans-portation on to Novorossiisk for export."[28]

Viktor Sheinis, a member of the State Duma commission chaired by Stanislav Govorukhin, which looked into the factors behind the war in Chechnya (Sheinis, like other moderates on the commission, refused to sign its slanted final report), has noted similar violations: "In Groznyi, there is a petroleum-processing plant which produces a unique type of aviation oil. This plant remained active. Petroleum processing could be carried out only with the provision of Russian oil. We have documentary evidence of how, over the course of a rather long period, oil went, completely officially, from Russia to Groznyi . . . [A] significant part of this oil product went for export, and also assured the well-being of the Dudaev regime and its armaments."[29] In addition to producing the scarce aviation lube oil (type MS-20) referred to by Sheinis, the Groznyi plants were also the sole manufacturer within the Russian Federation of paraffin, a product much in demand, and one which now needs to be imported into Russia.[30]

This highly corrupt oil and petroproducts export system, *Jane's* concludes, was being protected de facto by such high-ranking Russian officials as General Aleksandr Korzhakov, head of Yeltsin's Presidential Security Service, Oleg Soskovets, first deputy prime minister, Oleg Davydov, foreign trade minister, and Yuri Shafranik, minister of fuel and energy. In 1994, however, Korzhakov and Soskovets would (as we shall see in chapter 5, pp. 203–04) turn on Dudaev and his regime and emerge as leading figures in the Russian "party of war."[31]

Stephen Handelman, the author of a useful study on the burgeoning of crime in post-communist Russia, has observed concerning the weapons black market in Chechnya: "[F]or all their money, even the Chechens were, in the end, only junior partners in the [Russian] military's expanding commercial operations . . . [I]t was impossible to disregard evidence that military criminal enterprise was condoned, if not encouraged, by officials in the [Russian] defense establishment."[32]

The Institute of Strategic Research of the Russian Foreign Ministry's Moscow State Institute of International Relations (MGIMO) claimed in early 1996 that the Russian military's "narco-mafia" and Dudaev had worked out an agreement for the unobstructed passage through Chechnya of drugs brought in from Afghanistan and Tajikistan. This

[28] Ibid.   [29] In *Russkaya mysl'* (Paris), 2–8 March 1995, p. 3.
[30] In Ebel, "History and Politics," 4.
[31] In Holoboff, "Oil and the Burning," 256. On the "party of war," see John B. Dunlop, "The 'Party of War' and Russian Imperial Nationalism," *Problems of Post-Communism*, March–April (1996), 29–34.
[32] Handelman, *Comrade Criminal*, p. 207.

route allegedly went from Baku through Groznyi to Rostov-on-Don, and then on to Western Europe. This lucrative arrangement fell apart in November 1994, the institute asserts, "when President Dudaev demanded a higher share of the Central Asian drug profit . . . [T]he Chechen leader did not agree to [Russian defense minister] Pavel Grachev's proposals. And in response to this, the Russian high command decided to strike a mortal blow against Dudaev [i.e., launched the December invasion]."[33]

This account, originating in an institute attached to Evgenii Primakov's Russian Foreign Ministry, must be treated with caution. The December 1994 invasion, all the available evidence suggests, was not the result of "a drug deal gone bad." But that there was collusion between corrupt Russian military personnel and Chechen officials to channel drugs through Chechnya on their way to Western Europe appears likely. As in the case of the illicit arms trade, both sides in the deal stood to make immense profits.

Specialist Sergei Arutyunov of the Institute of Ethnology in Moscow has concluded that, for more than three years, "certain Russian corrupted civil and army circles and 'mafiosi' businessmen" zealously exploited the de facto free economic zone which had been formed in Chechnya. And he continues: "But when Dudaev and his group became a menace, demanding a bigger share of illegal incomes or promising to blackmail, then the necessity arose to lure the President of Russia and the whole might of the Russian army and secret services into an attempt to eliminate Dudaev."[34]

Concerning the operation of Groznyi Airport during 1992–94, Emil' Pain and Arkadii Popov have asked pertinently: "Who gave permission for planes filled with contraband to fly in and out of Groznyi infringing Russia's air space . . . ? Obviously persons who received money for this and no small amounts of money . . . Why did Russia not establish at least an air blockade against such an openly hostile regime . . . ?"[35] High-ranking Russian officials, they intimate, colluded with the Chechen leadership to keep Groznyi Airport open. It seems clear, therefore, that those Russian nationalists such as Duma commission chairman Stanislav Govorukhin who derogate the Dudaev leadership as

---

[33] Dr. Evgueni Novikov, "Drugs from Afghanistan and Central Asia and the War in Chechnya," *Prism* (Jamestown Foundation, Washington, DC), 26 January 1996.

[34] S. A. Arutyunov, "Possible Consequences of the Chechenian [sic] War for the General Situation in the Caucasus Area," Conference on the War in Chechnya: Implications for Russian Security Policy, 7–8 November 1995, sponsored by the Department of National Security Affairs, Naval Postgraduate School, Monterey, California, unpublished paper.

[35] Pain and Popov, "Rossiiskaya politika v Chechne," *Izvestiya*, 8 February 1995, p. 4.

a "criminal regime" provide a classic example of hypocrisy, of "the pot calling the kettle black." Chechnya was no more of a criminal regime than was the Russian Federation.

This self-evident fact has been underlined by dispassionate Russian specialists in ethnic affairs. Leading ethnographer Valerii Tishkov, for example, has remarked with reference to Dudaev's period of rule: "I do not agree with the image of a 'Medellin cartel' or criminal zone which the president's [i.e., Yeltsin's] entourage foists upon society. This is an attempt in retrospect to justify the Chechen war." "In reality," Tishkov notes, "it is a myth. Criminality among Chechens is in no way higher than among Georgians or Russians in Moscow . . . There were many crimes committed there [in Chechnya], that is a fact. But in Russia, or even in Moscow, is it all peace and quiet?"[36]

In similar fashion, Sergei Arutyunov maintained in testimony before the Russian Constitutional Court: "I cannot agree with the claim that Dudaev unleashed a raging of criminal activity in the country. It was unleashed by the paralysis of the [Chechen] authorities, who quickly became corrupted . . . But let us be objective and frank: the very same paralysis of authority and the very same colossal growth in crime took place in central Russia, and in Moscow itself, and in many other regions of the Russian Federation."[37] To balance the misleading image of a Chechen "criminal regime," Arutyunov points to instances where the Chechen authorities did attempt to combat the upsurge in crime in the republic. Thus the Chechen and Stavropol' procuracies worked together to investigate individual crimes. And on the subject of train robberies, Arutyunov states: "I cannot say, for example, that the robberies of trains were approved by the Dudaev government. I cannot say that it did not try to struggle with this."[38] The Tishkov group has, in similar fashion, noted that "Dudaev himself insisted upon the criminal investigation of the minister of agriculture of the republic."[39] There were thus, apparently, levels of corruption among his subordinates that Dudaev was not prepared to abide.

Another related tendency prevalent among nationalistically inclined Russians has been to tar all Chechens with the epithet "Chechen mafia." Writing in late 1992, A. M. Ivanov sought to counter this defamatory tendency. "[T]oday," he reminisced, "we drove about Chechnya for hundreds of kilometers, and everywhere we saw how people were working in the fields, caring for livestock, and preparing fodder and wood for the winter, and building homes. Of course this was not the

[36] In *Novoe vremya*, 15 (1995), 22–23.   [37] In *Novoe vremya*, 29 (1995), 12–15.
[38] Ibid.   [39] Tishkov, et al., *Chechenskii krizis*, p. 22.

'Chechen mafia' at work . . . [T]here is, to be sure, a Chechen mafia, but there is also a Chechen people, which should not be confused with it. One needs to fight with the mafia but live in friendship with the people."[40]

Toward an ethnocratic Chechen state

Once he had solidified his grip on power, General Dudaev began the construction of an ethnocratic Chechen state. This move was criticized by the Russian government, and rightly so – a concern for ethnic minorities should be a key marker of any aspiring new state – but, as Dudaev's public statements underlined, he saw this new policy as largely defensive in nature. The treatment of Chechens living in the Russian Federation served as a key indicator for Dudaev. As he put it during an August 1993 interview: "Look what they are doing to the Chechens in Russia itself. They are depriving them of housing – and whom are they depriving? Shepherds who feed entire hungry oblasts with their labor. The Cossack Assembly [skhod] decides to deport the Chechens, to confiscate their property for the benefit of the [Cossack] settlements, to take away their livestock . . . We have hundreds of such facts from Astrakhan', Rostov, and Volgograd oblasts, from Stavropol' and Krasnodar krais. But our patience is not limitless."[41]

Perceived mistreatment of Chechens in Russia was thus a factor behind Dudaev's decision to focus exclusively upon the well-being of Chechens living in Chechnya. It should also be noted that public opinion polls taken among Russians in the post-1991 period document a marked rise in animosity toward Chechens and other "peoples of the Caucasus."[42]

In testimony before the Russian Constitutional Court in July 1995, Sergei Arutyunov independently confirmed that Dudaev's allegations against the Cossacks were not without truth: "Perhaps the heaviest blow to normal mutual relations [between Russians and Chechens]," he observed, "was administered by the appearance of Cossack bandit – the term indeed applies to them – formations, which already in 1991–92 put up pickets, beat up people according to their nationality, dragged children out of cars under the barrels of automatic weapons, robbed

[40] A. M. Ivanov, "Vid na Rossiyu iz Chechni," *Russkii vestnik*, 41–44 (1992), 9.

[41] In *Izvestiya*, 21 August 1993, pp. 1, 4. On the expulsion of Chechens from Volgograd oblast' in early 1992, see Yandarbiev, *Checheniya*, p. 137.

[42] For the results of these polls, see John B. Dunlop, "Russia: In Search of an Identity?," in Ian Bremmer and Ray Taras, eds., *New States, New Politics: Building the Post-Soviet Nations* (Cambridge, UK: Cambridge University Press, 1997), pp. 60–62.

automobiles, and so forth, all of which met with no counteraction on the part of the law enforcement organs."[43]

As has been noted, Cossacks dwelling in southern Russia had been catalyzed and energized by the 1991 Russian law on "repressed people," which legitimized their demands that they be accorded priority before other ethnic groups living in the region. In 1992, Yeltsin had issued a decree which essentially restored the Cossacks' previous status within the tsarist Russian Empire as territorially based paramilitary units in the North Caucasus.[44] In the opinion of ethnic affairs specialist Ol'ga Vasil'eva: "The differentiation between Russian and non-Russian national movements in the North Caucasus is a consequence of the policy pursued by the federal authorities [in Moscow]. Thus, the confrontation between the mountain peoples and the Cossacks in-creased after the President of the Russian Federation had signed a number of decrees on the rehabilitation of the Cossacks as a military class [soslovie]. A rise of Russian nationalism can, in its turn, bring about a new intensification of national movements in the North Caucasus."[45]

Because of problems experienced by the North Caucasus Military District in maintaining requisite force levels, the Cossacks were needed to provide military manpower for the southern flank of a weakened Russian state. As early as 1990, the Cossacks also began loudly calling for the return to Stavropol' krai of the Kargalinskii, Naurskii, and Shelkovskii districts of Checheno-Ingushetiya – given to that autono-mous republic in 1957 by Khrushchev in an attempt demographically to weaken the Chechens and Ingush.[46]

By mid-1994, tensions between Cossacks and Chechens, stoked by elements in the upper levels of the Russian government, had reached a near-fever pitch: "On 5 August," the newspaper *Moskovskie novosti* reported, "a pogrom was carried out at the [Chechen] farmsteads of the village of Galyuganovskaya, Stavropol' krai, which is on the border with Chechnya . . . [O]n the fifth, there arrived Cossacks – not local ones – and people in camouflage military uniforms. They beat everyone who crossed their path, put people up against a wall, robbed them, and ripped earrings out of the ears of young girls and women. Seventeen-year-old Viskhan Pashaev was killed by two shots to the head . . . They tried to abduct the daughter of one woman, and by a miracle she

[43] In *Novoe vremya*, 29 (1995), 12–15.
[44] In Hill, *"Russia's Tinderbox"*, pp. 36–37.
[45] See Ol'ga Vasil'eva, "North Caucasus," in Klaus Segbers and Stephan de Spiegeleire, eds., *Post-Soviet Peoples* (Baden-Baden, Germany: Nomos, 1995), vol. II, p. 439.
[46] See Hill, *"Russia's Tinderbox"*, pp. 46, 67–73.

managed successfully to plead with them to let her go . . . The Cossacks shouted loudly that they submit only to Yeltsin."[47]

In light of this aggressive behavior conducted against Chechens by Cossacks living in the Russian Federation, and in view of growing Cossack territorial claims on Chechnya's northern regions, it seems hardly surprising that Dudaev and his circle exhibited little sympathy or interest in the Cossacks or in ethnic Russians living in Chechnya. When, in August 1993, he was asked why he was not paying pensions to Cossack and Russian retirees living in Chechnya, Dudaev responded angrily: "Why don't the Cossacks and Russians who live here ask the Russian authorities, 'Where are our pensions?' Instead they demand them of Dudaev. And Dudaev himself does not receive the pension which he earned for serving thirty years in the armed forces."[48] For the Chechen president, Russians living in his republic were simply not his responsibility, but were instead a problem for the Russian Federation.

As he moved forward in his efforts to construct an ethnocratic Chechen state, Dudaev was confronted, as two Russian journalists noted in March 1993, with key problem areas in the northern regions of the republic: "[T]he Cossacks," they wrote, "are completely capable of becoming a 'party of influence' in both Russia and Chechnya . . . The 'Nogai factor' is also dangerous for Chechnya. There are not so many Nogai in Chechnya itself – about 7,000. But the Nogai national movement demands the unification of the people within the framework of Dagestan or Stavropol' krai and has pretensions to the Chechen part of the Nogai steppe."[49]

One clear option for Russians and Cossacks living in Chechnya was to migrate to the Russian Federation. Between 1979 and 1989, as has been noted, about 20,000 Russians and so-called Russian-language populace departed from Chechnya. From June 1990 to June 1991, another 20,000 people left, while between the summer of 1991 and the summer of 1992 the outflow from the republic increased to about 50,000.[50] In his address to the Russian Constitutional Court in July 1995, Sergei Shakhrai asserted that "over the past three–four years, about 250,000 people who have abandoned the Chechen Republic have moved to various regions of Russia."[51]

In his essay, "The Chechen Model of Ethnopolitical Processes," Vadim Korotkov has traced what happened to ethnic Russians and

[47] In *Moskovskie novosti*, 33, 14–21 August 1994, p. 11.
[48] In *Izvestiya*, 21 August 1993, pp. 1, 4.
[49] Vladimir Kolosov and Rostislav Turovskii, "Tak li uzh grozen Groznyi," *Novoe vremya*, 12 (March 1993), 13.
[50] In *Russkii vestnik*, 41–44 (1992), 9.
[51] For the text of Shakhrai's address, see *Rossiiskie vesti*, 12 and 13 July 1995.

Cossacks who chose to remain in the Chechen Republic. The fact that
the Chechen national movement headed up by Dudaev was directed
against the Moscow "center" and against its representatives in
Chechnya, he notes, produced an inevitably negative effect on the
Russian populace of the republic. "Representatives of ethnic Russians
were removed from the decision-making sphere and were squeezed out
of leadership posts in the sphere of economic administration, as well as
from the organs of judicial and legislative power. Various methods of
pressure, including the use of force, were employed in this process." The
"anti-imperial" campaign waged against Moscow by the Chechen mass
media also served to stimulate a negative attitude toward the Russian
populace on a day-to-day level. The growing crime rate in the republic
began to take on a "national selective character," especially in the area
of housing, where some Russian homes were directly seized. Leading
representatives of the Russian-language populace in Chechnya were
murdered: for example, university rector Kan-Kalik; Dean Udodov;
Judge Samsonova; the employee of the cabinet of ministers San'ko; a
correspondent for the press service "Express-Chronicle," Krikor'yants,
and "many others."[52]

The lack of effectiveness of the law enforcement organs in Chechnya
left the Russian-language populace unprotected and adrift. "The
Russian state withdrew from supporting legality in the region, and the
Chechen Republic for various reasons did not perform this task."[53]
Representatives of the Russian-language populace had previously been
concentrated in the industrial enterprises and in the state budget
organizations of Chechnya. The sundering of economic and financial
ties with Russia and the economic policies of the Chechen Republic led
to a squeezing-out of Russians from the process of privatization being
carried out there. The social and economic foundations of the Russians'
very survival suffered destruction. This resulted in "psychological
trauma" and in the political radicalization of elements of this populace.
As has been noted, many Russians sought to migrate to Russia. By mid-
1993, according to public opinion surveys, a majority of the 170,000
Russians remaining in Chechnya wanted to leave.

Accounts of the suffering of the Russian-language populace of
Chechnya have been intentionally and at times grotesquely exaggerated
by representatives of the Russian intelligence services, which were, of
course, actively engaged in seeking to undermine General Dudaev.
According to the former chairman of the FSK, Sergei Stepashin:
"[D]uring the three years of Dudaev's rule 350,000 were driven out of

[52] Korotkov, "Chechenskaya model'."   [53] Ibid.

the republic [this is 100,000 more than Sergei Shakhrai's above-cited estimate which was presented to the Constitutional Court] and 45,000 persons were killed [a staggering exaggeration – the true figure might be fewer than 100]."[54] In similar fashion, the above-cited compilation, *A Criminal Regime*, assembled by the public affairs departments of the FSK, MVD, and Defense Ministry, proclaims shrilly: "The murders of Russian people in Chechnya take place every day. The morgues in Groznyi are filled to overflowing with corpses, many of which have been disfigured." But what, the volume's anonymous authors proceed to ask themselves, about the argument that Chechen criminals also kill Chechens? "It could be objected," they are prepared to admit, "that they also kill Chechens. Yes, they do. But the Chechens basically perish in disputes among themselves, in the struggle for power and for spheres of influence in business." The volume's authors conclude by excoriating what they term "genocide against the Russian part of the population."[55]

While material disseminated by the Russian special services has to be utilized with extreme care – much of it obviously constitutes disinformation – one of the documents contained in a so-called *White Book* of materials circulated by the Russian FSK seems deserving of comment: namely, the text of an open letter addressed to President Yeltsin, with copies to Prime Minister Chernomyrdin and to other high-ranking Russian officials, allegedly signed by 49,244 inhabitants of the Naurskii and Shelkovskii districts located in the north of the republic.[56] This document – which appears to be authentic, though its text may have been interpolated by the FSK – began circulating in January 1995, i.e., in the month following the Russian military invasion of Chechnya.[57]

Noting that the Naurskii and Shelkovskii regions previously belonged to Stavropol' krai in the Russian Federation, the nearly 50,000 signatories of the letter contend that they have been subjected to intolerable persecution by the Chechen government: "They have deprived us of Sunday as a holiday and replaced it with Friday," they complain. "The teaching in school is conducted in the Chechen language." The signatories also claim to have been subjected to economic oppression: "For two years we have not received our wages, and old people have not gotten their pensions. We constantly hear proposals and threats that we get out of here to Russia. But we are in Russia."

[54] In *Belaya kniga*, vol. II, p. 74. See also the letters received from Russians and Cossacks living in Chechnya which were published by the Govorukhin Commission: *Komissiya Govorukhina* (Moscow: Laventa, 1995), pp. 151–64.

[55] In *Kriminal'nyi rezhim*, pp. 43–44.

[56] "Prezidentu Rossiiskoi Federatsii El'tsinu B. N.," in *Belaya kniga*, vol. I, pp. 38–41.

[57] See OMRI (Open Media Research Institute, Prague, Czech Republic) *Daily Digest*, 24 January 1995.

"[W]ith the coming to power of Dudaev," the signatories assert, "we have turned from masters of the district into reservation dwellers." The names of sixteen persons allegedly killed by Chechen hoodlums are then given, and it is said that the names of "many, many others" could be added to this list. "They [Chechens] break into homes, administer beatings, and demand money and gold which we have never had. They tie old people to chairs . . . after robbing them." And the signatories urge: "These two districts provide 60–70 percent of the profit of the republic. Return these districts to Stavropol′ krai, and the rest of Chechnya will crawl to Russia on its knees."[58]

It is difficult to determine how accurate the charges contained in this document are. The authors, it should be underlined, waited until the Russian invasion to compose their letter, and it was circulated by the FSK, hardly an impartial party. On the other hand, one suspects that at least some of the abuses the authors detail did take place, since it seems likely that Chechens living in the northern districts of the republic (and Chechens outnumbered Russians even there) would have strongly resented the Russians' desire to detach that area from Chechnya and return it to Stavropol′ krai.

One curious event should be briefly noted before we leave the subject of Russian–Chechen relations in the period 1992–94. On 28 August 1994, Nikolai Kozitsin, ataman of the Don Cossack Host, signed a treaty with General Dudaev and with the Chechen government. Retired KGB major general Aleksandr Sterligov, a shadowy figure involved in Russian nationalist politics, was reportedly a key figure behind the signing of this treaty. Kozitsin's actions were then roundly condemned as treachery by other Cossack organizations in Russia.[59] According to two specialists on the Russian Cossacks, S. Ivankov and M. Malyutin, Kozitsin's actions had a purely monetary explanation – he was effectively bribed by corrupt business circles in Moscow and by the "local 'gangsterocracy'" in Chechnya.[60]

---

[58] "Prezidentu Rossiiskoi Federatsii El′tsinu B. N."

[59] On this, see Ostankino Television, 9 September 1994 in Radio Free Europe–Radio Liberty (RFE–RL), *Russia and CIS Today*, 12 September 1994, pp. 0649/20–22; *Kommersant*-daily, 27 August 1994, p. 3; *Trud*, 9 August 1994, pp. 1, 2; and *Izvestiya*, 30 August 1994, p. 2.

[60] S. Ivankov and M. Malyutin, "Cossacks as a Russian Nation-Wide and Regional Political and Economic Factor," in Segbers and de Spiegeleire, *Post-Soviet Puzzles*, vol. III, pp. 650–51.

Chechnya and the Confederation of Peoples of the Caucasus

In addition to seeking to achieve the secession of Chechnya from Russia, General Dudaev, like other nationalists in the North Caucasus region, wanted to recreate the independent North Caucasus State, or Mountain Republic, which had been founded on 11 May 1918. Independent Chechnya was thus not envisioned by Dudaev or by his entourage as "going it alone"; rather its perceived role was to be part of a considerably larger political and geographical entity.

In an interview published in the 6 March 1994 issue of the Turkish newspaper *Zaman*, Dudaev confided: "My plan foresaw the creation of a union of Caucasus countries directed against Russian imperialism, signifying a united Caucasus. Our chief goal was the achievement of independence and liberation, acting together with the Caucasus republics which have been oppressed by Russia over the course of 300 years. After that, we proposed together to exploit the rich natural resources and oil of the Caucasus and transport it across Turkey to world markets."[61] According to documents which were reportedly found in Groznyi following the Russian invasion of December 1994, it emerges that this new Mountain Republic was to include Abkhaziya, North and South Ossetiya (despite the fact that a majority of that region's populace was Christian), Kabardino-Balkariya, Adygeya, Karachaevo-Cherkessiya, Dagestan, and possibly Azerbaijan as well. Some territorial units, including apparently Ingushetiya (which was presumably to be absorbed by Chechnya), were to lose their autonomous status.[62]

In his second volume of memoirs, Zelimkhan Yandarbiev writes concerning a meeting of the round-table "Caucasus Home [Kavkazskii dom]" which began its work on 4 September 1992. Representatives taking part in the round-table, he reports, came from Azerbaijan, Armenia, Georgia, Karachaevo-Cherkessiya, Kabardino-Balkariya, Dagestan, Ingushetiya, Ossetiya, and Abkhaziya. In the summary statement issued by the participants in the round-table, some of the points which were underscored concerned: "the need to create a confederation of peoples and states of the Caucasus"; "the need to create a single system of collective security for the Caucasus"; and "the need for the speediest possible withdrawal from the territory of the Caucasus of the armed forces of all non-Caucasus states." In Yandarbiev's view, the round-table made "a real attempt to unite the Caucasus – both its peoples and states."[63]

[61] Cited in *Chechenskaya tragediya*, p. 59.   [62] Ibid., pp. 58–59.
[63] Yandarbiev, *Checheniya*, pp. 175–76.

Russian nationalist authors have violently assailed General Dudaev's vision of a revivified Mountain Republic as constituting a kind of "Nazism." Thus Sergei Roi, deputy editor of the journal *Moskva*, has fulminated: "The ideology of Dudaev's regime rested on two planks – Islam and a Chechen version of Nazism, both of which helped to overcome clan (*teip*) fragmentation and to achieve a degree of political cohesion. The reason I speak of Chechen Nazism, not of separation or simply nationalism, is its extremely aggressive, expansionist nature manifesting itself, for example, in plans for a 'Greater Chechnya,' stretching from the Caspian to the Black Sea, and on Dudaev's insistence that Chechens are the 'ethnically central nation of the Caucasus.'"[64]

Roi's invective seems wide of the mark. The idea of reviving the Mountain Republic of 1918 was scarcely a neo-Nazi scheme, and it seems clear that this republic was envisioned as a confederation of equal states rather than as an imperial "Greater Chechnya." It could more plausibly be argued that it was ethnic Russians, like Sergei Roi, who were aggressively seeking to retain Russia's position as the "ethnically central nation of the Caucasus."

The cauldron of Abkhaziya

The original impulse for resurrecting the 1918 Mountain Republic belongs not to the Chechens but rather to the Abkhazians, a largely Muslim people whose historic territory lay in northwest Georgia, adjacent to the Black Sea. In August 1989, the Assembly of the Mountain Peoples of the Caucasus was constituted at a meeting held in the Abkhazian capital of Sukhumi. The meeting was attended by delegates from the Abkhaz, Adygei, Abaza, Ingush, Kabard, Cherkess, and Chechen informal movements. A year later, the assembly had become significantly radicalized. In the autumn of 1990, a confederative treaty was signed, on the basis of which the assembly was declared to be the legal successor of the 1918 Mountain Republic and was entrusted with the task of restoring the sovereign statehood of the North Caucasus. In October 1992, at a congress held in Groznyi, the assembly officially changed its name to Confederation of Peoples of the Caucasus (and subsequently came to be known by the Russian initials of its name: KNK).[65]

---

[64] Sergei Roy, "Chechnya and Russia Before and After Budyonnovsk," *Moscow News*, 26, 7–13 July 1995, p. 5.

[65] Hill, *"Russia's Tinderbox"*, pp. 25–26, and Ann Sheehy, "Power Struggle in Checheno-Ingushetiya," RFE-RL, *Report on the USSR*, 15 November 1991, p. 21. On the

After 1991, leadership of the KNK passed, de facto, from the Abkhazians to the greatly more numerous Chechens. In November 1991, Yusup Soslambekov (b. 1956), a Chechen, was chosen chairman of the assembly's parliament. Reflecting the strong secessionist view of the Chechen leadership, the KNK emphatically rejected Russia's Federation Treaty of March 1992.

As Fiona Hill has noted, the KNK was motivated by strong geopolitical ambitions: "The KNK's stated objective is to restore the 1918 Mountain Republic of the North Caucasus as a confederation stretching from the Black Sea to the Caspian, with the capital in Sukhumi, Abkhazia, on the basis of a shared historical experience in the Caucasian wars of 1817–64 and a common cultural heritage rooted in Islam." And she goes on to observe: "In theory, such a confederation would exercise full control over the key Black Sea–Caspian Sea axis and the transportation and communication links between Russia and Transcaucasia (and hence Turkey and Iran) to the south – at the expense of Russia's strategic position in the region."[66]

The newly formed Confederation received a stern testing when, in July 1992, the Abkhazian legislature voted to reinstate that region's 1925 constitution, effectively asserting its sovereignty from Georgia. Abkhaziya also asked Russia either to make it a protectorate or to annex it outright. These moves soon triggered a full-scale war with the Georgian government led by Eduard Shevardnadze, who had replaced nationalist Zviad Gamsakhurdia earlier that same year. (Many of Gamsakhurdia's followers had fled to Abkhaziya, where they fought with the Abkhazians against the Georgian troops.)[67]

At first, the better-armed Georgian national guard succeeded in pushing back the Abkhazian forces and in recapturing the city of Sukhumi on the Black Sea coast. In August 1992, however, the leaders of the KNK declared a mobilization of volunteers throughout the republics of the North Caucasus to help Abkhaziya.[68] In the autumn of 1992, the Abkhazians, led by Vladislav Ardzinba, launched a successful counteroffensive, which resulted in a major defeat for the Georgian forces. As we shall see, this stunning victory was achieved with strong assistance from both the Chechens and the Russian military. Eventually, 200,000 Georgians living in Abkhaziya were "ethnically cleansed" and

---

involvement of Chechen volunteers in the Abkhaz struggle, see Zelimkhan Yandarbiev, *V preddverii nezavisimosti* (Groznyi: author publication, 1994), p. 33, and Yandarbiev, *Checheniya*, pp. 170–72, 208.

[66] Hill, *"Russia's Tinderbox"*, pp. 26–27.

[67] On Gamsakhurdia's death in January 1994 and the solemn removal of his remains to Chechnya, where they were reburied, see Yandarbiev, *Checheniya*, pp. 290–94.

[68] Timur Muzaev, *Chechenskaya respublika* (Moscow: Panorama, 1995), pp. 119–20.

forced to flee the area. President Shevardnadze of Georgia was com-
pelled to yield to Moscow's pressure and to join the CIS, including its
collective security system. A ten-year treaty of friendship and cooperation with Moscow was signed.[69]

It is worth scrutinizing both the Chechen and the Russian roles in this
conflict. Emil' Pain and Arkadii Popov have written: "[T]he fact of the
participation of Chechen armed detachments in the Georgian–Abkhaz
war of 1992–93 is commonly known. The basic military successes of the
Abkhaz side were achieved precisely with the help of the Chechen
battalion, which was called 'Abkhaz' in honor of its victories." The top
commanders of the KNK units, they note, "were always Chechens from
Dudaev's entourage – Isa Arsamikov, then Shamil' Basaev."[70] If Pain
and Popov are correct – and I believe that they are – then it was the
Chechens who played perhaps the key role in defeating Shevardnadze's
Georgian military forces. It should be noted that Zelimkhan Yandarbiev
has written that "up to 150 Chechens" died fighting as volunteers in
Abkhaziya.[71]

But did the Chechens act alone in achieving this victory? What, if any,
was the role of the Russian Federation in bolstering the Abkhazian
secessionists? As Stanislav Lunev, a retired colonel in Soviet military
intelligence (the GRU) has written: "[S]tarting in 1992, the new
Russian leadership began to conduct the old Soviet policy of 'divide and
conquer' in the countries of the so-called 'near abroad.' Separatist forces

[69] See Rossen Vassilev, "Georgia's Ethnic Conflicts," *Prism*, part III, 23 February 1996.
For a detailed and useful discussion of the Abkhaz conflict, see Gueorgui Otyrbi, "War
in Abkhazia," in Roman Szporluk, ed., *National Identity and Ethnicity in Russia and the
New States of Eurasia* (Armonk, NY: M. E. Sharpe, 1994), pp. 281–309, and Fiona Hill
and Pamela Jewett, *"Back in the USSR": Russia's Intervention in the Internal Affairs of the
Former Soviet Republics and the Implications for United States Policy Toward Russia*
(Cambridge, MA: John F. Kennedy School of Government, Harvard University,
Strengthening Democratic Institutions Project, January 1994), pp. 45–60. See also
Catherine Dale, "The Case of Abkhazia (Georgia)," in Lena Jonson and Clive Archer,
eds., *Peacekeeping and the Role of Russia in Eurasia* (Boulder, CO: Westview Press,
1996), pp. 121–37, and Ariel Cohen, "Revisiting Russia's Turbulent Rim," in Uri
Ra'anan and Kate Martin, eds., *Russia: A Return to Imperialism?* (New York: St.
Martin's Press, 1995), pp. 93–96. See also Paul B. Henze, *Islam in the North Caucasus:
The Example of Chechnya*, P-7935 (Santa Monica, CA: RAND, 1995), pp. 32–34, and
Henze, *Russia and the Caucasus*, P-7960 (Santa Monica, CA: RAND, 1996), pp. 8–12;
and *The Caucasus and the Caspian: 1996–1997 Seminar Series* (Cambridge, MA: John F.
Kennedy School of Government, Harvard University, Strengthening Democratic
Institutions Project, 1997), pp. 4–40. See, too, Alexei Zverev, "Ethnic Conflicts in the
Caucasus, 1988–1994," and Ghia Nodia, "Political Turmoil in Georgia and the Ethnic
Policies of Zviad Gamsakhurdia," in Bruno Coppieters, ed., *Contested Borders in the
Caucasus* (Brussels: VUB Press, 1996), available on the Internet at:
gopher://marvin.stc.nato.int:70/11/secdef/cipdd/COP.
[70] Pain and Popov, "Rossiiskaya politika v Chechne," *Izvestiya*, 8 February 1995, p. 4.
[71] Yandarbiev, *Checheniya*, p. 172.

in Moldova, Georgia, and other former union republics were supported by the Russian special forces, with the blessing, and at the insistence, of the country's highest military and political leadership. In these republics, detachments, officially called 'diversionary groups,' were trained and prepared under Russian control. At first, these detachments really served Russia's interests, creating zones of instability in newly independent states."[72]

Excursus on Shamil' Basaev and the Abkhaz Battalion

The now-legendary commander of the Abkhaz Battalion, Shamil' Basaev, was born in 1965 in the Chechen mountain village of Dyshni-Vedeno. He holds a secondary but not a higher education, and after 1983 was employed as a common laborer. In November 1991, as has been noted, at the time of a threatened Russian invasion of Chechnya, he and two other fighters hijacked a Russian plane to Turkey. While he had no formal military training, Basaev early on showed a keen aptitude for the conducting of military operations. In 1992, he served as first the commander of a company and then of a battalion of Chechen *spetsnaz*. In August 1992, he went as a volunteer to Abkhaziya, where he eventually rose to the rank of commander of KNK forces and deputy minister of defense of Abkhaziya.[73]

Elizabeth Fuller of the Open Media Research Institute in Prague, citing a Russian publication, has written: "Abkhaz tactics during the fifteen-month war [with Georgia] were coordinated by Russian military intelligence."[74] One of the forces used by the GRU in this struggle consisted of Cossack volunteers. As S. Ivankov and M. Malyutin have noted in an article on the Russian Cossacks: "'Enlistment' of the most active units of the Cossack Army in all zones was carried out in the traditional Cossack way: through participation in border wars, first in the Dniestr region, then in Abkhaziya and in Serbia. According to Federal Counterintelligence Service [FSK] data, a total of about a hundred thousand Cossacks passed through this conveyer belt."[75]

In Abkhaziya, the authors continue, "according to FSK data, upwards of eight [Cossack] battalions fought in shifts." Despite this heavy Cossack presence, however, "even in Abkhaziya they [i.e., the Cossacks] did not achieve very much in comparison with the Confedera-

---

[72] Stanislav Lunev, "Chechen Terrorists – Made in the USSR," *Prism*, part III, 26 January 1996.
[73] In Muzaev, *Chechenskaya respublika*, p. 59.
[74] Elizabeth Fuller, "Shamil Basaev: Rebel with a Cause?," *Transition*, 28 July 1995, p. 47.
[75] Ivankov and Malyutin, "Cossacks," pp. 653–54.

tion of Mountain People."[76] It was Basaev's Abkhaz Battalion, and not the Cossack units, which took the city of Sukhumi in October 1993, crushing and humiliating the Georgian military.

One of the reasons that Basaev was successful in this operation was that he had reportedly received training from the Russian GRU. As the former GRU colonel Stanislav Lunev has noted: "Shamil' Basaev's detachment went through not only training, but was also 'broken in' under fire in Abkhaziya under the direction of GRU specialists, whose professionalism and individual courage received the highest marks from the Chechen terrorist himself."[77]

Sergei Arutyunov has sought to elucidate the reasons for the Russian military's decision to make use of the Chechens in Abkhaziya: "The Russian military stationed in Abkhaziya," he writes, "decided to support the Abkhazian side for several reasons: Abkhazians not only behaved correctly to [sic] them, but had declared they were in favor of a revival of the Soviet Union, where Abkhaziya could be one of the Union republics. Interestingly and significantly, the same position was adopted by Dudaev in Chechnya still earlier, and this may explain to some extent initially a rather tolerant attitude to him on the side of many Russian military, ex-military and pro-military . . . Besides, the Russian military, quite expectedly, were consumed with their hatred for Shevardnadze [i.e., for helping to destroy the USSR]."[78]

Shamil' Basaev has confirmed the fact of his earlier cooperation with the Russian military: "While still in Abkhaziya," he recalled in mid-1995, "I had contact with Russian generals and officers."[79] Beginning in 1994, he would put this training to use against the very Russians who had provided it to him in the first place.

During the summer of 1995, President Shevardnadze of Georgia suggested during an interview given to *Moscow News* that the Russian state had been reaping the fruits of its foolish and counterproductive Abkhazian strategy: "Had there been no Abkhaz tragedy," he remarked, "it might have been possible to avoid the tragedy in Chechnya. Take the example of Sukhumi [in October 1993]. Thousands of Chechens fought there and went through the schooling of a terrible war. They realized there that war is a political method of pressure. Who was behind them? Let's look into this matter. Did Dudaev alone maintain such a number of people? One group fights for three to four months, then they are provided with uniforms and arms, then another group is sent – all in all

[76] Ibid., pp. 655–56.   [77] Lunev, "Chechen Terrorists."
[78] Arutyunov, "Possible Consequences."
[79] Marina Perevozkina, "Shamil' Basaev: govorite gromche!," *Russkaya mysl'*, 20–26 July 1995, p. 2.

6,000–7,000 people. This is the way they [the Chechens] were hardened."[80] (Shevardnadze's figures for the number of Chechens involved in the fighting appear to be inflated.)

By late 1996, the stance of the Chechen leadership toward Georgia under Shevardnadze had completely changed. The then Chechen prime minister (and former military chief-of-staff) Aslan Maskhadov and then acting president Zelimkhan Yandarbiev told Georgian journalists that they were seeking a meeting "any time, any place" to overcome differences with Georgia and to become "real allies" and "strategic partners" with them. The two Chechen leaders (unconvincingly) blamed Moscow for having misled the Chechens into supporting Abkhaziya's secessionist war against Georgia. "Unfortunately," Maskhadov confided, "we were slow to understand that the Kremlin involved us in that conflict by telling us to help the Abkhaz as our Muslim brothers. That was a dirty policy directed not only against Georgia but, as it turned out, against us."[81] Efforts then began to hold a meeting between Yandarbiev and Shevardnadze. The latter cautiously welcomed the overtures from the Chechens while signaling that he would not be drawn into an anti-Russian front.[82]

It appears that, in 1992 and 1993, the Russian GRU also employed Chechens as fighters in other small regions which were seeking to break away from newly independent states located in the "near abroad," particularly in Georgia. In his July 1995 address to the Russian Constitutional Court, for example, Sergei Shakhrai noted that "the backbone of the illegal armed formation of Dudaev was composed of units which had had combat experience in . . . Abkhaziya, Georgia, Ossetiya, and Moldavia."[83] The future Chechen secessionist fighters had thus, at least in part, been trained by the Russian military.

By the autumn of 1994, the Confederation of Peoples of the Caucasus had lost much of its strength due to its own internal contradictions. The harsh ethnic conflict which had broken out in 1992 between North Ossetians and Ingush served to weaken the unity of the KNK. "[T]he conflict," Fiona Hill has written, "was a great blow to the KNK's plans to create a Mountain Confederation in the North Caucasus."[84] And while the Confederation sought to allay fears among Russian Cossacks in the region by acknowledging the Cossacks as being "among the indigenous Caucasians," it was unable to overcome a perception among Cossacks that it in effect represented an anti-Russian force. The KNK

[80] Interview with Shevardnadze in *Moscow News*, 29, 28 July–3 August 1995, p. 4.
[81] In *Monitor* (Jamestown Foundation, Washington, DC), 7 November 1996.
[82] In *Monitor*, 21 November 1996.   [83] In *Rossiiskie vesti*, 13 July 1995, p. 2.
[84] Hill, *"Russia's Tinderbox"*, p. 51.

also found itself increasingly isolated among the Muslim peoples of the North Caucasus: "[T]he majority of the national movements in the North Caucasus have been in favor of remaining within the Russian Federation."[85] By late 1994, the Chechens had been thrown back upon themselves and upon their own resources, both military and spiritual. Their movement had now been defined as in essence a national one, not one with a larger Caucasus-wide dimension.

Dudaev, the clans, the council of elders, and Islam

During the nineteenth-century Caucasus War, Imam Shamil', a strict adherent, as we saw in chapter 1 (pp. 26–27), of the Naqshbandi *tariqat*, had proclaimed the need to construct a theocratic state and had attempted to erase clan distinctions, wiping out the *adat*, or customary law, and replacing it with the *sharia*, or Islamic law. In contrast to Shamil', who tried to destroy the clan hierarchy, specialist Sulim Nasardinov has written, "Dzhokhar Dudaev made a stake on the rebirth of clans in a bid to draw on their traditional prestige for support. The institutions of state authority, which regulated societal life, were abolished, and the role of traditional institutions such as the Council of Elders naturally increased."

None of these measures, however, Nasardinov concluded, had resulted in the strengthening of Chechen statehood. "The Soviet system of administration," he summed up, "was destroyed, but the patriarchal one was not reestablished." Beginning in 1988, Nasardinov went on, "The Soviet *nomenklatura* started giving way to a new elite [in Chechnya]. The latter was profoundly echeloned in society because it relied on clans. In parallel, a system of religious communities (*virds* [or wirds] united in *tarikats* [tariqats] . . .) was developing. Drawing on finances, the new elite has been 'raising' its own clans while the *virds* were providing them with religious charisma." Thus, despite the upheavals rocking the republic, Nasardinov underlined: "Chechen society has preserved its traditional clan and *vird* structure that regulates social processes."[86]

The rise in influence of the Council of Elders during the Dudaev period was remarked upon by other close observers of the Chechen scene. In December 1994, on the eve of the Russian invasion, it was reported that there were a total of 7,000 village elders in Chechnya who had made the parliament building in Groznyi their headquarters. "The

[85] Ibid., pp. 29, 38.
[86] Sulim Nasardinov, "Will Chechnya Become Fundamentalist?," *Moscow News*, 20, 26 May–1 June 1995, p. 2.

Chechen Council of Elders," one account noted, "is trying to reconstitute itself as an arbiter in disputes between people of different *teips*, the clans to which every Chechen belongs."[87]

One specialist on Chechnya, Khamid Delmayev, has noted that the clan structure of Chechnya and the institution of the Council of Elders actually militated against one-man rule such as was practiced by Dudaev: "The ethnic tradition [of Chechnya]," he wrote, "is the inter-clan consent which is being consolidated on the approximately equal representation in power structures. The cultural tradition is the Council of Elders . . . Chechnya can only be a parliamentary republic with a parliament elected from single-mandate constituencies that will have to be parceled out according to clan traditions."[88]

Dudaev, as has been noted, eschewed emulation of Shamil''s nine-teenth-century strategy of requiring observance of the *sharia*. Unlike Shamil', he was not an adherent of the Naqshbandi *tariqat*; like most mountain and many lowland Chechens, he belonged to the influential Qadiriya *tariqat* (Kunta Haji *vird*). As we saw in chapter 1 (pp. 31–33), that brotherhood was less strict and more admixed with pagan elements than was the Naqshbandiya professed by Shamil'. Once ensconced in power, Dudaev actively attempted to "turn Chechen Islam into an instrument for the manipulation of mass awareness."[89]

Given the numbers of observant Muslims among Chechens, there was every reason for Dudaev to attempt to turn Islam into such a pliant instrument. Citing regional surveys which had been conducted in the Russian Federation in late 1993, Susan Goodrich Lehmann of Columbia University has noted that "seven in ten Chechens say that they not only believe in, but practice Islam." By contrast, less than one-fifth of Tatars, Bashkirs, Balkars, and Kabardintsy did so. Lehmann also pointed out that, among Chechens, "[M]en and women are equally likely to observe Muslim religious practices, and a majority of young people do so as well," and that "The differences in observance by educational level are also much more modest among the Chechens than in the other [national] groups investigated." One of the reasons for the continued strength of Islam among Chechens, Lehmann speculated, was the prevalence among them of Sufism: "Because Sufism is clan-based and less closely linked with mosques and other formal Muslim

---

[87] "Chechen Elders Aim for Leadership," *Moscow Times*, 11 December 1994, p. 17.

[88] Khamid Delmayev, "Will Chechnya Become a Clan-Governed Republic?," *Moscow News*, 34, 1–7 September 1995, p. 3.

[89] Yurii Kul'chik, "Dva islama: odna Chechnya," *Smena*, 12 May 1994, p. 4. On Islam in Chechnya, see also Henze, *Islam in the North Caucasus*, pp. 24–27.

institutions, it was better able to withstand the Communists' efforts to undermine Islamic beliefs and practices."[90]

It should be emphasized here that it was only in mid-November 1994, when a Russian military invasion of Chechnya appeared increasingly likely, that Dudaev finally "proposed that his self-declared independent republic of Chechnya become an Islamic state, introducing *sharia* law and forming an Islamic battalion to 'counter Russian aggression.'"[91] This decision was effectively forced upon him by the Russian state.

Dudaev confronts growing political opposition

Throughout 1992–94, Dzhokhar Dudaev found himself increasingly enmeshed in a fierce struggle for power with rival Chechen leaders, some of whom began to receive covert economic and military support from Moscow. Among those who turned against Dudaev, according to specialist Timur Muzaev, were "the national intelligentsia, the economic leaders, and a majority of entrepreneurs."[92] The marked failure of Dudaev's economic program served as a major factor underlying the mounting disillusionment of many educated Chechens. As early as March 1992, elements among the Chechen opposition had created a so-called Coordinating Committee for the Reestablishment of a Constitutional System in the Chechen–Ingush Republic.

On 31 March, a detachment of armed men from this shadowy committee, numbering some 150 persons, launched an attempted coup by seizing the television and radio stations in Groznyi. Its anonymous leadership then demanded the immediate resignation of Dudaev. During the second half of the day, however, Dudaev, sensing and exploiting the indecisiveness of the coup-plotters, brought up loyal troops and suppressed the rebellion, whose organizers and participants then took refuge in the Nadterechnyi district in the north of the republic, headed by its anti-Dudaev leader Umar Avturkhanov.[93] These shadowy putschists may well have received some support from the Russian government.

In November 1992, the Russian military came close to invading Chechnya but was checkmated by Dudaev and forces loyal to him (discussed in chapter 5, pp. 173–78). In light of his increasingly strained relations with Russia, Dudaev became less and less willing to tolerate

---

[90] Susan Goodrich Lehmann, "Islam Commands Intense Devotion Among the Chechens," *Opinion Analysis: USIA*, US Information Agency, Washington, DC, M-112-95, 27 July 1995.
[91] In *Moscow Times*, 27 November 1994, p. 14.
[92] Muzaev, *Chechenskaya respublika*, p. 170.   [93] Ibid.

domestic opposition within Chechnya, apparently believing that this opposition was being assisted and financed, at least in part, by Moscow.

One of those who turned against Dudaev at this juncture was the previously mentioned Chechen entrepreneur and specialist in the oil industry, Yaragi Mamodaev, who had played a key role in Dudaev's coming to power in the autumn of 1991. In October 1991, Dudaev had named Mamodaev chairman of the Provisional Committee for the Administration of the People's Economy in the first government to be formed in "independent Chechnya"; in May 1992, Mamodaev was named first deputy prime minister of the Chechen Republic (i.e., de facto head of the republic's government).

At the beginning of 1993, Mamodaev began to sharply criticize Dudaev for incompetency in economic matters, and he also accused a number of Chechen ministers and high-ranking bureaucrats of stealing petroproducts. In February, Mamodaev demanded of Dudaev that he fire the security minister and the minister of the oil industry of Chechnya for large-scale theft and for the unlawful sale of petroproducts. In April, Mamodaev supported opposition demands that Dudaev surrender the post of prime minister; the following month, however, he was himself fired from his post by Dudaev. In May 1993, the rebellious Chechen parliament declared Dudaev removed from the post of prime minister, and empowered Mamodaev to form a "Government of Popular Trust." This move, in turn, led to the attempted forcible dissolution of the parliament by a Dudaev decree of 17 April.[94] The parliament, however, refused to dissolve, and in May elected anti-Dudaev leader Yusup Soslambekov its new chairman.[95]

In early 1993, Dudaev prepared amendments to the constitution of the Chechen Republic under which all real power in the republic was to be concentrated in the hands of its head of state. Under these amendments, the parliament, elected together with Dudaev in late 1991, was transformed into a toothless organ without rights whose chief prerogative became to confirm decrees issued by the president. On 17 April, a close Dudaev ally, Zelimkhan Yandarbiev, was by presidential decree declared to be the "acting vice president" of Chechnya.[96]

In June 1993, Dudaev formally declared the dissolution of the republican parliament, the Groznyi city assembly, and the Chechen Constitutional Court. At dawn on 4 June, the building of the city assembly was attacked by Dudaev forces making use of armor and automatic weapons; the building was successfully stormed, and its

[94] Ibid., pp. 76–77.   [95] Soslambekov, *Chechnya*, p. 25.
[96] On this episode, see Yandarbiev, *Checheniya*, p. 124.

deputies were dispersed.[97] A presidential dictatorship was thus established in Chechnya, though Dudaev attempted to conceal this fact by permitting a "curtailed" parliament to come into existence headed by his relative, Isa (Akh"yad) Idigov.[98] In place of the Constitutional Court, which was disbanded in May–June 1993, Dudaev, in January 1994, established a "constitutional collegium" of the Supreme Court, whose seven judges were to be named by himself.

Commenting on Dudaev's state coup, Emil' Pain and Arkadii Popov have written: "Having accused the leaders of the parliament and the entire opposition of a 'pro-Russian conspiracy' and of 'national betrayal,' Dudaev was permitted, without any visible harm to his charisma, in May–June 1993 to dissolve the new parliament, which had been elected together with him, as well as the Constitutional Court, which had tried to carry out a referendum concerning the organization of power in the Chechen Republic."[99]

The Chechen parliament was dissolved by Dudaev because it refused to be subservient to his will. According to one account: "The parliament of the Chechen Republic consists of forty-one deputies. Five support the head of state [Dudaev]. Fifteen are in opposition. The remainder vote in different ways."[100] Such a parliament was patently unacceptable to Dudaev.

Following Dudaev's state coup of 4 June 1993, the center of the opposition to him and to his regime moved from Groznyi city to districts of the republic whose clans disapproved of his policies. The lowland or plains regions of Chechnya became the primary loci of this opposition. Faced with this situation, Dudaev increasingly turned for support to the so-called mountain clans of Chechnya. In so doing, he played, according to Timur Muzaev, upon the "religiosity and political inexperience" of the highlanders, as well as upon their envy and dislike of the "rich *partocrat* plains people."[101]

On 19 January 1994, Dudaev published a decree officially renaming the Chechen Republic "the Chechen Republic–*Ichkeriya*."[102] As journalist Igor' Rotar' has noted, citing the opinion of Chechen philosopher and political scientist Vakhid Akaev: "Ichkeriya is a territory which comprises two mountainous districts of southern Chechnya, the Shatoi district and Vedeno district. By incorporating the word 'Ichkeriya' into the republic's official name . . . Dzhokhar Dudaev officially proclaimed

---

[97] For Yandarbiev's detailed account of the convulsive events of April–June 1993, see ibid., pp. 231–63.

[98] Muzaev, *Chechenskaya respublika*, p. 171.

[99] Pain and Popov, "Rossiiskaya politika v Chechne," *Izvestiya*, 9 February 1995, p. 4.

[100] *Megapolis-ekspress*, 8, 24 February 1993, p. 20.

[101] Muzaev, *Chechenskaya respublika*, p. 172.   [102] Ibid., p. 6.

the superiority of the mountain population over those Chechens who live in the plains."[103]

To return to events in 1993, early one Sunday morning in August, Chechen forces loyal to anti-Dudaev leader Bislan Gantamirov attempted to assassinate the Chechen president by firing a grenade launcher, a machine gun, and automatic weapons at the windows of his presidential office. Two of Dudaev's guards were slightly wounded. In a statement following the incident, Dudaev put the blame on the Russian special services: "Even if it was Gantamirov," he commented, "he was acting as a simple executor. According to our information, the act physically to remove me was headed up by the Russian general Aleinikov. All such diversions are prepared in the offices of the special services in Moscow."[104]

In late 1993 and early 1994, Dudaev came under threat from the leaders of his own elite military and police units. As one Russian journalist observed: "Dudaev has to negotiate with the commander of the Chechen *spetsnaz*, the head of the Groznyi OMON, the leader of the Abkhaz battalion, the commander of the Shali tank regiment, and the commander of a large detachment, Ibragim Suleimenov."[105] On the evening of 16 December, army units led by these commanders surrounded the presidential palace in Groznyi. "The units had been brought in by their commanders who had appeared on Groznyi television the previous day demanding that . . . Dudaev resign as prime minister, create a security council and ministry of defense, and hold parliamentary elections by the end of March [1994]."[106] Dudaev responded to this crisis by meeting with each of the military leaders separately and thus defusing the crisis by preventing them from joining together in a plot against him.

In his second volume of memoirs, Zelimkhan Yandarbiev has confirmed that Dudaev at this juncture came close to losing the support of his top commanders, including such stalwarts as Shamil' Basaev and Ruslan Gelaev (head of an elite Chechen *spetsnaz* regiment). Bislan Gantamirov and other "opposition" leaders, Yandarbiev writes, had convinced these commanders to take a public oath on Sheikh Mansur Square in Groznyi in which they "repudiated the use of coercive methods against one another and the people." "I assessed their actions," Yandarbiev fulminates, "as betrayal and treachery, as doing the job of

---

[103] Igor' Rotar', "The Chechen–Russian Stalemate," *Prism*, Part II, 3 November 1995.

[104] See *Nezavisimaya gazeta*, 10 August 1993, p. 3, and *Moskovskie novosti*, 35, 29 August 1993, p. 12A.

[105] Dmitrii Kholodov, "Pirova pobeda Dzhokhara Dudaeva," *Moskovskii komsomolets*, 5 January 1994, p. 3. The author of this article was assassinated in October 1994.

[106] *RFE–RL Daily Report*, 17 December 1993, p. 2.

the Russian special services." It would not be until November 1994, he concludes, that Basaev and other Chechen commanders would finally come to "recognize the true face of the Gantamirovs."[107]

The leading clans of Chechnya were likewise becoming increasingly restive. "The congress of clans set for the end of December [1993]," one journalist noted, "was not permitted by Dudaev, who encircled the center of the city with a unit of guards. Chechnya was on the verge of civil war."[108] The following month, January 1994, saw an attempt by a so-called Committee of National Salvation (of Chechnya), led by the commander Ibragim Suleimenov, to remove Dudaev from power in a coup. Suleimenov's organization fell upon pro-Dudaev forces located near the city of Groznyi. In February 1994, Dudaev's National Security Service, headed by Sultan Geliskhanov, a former MVD official, succeeded in arresting Suleimenov and thus put an end to the activities of this tenebrous "committee."[109]

Russia gets serious about ousting Dudaev

By the spring of 1994, two powerful opponents of the Dudaev regime based in Moscow, Doku Zavgaev, the former Communist Party leader of Checheno-Ingushetiya and now an official adviser to President Yeltsin, and Sergei Shakhrai, Russian deputy prime minister and minister of nationalities (and a Terek Cossack by background), managed to "convince the president of Russia and the heads of the 'power ministries' that the Federation should actively intervene in the events in Chechnya. By that time Zavgaev and Shakhrai had acquired additional arguments to support their position. Russia had gotten involved in the competitive struggle for the right to participate in the Azerbaijani oil project, the so-called 'project of the century.'"[110] In order to be profitably exploited by Russia, the vast oil deposits of the Caspian Region ("a second Kuwait") required a pacified Chechnya, since the existing oil pipeline extending from Baku to Novorossiisk on the Black Sea ran directly through Chechnya.

[107] Yandarbiev, *Checheniya*, pp. 285–89.

[108] Kholodov, "Pirova pobeda," p. 3.   [109] Muzaev, *Chechenskaya respublika*, p. 172.

[110] Maria Eismont, "The Chechen War: How It All Began," *Prism*, Part IV, 8 March 1996. In February 1997, the Federation Council of the Russian Federation approved Zavgaev for the post of Russian ambassador to Tanzania. (See *Izvestiya*, 13 February 1997.) For a discussion of the "oil dimension" of the December 1994 Russian military move into Chechnya, see Rosemarie Forsythe, *The Politics of Oil in the Caucasus and Central Asia* (London: Oxford University Press, Adelphi Paper No. 300, 1996). See also Yurii Fedorov, *Kaspiiskaya neft' i mezhdunarodnaya bezopasnost': analiticheskii doklad po materialam mezhdunarodnoi konferentsii*, 2 vols. (Moscow: Federatsiya mira i soglasiya, 1996).

The Nadterechnyi district of Chechnya, led by its mayor, Umar Avturkhanov, had, as has been noted, served for some time as the focal point of anti-Dudaev activity in the republic. (This was also the home territory, it should be remarked, of Yeltsin adviser Doku Zavgaev.) In December 1993, a so-called Provisional Council of the Chechen Republic was brought into existence, and Avturkhanov was elected as its chairman. Bislan Gantamirov (b. 1963), the former mayor of Groznyi, who had formed a second center of anti-Dudaev activity in his home district of Urus-Martan, was named commander of the armed forces of the Provisional Council. These two leaders, it soon emerged, enjoyed significant support from the Yeltsin leadership in Moscow.[111]

Soon a third powerful Chechen "opposition" leader, convicted murderer Ruslan Labazanov (b. 1967), allied himself with Avturkhanov and Gantamirov. Labazanov had studied at the Krasnodar Institute of Physical Culture and had become a master of the Eastern martial arts. He was sentenced for murder in 1990 in Rostov-on-Don but led a successful prison break in November 1991. For a while, he was close to Dudaev and even held the rank of captain in his national guard. During 1992–93, Labazanov also engaged in the illegal sale of weapons.

In May 1994, Labazanov announced the creation of the Niiso (Justice) Party which adopted an openly anti-Dudaev stand. On 12 June, Labazanov's adherents held an anti-government rally on Sheikh Mansur Square in Groznyi, demanding the resignation of both the president and vice president of Chechnya. On the following day, 13 June, detachments of the Shali tank regiment and of the "Abkhaz" battalion, two units loyal to Dudaev, undertook the disarming of Labazanov's followers and stormed his headquarters. According to the anti-Dudaev opposition, between 180 and 300 persons perished in this operation; Labazanov, however, managed to escape arrest.[112]

On 27 May, a powerful remote-controlled car bomb came close to killing Dudaev in Groznyi. He and other Chechen officials blamed the Russian secret services for this attack, which, they said, had every appearance of having been the work of professionals. "*Rusism* [i.e., imperial Russianism]," Dudaev charged angrily, "has today become a world evil. It is a recurrent diversion, a provocation, a terroristic act, and an attempt on the life of the president, who is so hated by Russia

---

[111] Muzaev, *Chechenskaya respublika*, p. 44. In May 1996, it was announced that the Russian authorities had arrested Gantamirov for "embezzling billions of rubles allotted from the federal budget to finance the rebuilding of the Chechen Republic." See *Moscow News*, 17–18, 2–22 May 1996, p. 1.

[112] Muzaev, *Chechenskaya respublika*, pp. 50, 75–76; on Labazanov, see also "Okhotniki na Dudaeva," *Moskovskie novosti*, 36, 4–11 September 1994, p. 4.

today."[113] According to Dudaev's widow, Alla, the Chechen president happened purely by chance to be sitting in the third car in the procession rather than in the second car, which was his usual position;[114] the second car took the full impact of the blast, and thus it was the Chechen interior minister, Magomed El'diev, and his deputy who were killed rather than Dudaev.

On 3–4 June 1994, a "Congress of the Peoples of Chechnya" was held at the initiative of the Avturkhanov-led Provisional Council in the village of Znamenskoe, Nadterechnyi district. More than 2,000 delegates representing all districts in the republic attended. The participants in the congress "expressed a lack of trust in D. Dudaev and Z. Yandarbiev" and demanded that they resign their posts. It was proposed that the current Chechen parliament set a date for new elections to the highest organs of power in the republic. The congress also "declared the Provisional Council to be the sole legitimate organ of power on the territory of the Chechen Republic." On 30 June, the Provisional Council adopted a "decree on power" under which it proclaimed Dudaev removed from the presidency and affirmed that it had itself assumed "the entire plenitude of power in the Chechen Republic."[115]

During the same time period, the Provisional Council published a Decree on the Formation of a Government of National Rebirth and a Decree on the Setting of Elections to the People's Council of the Chechen Republic (without a specific date for the elections being specified). During July and August 1994, armed formations of the Provisional Council were created in both Nadterechnyi and Urus-Martan districts. On 11 August, the Provisional Council declared the formation of a new government of the Chechen Republic, with Ali Avadvinov being named as prime minister. On 25 August, the "procurator general" of the Provisional Council, Bek Baskhanov, issued an order for the arrest of General Dudaev, who was charged with having unlawfully seized power and with "a conspiracy with criminal groups."[116]

As journalist Maria Eismont has observed: "Umar Avturkhanov, head of the so-called Chechen Provisional Council . . . proved to be the best candidate for Moscow to support in Chechnya. The Provisional Council was composed mainly of former communist functionaries and associates of Zavgaev who had lost everything when Dudaev came to power . . .

[113] See Russian Television, "Vesti," 28 May 1994, in RFE–RL, *Russia and CIS Today*, 29 May 1994, p. 0383/12, and NTV, 4 June 1994, in RFE–RL, *Russia and CIS Today*, 6 June 1994, p. 0401/01.
[114] Interview with Alla Dudaeva, *Izvestiya*, 8 June 1995, pp. 1, 6.
[115] Muzaev, *Chechenskaya respublika*, pp. 44–45.   [116] Ibid., pp. 44–45.

[N]ew persons seeking to become the Chechen head of state appeared in the Kremlin, specifically the former USSR and petrochemistry [*sic*] industry minister, academician Salambek Khadzhiev. However, on 25 August 1994, the Russian government resolved to put its bets on Umar Avturkhanov and his Provisional Council."

And Eismont continues: "In accordance with a secret resolution of the Russian government, the Chechen Provisional Council was recognized as the 'only legitimate power structure in Chechnya.' Simultaneously, Umar Avturkhanov was promised all possible support in both the military and economic sphere. The Russian government began to pay wages and pensions to the people of the Upper Terek [i.e., Nadterechnyi] and Urus-Martan districts of Chechnya . . . Moscow also began to supply arms and ammunition to Avturkhanov. These supplies were very substantial: they included heavy armored vehicles and artillery installations. Moreover, a number of aircraft of the North Caucasus Military District were put at the disposal of the Chechen Provisional Council."[117]

Outlining his views on the desired nature of future Chechen–Russian relations, Avturkhanov stated that his Provisional Council wanted to emulate what Tatarstan and Bashkortostan had accomplished and to sign "treaties on the delimitation of powers" with Moscow. Under such an arrangement, Chechnya would remain firmly within the Russian Federation.[118] Avturkhanov boasted that 80 percent of the Chechen populace supported him, but independent checks by Russian journalists showed that few Chechens had ever heard of him.

While the final irrevocable decision by the Russian government to back Avturkhanov appears to have been taken in August 1994, it seems that a preliminary decision to support the anti-Dudaev opposition dates from the spring of 1994. As Valerii Tishkov has commented: "From the spring of [1994], there existed the so-called half-force [polusilovoi] variant of supporting and arming the Chechen opposition, excluding the use of the [Russian] army." Tishkov added: "I didn't see anything criminal in it [the half-force policy], inasmuch as it was not war."[119] Contrary to Tishkov's opinion, the "half-force" variant did lead, almost ineluctably, toward a "full-force" variant; Russia had started down a slippery slope leading to war.

That a pivotal decision had in fact been reached became clear from public statements made by Yeltsin in August. Thus, in response to one journalist's question, the Russian president replied that "he would not risk the use of force in Chechnya . . . [then] added with a sly smile: 'The

[117] Eismont, "The Chechen War."   [118] *Izvestiya*, 16 August 1994, p. 5.
[119] In *Novoe vremya*, 15 (1995), 22–23.

situation in Chechnya is changing. The role of the opposition is growing, and I would not say that we have no influence there.'"[120] Such statements by Yeltsin served to convince Dudaev and his circle that the Russian president now personally favored the use of active measures to remove Dudaev from power.

Thus, when a reporter for the newspaper *Trud* asked Dudaev if the head of the Provisional Council, Umar Avturkhanov, was "directly connected with the Russian special services," the Chechen president responded: "Well, of course." And when asked about the opposition paramilitary leader Ruslan Labazanov, Dudaev replied: "Labazanov is being used by the special services of Russia for definite aims."[121]

Similarly, Dudaev's secret police chieftain, Sultan Geliskhanov, claimed that the Russian FSK was spending 100 billion rubles "on Chechnya." That money, he said, was being used to underwrite "the organization of diversion, terror, sabotage, propaganda, and also a direct military incursion onto the territory of Chechnya."[122]

These words by Chechnya's leaders were accompanied by a series of defensive actions. On 10 August, a "people's congress" was convoked by Dudaev in Groznyi. The congress was held amid an atmosphere described as being "close to martial." At this congress, leaders of the Chechen opposition, such as Doku Zavgaev and Ruslan Khasbulatov, were declared to be "enemies of the nation" while Umar Avturkhanov and the Provisional Council headed by him were "sentenced to death in absentia."[123] Dudaev signed a decree authorizing a "full mobilization" of all Chechen combat forces and introduced emergency rule onto the territory of Nadterechnyi district, Avturkhanov's home base, dating from 12 August.[124]

In August and September 1994, Dudaev's units began to administer a series of sharp military blows to their heavily armed opponents. On 31 August, for example, the elite "Abkhaz" battalion took control of the Rostov–Baku Highway, which had been controlled for more than a month by followers of Ruslan Labazanov; and, on 3 September, detachments loyal to the Chechen president drove the Labazanov group out of the city of Argun.

Also in early September, forces of Avturkhanov's Provisional Council began an operation aimed at taking control of the capital of Groznyi. Some twenty kilometers outside the city, Russian helicopters made four attacks on three Chechen villages, firing rockets at the settlements. A

[120] In *Washington Post*, 12 August 1994, p. A33.
[121] In *Trud*, 9 August 1994, pp. 1, 2.
[122] In *Nezavisimaya gazeta*, 10 August 1994, p. 1.
[123] In *Izvestiya*, 12 August 1994, p. 1.   [124] In *Izvestiya*, 13 August 1994, p. 2.

tank column of twelve vehicles, reportedly "manned by Russian crews," also took part in this fighting. Dudaev's forces claimed to have destroyed one tank and to have seized one armored vehicle during the battle. They also took eight soldiers captive, including some "Russian soldiers."[125]

In late September, Umar Avturkhanov admitted for the first time that the anti-Dudaev forces possessed "a large number of MI-24 and MI-8 helicopters."[126] In mid-November, there were reports of the Provisional Council, "backed by tanks, armored vehicles, and helicopters," attacking and defeating Dudaev forces in the village of Bratskoe. During an interview on 19 November, Dudaev referred directly to "the beginning of the Second Russian–Caucasian war."[127] By early December, shortly before the invasion of Chechnya, the Provisional Council admitted to "having received forty billion rubles in cash from the Russian government" as well as to having obtained about seventy tanks and also some helicopter gunships together with crews.[128]

(As a footnote, it should be remarked that, in the opinion of specialists Emil' Pain and Arkadii Popov, the Yeltsin leadership waited too long to side decisively with the Chechen opposition. As they wrote in early 1995: "Today, for some reason, it is common to say that the whole Chechen opposition was 'invented' by the Kremlin and did not have support in society. That is absolutely untrue . . . In reality, in 1993 the opposition to Dudaev did not consist solely of the former [communist] *nomenklatura* . . . but also of a majority of the members of the parliament of the Chechen Republic elected at the end of 1991; of the Constitutional Court; of the heads of city and district administrations; of the leaders of almost all parties and movements; and of the heads of clans and the clergy." The authors proceed to indict the Kremlin for "an inability or disinclination to have dealings with the Chechen opposition" before August 1994.)[129]

Khasbulatov's gambits

On 1 March 1994, following his release from Lefortovo Prison in Moscow after having been amnestied by the Russian parliament for his part in an attempted coup d'état staged in Moscow in October 1993, former speaker of the Russian parliament Ruslan Khasbulatov arrived in Chechnya and took up residence in the village of Tolstoi-Yurt, located

[125] *Nezavisimaya gazeta*, 3 September 1994, pp. 1, 3.
[126] Ekho Moskvy radio, 29 September 1994, in RFE–RL, *Russia and CIS Today*, 30 September 1994, p. 0700/17.
[127] RFE–RL, *Daily Report*, 21 November 1994, p. 1.
[128] In *Moscow News*, 48, 2–8 December 1994, p. 1.
[129] Pain and Popov, "Rossiiskaya politika v Chechne," *Izvestiya*, 9 February 1995, p. 4.

within Groznyi district, to the north of the Chechen capital. During March and April 1994, Khasbulatov began traveling around the villages of Chechnya, talking to large crowds and taking political soundings.

Zelimkhan Yandarbiev, a harsh critic of Khasbulatov, has admitted in his memoirs that, in the spring of 1994, the former speaker of the Russian Supreme Soviet enjoyed considerable popularity among Chechens. In October 1993, at the time of the bloody clashes in Moscow, protest meetings, he recalls, had been organized in support of Khasbulatov in Chechnya, and committees in his defense had been formed; even Dudaev had felt politically required "to come out in defense of R. Khasbulatov." When Khasbulatov arrived in Groznyi in March 1994, he had been met by "a large number of people"; Dudaev, too, had been forced to take Khasbulatov's popularity among Chechens into account and had sent a delegation to the airport to greet him.[130]

As Khasbulatov has observed in his short book on the Chechen crisis: "By the spring and summer of 1994, the social base of Dudaev's adherents had shrunk to a minimum. Ninety percent of the populace were going hungry. Against this background, the parasitic ruling clique in Groznyi elicited general hatred. This was immediately seen by everyone who analyzed the situation, as soon as I returned to Chechnya."

Khasbulatov began visiting the towns and villages of Chechnya, including remote ones: "These mountains," he writes, "had not previously known gatherings of 100,000 people in one place. Learning that I had been in the mountain valleys of Kharacha, Benoi, Vedeno, and Shatoi, more than 100,000 people came to a meeting (the villages of Shali, Urus-Martan, Staraya Sunzha). Not to speak of the plains, where 100,000, 200,000, 300,000 people gathered."[131]

Returning to Moscow, Khasbulatov, on 18 July 1994, issued a declaration "On the Situation in the Chechen Republic" in which he called for a peaceful resolution of the political conflict in Chechnya. On 3 August, he issued another declaration "Concerning Dangerous Maneuvers Around the Chechen Crisis," in which he categorically protested "against those making preparations for the occupation of the Chechen Republic."[132] On 8 August, Khasbulatov returned once again to Tolstoi-Yurt in Chechnya, where he would remain until the eve of the Russian military invasion in December.

In Khasbulatov's opinion, he and his "peacemaking mission" represented the sole hope of avoiding a bloody clash between Chechens and Russians. As a formerly imprisoned political opponent of Yeltsin, he

[130] Yandarbiev, *Checheniya*, pp. 284–85, 294.
[131] Khasbulatov, *Chechnya*, p. 25.   [132] Muzaev, *Chechenskaya respublika*, p. 48.

could hardly be suspected of being a puppet of the Russian government unlike, say, Umar Avturkhanov. On the other hand, he had no clan or other connections to Dudaev. For those Chechens seeking sovereignty, but also desiring a workable relationship with Russia, Khasbulatov might well have appeared to be an ideal candidate. His notoriety served to attract large crowds to hear him but so, presumably, did his perceived "centrist" message. (It seems likely, incidentally, that Khasbulatov has exaggerated, and perhaps by a great deal, the numbers of Chechens who came to hear him speak.)

Since Yeltsin and the Russian leadership detested Khasbulatov, however, they drew, in the latter's opinion, a faulty and dangerous conclusion: "In Moscow, they reached this conclusion: 'Since from 100,000 to 400,000 are attending Khasbulatov's meetings, that is no joke. Dudaev's regime must be falling.' They then hurriedly recognized the 'opposition' headed by Avturkhanov and began to arm it . . . After my Declaration [of 18 July], when the Provisional Council had been recognized by Moscow, Avturkhanov began to avoid meeting me, citing the fact that Moscow forbade him to see me and was advising him to oppose me as much as he was opposing Dudaev . . . 'Don't even think of bringing Khasbulatov to power,' Chernomyrdin supposedly told him, according to Avturkhanov's words."[133]

Khasbulatov, however, continued with his "peacemaking" activities, which he undoubtedly hoped would propel him to the Chechen presidency. On 9 and 10 August, he formed a "peacemaking group," consisting of a number of leading and respected Chechen figures, such as Magomed-bashir-Khadzhi Arsanukaev, the first mufti to be named in Dudaev's Chechen Republic; Arsanukaev had been forced to submit his resignation in 1993 under pressure from Dudaev.[134]

According to Khasbulatov, his approach came to enjoy considerable success among Chechens. The settlement of Tolstoi-Yurt, fifteen kilometers north of Groznyi, where he had taken up residence, became "a center of pilgrimage of the populace." Even before he began his activities, Khasbulatov notes, "the whole northern part of the republic did not, on the whole, support the Groznyi regime." Now, after his efforts, "practically the whole southwestern part of the republic – the Urus-Martan district – was now openly against the regime."[135]

[133] Khasbulatov, *Chechnya*, pp. 30–31.
[134] For the membership of the "peacemaking group," see ibid., pp. 32–33. On Arsanukaev, see Muzaev, *Chechenskaya respublika*, p. 58.
[135] Khasbulatov, *Chechnya*, pp. 33, 36.

The "opposition" takes Groznyi, then lets it go

As Khasbulatov recalls, matters came to a head in mid-October 1994: "When, on 15 October, an order was suddenly given by Avturkhanov and Gantamirov to attack Groznyi, we had by that time carried out an enormous work with the populace . . . and not only with the populace; we had become acquainted with practically all of Dudaev's commanders." On 13 October, he remembers, he had had a meeting with several of Dudaev's commanders. Then came the surprising news that Avturkhanov and Gantamirov had broken into the city.

"People came to me," Khasbulatov recalls, "and asked: 'What should we do? Fight with them [Avturkhanov and Gantamirov] or not?' I said: 'No, for God's sake, don't fight. Let's try to resolve the question without large-scale bloodshed.'" And he concludes his account of the incident: "Therefore it is no accident that only seven persons in all were killed in the taking of Groznyi on 15 October 1994."[136] The fact that all of the combatants had been Chechens and that no Russians had been involved in the fighting was a key to the striking lack of bloodshed. Whatever their mutual animosities, Chechens apparently had no desire to be involved in the "large-scale bloodshed" of other Chechens. This almost bloodless taking of Groznyi therefore offered excellent prospects for a settlement with Russia.

Because of Russian political miscalculation, however, an extraordinary opportunity was missed: "The city," Khasbulatov writes, "had been taken de facto on the 15th, but then Avturkhanov and Gantamirov suddenly abandoned it at 4:00 p.m., leaving behind their people's militia and their equipment. What happened?" Flying to Mozdok in North Ossetiya to meet with Moscow-based FSK general Evgenii Savost'yanov and Avturkhanov and Gantamirov, Khasbulatov learned, he writes, that the two opposition leaders had sought the introduction into Groznyi of tanks and Russian forces. This, he reports, made him furious: "I don't know what you are saying," he shouted, "there should be no introduction of Russian troops."[137] As Khasbulatov was well aware, such a move would have induced many Chechens to rally around their president against a foreign invader.

Several days later, Khasbulatov recalls, he was visited by one of the leaders of the local FSK who had worked in the town of Znamenskoe in the Nadterechnyi district. The FSK officer told him: "You know, I

[136] Ibid., p. 37.
[137] Ibid., pp. 37–38. For Yandarbiev's somewhat evasive account of the 15 October events – which he mistakenly dates as having taken place on 15 November – see Checheniya, p. 341.

found out that the order to leave the city on 15 October was not given by E. Savost'yanov; he did not know about it. Avturkhanov telephoned Moscow and said: 'We have seized the city, and there is almost no resistance. What should we do?' And they said: 'Get out, leave the city.' According to this [FSK] man, Moscow was more interested in to what degree the operational points and the people of Khasbulatov had suffered in Groznyi. It seems to me that during the thrust into the city they expected there to be large bloodshed. But, as a result of our work, blood did not flow. Only seven people in all were killed. That did not suit those who wanted to send in the troops."[138]

The Tishkov group has expressed agreement with Khasbulatov's point that the debacle which occurred on 15 October represented a key turning point. "Until now [i.e., 1995]," they write, "it remains unclear why, on 15 October 1994, the forces of the opposition, having taken Groznyi de facto (with losses on both sides totaling seven persons in all), upon a command from Moscow then left the city, which later gave Dudaev a chance to present this as his victory over Russia and to consolidate his regime." In general, they award Khasbulatov's strategy quite high marks. While he favored arming the opposition, Khasbulatov resolutely opposed "direct military interference by Russia in the conflict." By October 1994, Khasbulatov may indeed, as he claims, have established contacts with most of Dudaev's field commanders, "including the commander of the Abkhaz battalion." Khasbulatov well understood that "The threat of war – and not war itself – was the most preferable variant." All of Khasbulatov's useful spadework, however, failed because of the implacable animosity of the Yeltsin leadership toward him. As Khasbulatov put it in hearings before the State Duma: "The federal forces upheld the principle, 'Let the whole Caucasus explode so long as Khasbulatov does not come to power.'"[139]

It should be noted here that Maria Eismont, a leading Russian journalist for the newspaper *Segodnya*, believes that Khasbulatov may have been considerably more involved in the 15 October events than he has admitted. "On 15 October 1994," she writes, "Khasbulatov, with the support of Chechen opposition force commander Bislan Gantamirov, undertook his own attempt to storm the city of Groznyi. Gantamirov's units, supported by those of Khasbulatov's 'peacekeeping group,' entered Groznyi. They met almost no resistance and even managed to occupy a number of administrative buildings. However, neither Umar Avturkhanov, nor the North Caucasus Military District aviation provided even the slightest support for them, and on the same

---

[138] Khasbulatov, *Chechnya*, p. 38.   [139] Tishkov, et al., *Chechenskii krizis*, pp. 27–29.

day Bislan Gantamirov ordered his units to leave the city."[140] Future historians will have to sort out the discrepancies in these accounts in an effort to determine what actually took place on 15 October in Groznyi.

With the collapse of these promising developments on 15 October, the so-called half-force variant simply collapsed. Key factors in its collapse, the Tishkov group writes, "were the unsuccessful actions of the Chechen opposition, whose leaders (Avturkhanov, Khadzhiev, Khasbulatov) were unable to work in collaboration with one another, while Moscow, in turn, feared the possibility of Khasbulatov's coming to power in Chechnya."[141]

In the wake of the bizarre collapse of the 15 October invasion, Moscow took a decision to strengthen the Chechen opposition and its reputation. On 24 November, a "Government of National Rebirth [of Chechnya]" was brought into existence under the aegis of the Provisional Council. This time it was Salambek Khadzhiev who emerged as prime minister, and Abdula Bugaev and Bislan Gantamirov as deputy prime ministers. Significantly, two Slavs – Grigorii Khoperskov and Vladimir Shumov – were named respectively chairman of the Chechen FSK and acting minister of Chechen internal affairs.[142] With this new "government of national rebirth" in place, Russia was now in a position to launch the ill-fated assault on Groznyi of 26 November.

[140] Eismont, "The Chechen War."
[141] Tishkov, et al., *Chechenskii krizis*, p. 28.
[142] Muzaev, *Chechenskaya respublika*, pp. 45–46.

5   Russia confronts secessionist Chechnya, 1992–1994

> If we used force in Chechnya, it would spark an uprising in the Caucasus and lead to such turmoil, so much bloodshed, that no one would forgive us afterward.   Boris Yeltsin in August 1994[1]

> The post of minister [of nationalities] was occupied by persons who had been raised in the Caucasus and who considered themselves to be specialists in inter-ethnic relations. But it is not enough to be born in the Caucasus to be an expert on the Caucasus.
>   Valerii Tishkov, former chairman of the Russian State Committee
>   on Nationality Affairs[2]

In the previous chapter, we looked at events taking place during the tumultuous years of 1992–94 largely from the perspective of the separatist Chechen leadership. In the present chapter, our task will be once again to scrutinize this period, but this time chiefly through the eyes of the Yeltsin leadership. As we shall see, the Russian government appeared to lurch convulsively, and often unpredictably, from a conciliatory to a hard-line approach to the Chechen problem until the spring of 1994, when support for a coercive solution began to receive increasing backing at the top.

Russia arms Chechnya

It will be recalled that USSR deputy defense minister Pavel Grachev had traveled to Groznyi in early December 1991 for talks with General Dudaev. The Chechen president had agreed at the time to facilitate a withdrawal of Russian troops from the republic "if a part of their arms and military hardware were handed over to him."[3] Evgenii Shaposhnikov, at that time USSR defense minister, has claimed that Dudaev

---

[1] In the *Washington Post*, 12 August 1994, p. A33.
[2] In *Novoe vremya*, 15 (1995), 22–23.
[3] In *Rossiiskie vooruzhennye sily v chechenskom konflikte: analiz, itogy, vyvody (analiticheskii obzor)*, 1st edn. (Moscow: Holveg, 1995), p. 9.

proposed to Grachev "a 50–50 split" of the armaments based in Chechnya but that he, Shaposhnikov, had firmly refused this offer.[4]

In May 1992, General Grachev was named Russian defense minister by President Yeltsin, and, during the same month, he sent a senior officer, General Ochirov, to Chechnya for talks with Dudaev. There was a pressing need for such talks since, in the wake of the failed 31 March 1992 Moscow-backed putsch (more on this incident on pp. 170–72), the Chechen nationalists urgently wanted the Russian troops out. During the course of their negotiations, Dudaev and Ochirov agreed that the Chechen president would give back half of the weapons on Chechen soil. Ochirov reported this arrangement back to the Defense Ministry by a coded telegram dated 22 May.[5]

In a directive issued on 28 May 1992, Grachev then ordered that 50 percent of the Russian military equipment located in Chechnya be handed over to the forces of General Dudaev.[6] Earlier, Grachev had argued for acceptance of such a position during a closed session of the Russian Security Council. In June 1992, the North Caucasus Military District was ordered to withdraw Russia's 50 percent of the weaponry to other regions of the Russian Federation. Under threat of "armed actions on the part of the Chechens," however, the Russian troops stationed in Chechnya were forced hurriedly to leave the republic and to abandon their weapons.[7]

In early 1992, Chechen fighters had begun to make raids upon Russian weapons storage depots in Chechnya. On 7 February, the facilities of the 93rd Radio-Technical Regiment were attacked, and forty-three tons of ammunition and 160 firearms were stolen. On the same day, Chechen fighters attacked the 382nd Training Aviation Regiment and seized 436 automatic weapons and 265 pistols, as well as ammunition for them. On 8 February, two complexes of the 173rd Military District Training Center were attacked, and a large amount of equipment and property was taken.[8] Oddly, no one appears to have been killed or wounded in these raids (or "raids").

Russian military personnel stationed in Chechnya appeared to be coming under increasing threat from Chechen national radicals. The

---

[4] Pyotr Yudin, "Source of Chechen Arms Sparks Rift," *Moscow Times*, 25 December 1994, p. 32.

[5] *Izvestiya*, 12 January 1995, p. 5. See also the statement by Deputy P. P. Shirshov at a session of the Council of Federation in *Chechnya: tragediya Rossii* (Moscow: Izdanie Soveta Federatsii, 1995), pp. 40–41.

[6] *Moskovskii komsomolets*, 18 January 1995, cited in *Rossiiskie vooruzhennye sily*, p. 12.

[7] *Rossiiskie vooruzhennye sily*, pp. 12–13.

[8] *Chechnya: tragediya Rossii*, p. 40.

government of Chechnya issued an ultimatum in which it demanded the withdrawal of all Russian troops from the republic. On 31 March 1992 – the date of the failed putsch – the Chechen parliament had passed a resolution under which all military centers, armaments, and equipment of the armed forces of the CIS were to be taken under the jurisdiction of the Chechen Republic.[9] On 6 June, General Dudaev demanded that all Russian forces be withdrawn from Chechen territory without their weapons and equipment in the course of twenty-four hours.

According to the Chechen information minister, Movladi Udugov, this action was taken by the Chechen authorities in response to a declaration made by the minister of defense of the Russian Federation, Pavel Grachev, which was broadcast over the Ostankino television network, concerning "his readiness to introduce paratroop units into Chechnya for the defense of [Russian] military personnel and their families."[10] The presence of Russian tank, artillery, rocket, and aviation units on Chechen soil, Udugov said, represented a serious threat to the republic's security. On the orders of Defense Minister Grachev, "in order to avoid bloodshed," all Russian military personnel and their families were then forthwith evacuated from Chechnya.[11]

According to former USSR defense minister Shaposhnikov, who later also served as CIS armed forces commander, an attempt was made by Grachev in June 1992 to remove Russia's agreed-upon 50 percent of the armaments from Chechnya. An estimated 10,000–20,000 firearms were in fact successfully withdrawn from Chechnya, but when a Russian military aircraft arrived in Groznyi to take out more weaponry, it was blockaded by Chechen fighters, and the 50–50 arrangement was in effect annulled. At this point, the Russian military had another option before it: namely, to blow up the weapons rather than turn them over to the Chechens. "According to the testimony of [Russian] combat engineers," one investigative report on the military dimension of the Russian–Chechen conflict has noted, "'Everything was carefully prepared to be blown up and destroyed, but, unexpectedly, there arrived a command – 'Leave everything as it is, blow nothing up, and leave.'"[12] This order is said to have originated with Defense Minister Grachev.

[9] Ibid., p. 41.
[10] "Ofitsery vydvoreny za predely Chechny," *Izvestiya*, 8 June 1992, p. 3.
[11] In the Govorukhin Commission report, *Pravda*, 2 March 1996, p. 2. For the full text of this report, see *Komissiya Govorukhina* (Moscow: Laventa, 1995). The chairman, S. S. Govorukhin, and five other members of the commission chose to sign the report. The deputy chairman, V. A. Nikonov, and three other members – Yu. E. Voevoda, B. A. Zolotukhin, and V. L. Sheinis – elected not to.
[12] *Rossiiskie vooruzhennye sily*, p. 12. According to the 12 January 1995 issue of *Izvestiya*, 19,801 firearms in total were withdrawn (p. 5).

It should be remarked that there has been considerable discussion in the Russian press concerning the extent to which the Russian arsenal was handed over to the Chechens under duress, and the degree to which this was done in response to monetary incentives. Specialists Emil' Pain and Arkadii Popov have written: "The version of the 'bold robbery' [of the Russian arsenal in Chechnya] is countered by the version of an 'amicable' agreement to hand over the weapons for an appropriate reward. Many eyewitnesses maintain that it is this second version which is correct, and that the wild organized attacks [on the arsenals by the Chechens], together with whoopings and shouts, were nothing more than a spectacle staged to divert suspicion away from enterprising merchants in epaulettes."[13]

According to one well-informed anti-Dudaev Chechen leader, Yusup Soslambekov, "a significant part of the firearms and auto transport of the Russian [military] command (ranging in rank from division commander, to company commander, to battalion commander) was sold in advance to the local populace. The remaining part was handed over to Dudaev."[14] Dudaev's acting vice president, Zelimkhan Yandarbiev, has similarly asserted that the Russian military command and officer corps based in the Chechen Republic, "exploiting the collapse of the USSR and the transitional period in Checheniya, sold everything that they could get their hands on."[15]

Whatever the reason for the failure to remove the Russian armaments, one thing seems clear: the Chechens had seized or had secretly purchased a daunting arsenal of weapons. Several lists of this military equipment have been published in the Russian press; these lists differ in some details, but all of them serve to underline the magnitude of the weaponry which was henceforth to be in the hands of Dudaev and his men. According to a report by the Russian State Duma's Govorukhin Commission, to take one example, Dudaev's forces succeeded in appropriating the following: 260 airplanes; 42 tanks; 48 armored vehicles; 44 lightly armored vehicles; 942 automobiles; 139 artillery systems; 89 anti-tank devices; 37,795 firearms, including 24,737 automatic weapons, 10,119 pistols, and 1,682 machine guns; and 1,257 rifles."[16] While impressive, these figures could be somewhat understated. According to the newspaper *Izvestiya*, more accurate figures would be: 426 planes, including 5 military aircraft; 2 helicopters; 42 tanks; 92

---

[13] In "Rossiiskaya politika v Chechne," *Izvestiya*, 8 February 1995, p. 4.

[14] Yusup Soslambekov, *"Chechnya (Nokhchicho') – vzglyad iznutri"* (Moscow: author publication, 1995), p. 32.

[15] Zelimkhan (Zelimkha) Yandarbiev, *Checheniya – bitva za svobodu* (L'vov, Ukraine: Svoboda narodiv [sic] and Antibol'shevitskii blok narodov, 1996), p. 166.

[16] *Pravda*, 2 March 1996, p. 2.

armored vehicles; 139 artillery pieces; 101 anti-tank guns; 27 anti-aircraft guns; 37,795 firearms; and 27 railway cars of ammunition.[17]

This was a huge armory, but it was far from all of the weapons that the Dudaev forces came to possess. Even before the takeover of Russian military arms and equipment on Chechen soil, Dudaev had managed to acquire significant numbers of weapons. Subsequently, in the period leading up to the Russian invasion of December 1994, Dudaev continued to purchase all the military hardware that he was able to. It appears that corrupt elements in the Russian military were prepared to aid him in this task. Viktor Sheinis, a member of the Govorukhin Commission, has recalled: "At the hearings [of our commission] it was briefly mentioned that Dudaev had been given a part of the weapons of the Trans-Baikal Military District, that is, of what was withdrawn from Mongolia."[18] This gift to Dudaev by elements in the Russian military – if it took place – must have been made for hard cash.

Negotiations during 1992

In March 1992, a professional ethnographer, Valerii Tishkov, was appointed chairman of the State Committee on Nationality Policy (Goskomnats, essentially a ministry), and he then began to seek inventive solutions to Russia's manifold problems with minorities. Exasperated by the government's often contradictory public statements on ethnic questions, however, Tishkov submitted his resignation after just seven months on the job. In October 1992, Sergei Shakhrai (b.. 1956), a jurist by training and a leading adviser to Yeltsin, was named as Tishkov's replacement. The title of Shakhrai's position was upgraded to minister of nationalities, and he was also made a deputy prime minister.[19] Though he was a gifted, even a brilliant official, Shakhrai, a Terek Cossack by background, bears, as we shall see, much of the responsibility for the outbreak of the Chechen war in December 1994.

Also in March 1992, the separatist dangers which had been besetting the Russian Federation during 1991 and early 1992 were, for the first time, diminished with the signing of a Federation Treaty. The dispute

---

[17] *Izvestiya*, 12 January 1995, p. 5. For other lists of the materiel which was taken over, see *Rossiiskie vooruzhennye sily*, pp. 13–15; *Belaya kniga. Chechnya, 1991–1995: fakty, dokumenty, svidetel'stva*, 2 vols. (Moscow: Tsentr obshchestvennykh svyazei FSK Rossii, 1995), vol. I, pp. 7–8; *Novoe vremya*, 2–3 (1995), 14–15; and *Chechnya: tragediya Rossii*, p. 41.

[18] In *Russkaya mysl'*, 2–8 March 1995, p. 3.

[19] On Shakhrai, Tishkov, and Russian nationality policies, see John B. Dunlop, "Gathering the Russian Lands: Background to the Chechnya Crisis," *Working Papers in International Studies*, I-95-2, Hoover Institution (Stanford University, January 1995).

over which Russian territorial entities should qualify for the designation "subject of the federation" had been so sharp that it had proven necessary for the Russian government to negotiate three separate treaties (which came collectively to be known as a Federation Treaty): one treaty for the autonomous republics; one for the oblasts and krais; and one for autonomous districts. These three treaties taken together sketched out a division of authority between Moscow and the regions and specified which functions should be exercised by the "center" alone, which should be performed jointly, and which should be devolved wholly to the republics and regions. The three treaties were signed at the end of March. Two "subjects of the federation" stubbornly refused to sign the treaty: Tatarstan and Chechnya.[20]

In June 1992, the Russian parliament formally recognized the division of the former Chechen–Ingush Republic into two separate autonomous entities: the Republic of Chechnya and the Republic of Ingushetiya.[21] Ingushetiya, unlike Chechnya, exhibited little apparent desire to separate from Russia.

During the course of his July 1995 presentation to the Russian Constitutional Court, Sergei Shakhrai noted that more than ten meetings and consultations had been held between representatives of the Russian Supreme Soviet and the Chechen parliament and government during calendar year 1992. One of the meetings singled out by Shakhrai for attention occurred in Sochi from 12 to 14 March.[22] According to the official signed protocols of this meeting, agenda items scheduled by the two sides for future discussion included political, legal, and economic questions, and problems of collective security. (The protocols were signed by V. Zhigulin, deputy chairman of the Council of the Republic of the Russian Supreme Soviet, and by Zelimkhan Yandarbiev, head of the delegation of the Chechen Republic.)

A key point in the signed March protocols referred to "the recognition of the political independence and state sovereignty [o priznanii politicheskoi nezavisimosti i gosudarstvennogo suvereniteta] of the Chechen Republic; and the determining of the political-legal form of mutual

---

[20] On this, see Elizabeth Teague, "Center–Periphery Relations in the Russian Federation," in Roman Szporluk, ed., *National Identity and Ethnicity in Russia and the New States of Eurasia* (Armonk, NY: M. E. Sharpe, 1994), pp. 34–35. For the texts of the treaties and agreements signed on the delimitation of powers by the Russian government under Yeltsin with the various "subjects of the Federation," see *Sbornik dogovorov i soglashenii mezhdu organami gosudarstvennoi vlasti Rossiiskoi Federatsii i organami gosudarstvennoi vlasti sub"ektov Rossiiskoi Federatsii o razgranichenii predmetov vedeniya i polnomochii* (Moscow: Izdanie Gosudarstvennoi Dumy, 1997).

[21] See Teague, "Center–Periphery Relations," p. 54, n. 42.

[22] In *Rossiiskie vesti*, 12–13 July 1995.

relations between the Chechen Republic and the Russian Federation."[23] As can be seen, at this juncture, Russian and Chechen representatives were seeking to negotiate an agreement which would have provided for Chechnya's "independence and sovereignty," but which would also have facilitated the development of "collective security" and close political, legal, and economic ties between two sovereign entities.

Moscow backs a shadowy putsch

As was noted in chapter 4 (p. 149), on 31 March 1992, Moscow-backed opposition forces in Chechnya attempted to carry out an armed coup against Dudaev. The date was hardly chosen at random: 31 March was the day on which the Russian "subjects of the federation" were scheduled to sign the new Federation Treaty. It was, one presumes, seen as especially fitting that the pro-secession Dudaev government should be toppled on that day.

Yusup Soslambekov, at the time a Dudaev ally, has written: "[I]n Moscow they organized an opposition for us in the person of the current leaders of the 'Committee of National Concord,' the 'Government of National Rebirth,' and the 'Daimokhk' movement." At dawn on 31 March, this self-styled opposition, Soslambekov continues, "armed to the teeth with the latest weapons (where these weapons had come from was not hard to guess) seized the television center, the radio station, and a number of administration buildings of the city of Groznyi."[24] The fact that the leaders of these organizations had been delivering "pro-Russian speeches" and were clearly fronting for the Russian government induced many Chechens, including Soslambekov, to rally around their elected president, Dudaev, in order to defeat the putsch.

In his second volume of memoirs, Zelimkhan Yandarbiev writes that a column of buses coming from Nadterechnyi district and "filled with armed putschists" arrived at the center of Groznyi at about 9:00 a.m. on 31 March. The coup plotters then proceeded to seize the central radio and television stations. By this time, Yandarbiev recalls, "Moscow was already transmitting disinformation concerning the seizure of power by the 'opposition' in Groznyi and the forthcoming signing of the Federation Treaty by D. Zavgaev in the name of the Chechen Republic." Soon, however, Chechen national guards loyal to Dudaev succeeded in driving the putschists out of the radio station; a large crowd which had gathered

---

[23] For the text of the protocol of 14 March, see Yandarbiev, *Checheniya*, pp. 127–28. On the protocol, see also Sanobar Shermatova, "Chetvertaya popytka?," *Moskovskie novosti*, 24, 16–24 June 1996, p. 8.

[24] Soslambekov, *Chechnya*, p. 21.

in Freedom Square in support of independence advanced on the television center, and the rebels fled abandoning their weapons. "The leaders," Yandarbiev concludes his account, "fled to Moscow, to D. Zavgaev and his masters."[25]

As Yandarbiev has underlined, Moscow had become a most unpredictable negotiation partner. On 14 March, a high-ranking official of the Russian Supreme Soviet, V. Zhigulin, had signed an agreement in which Chechen "independence and sovereignty" were solemnly recognized; on 31 March, however, other Moscow officials had backed an armed "opposition" putsch aimed at overthrowing the Dudaev leadership. Once that coup had visibly failed, then Moscow was forced to "continue the dialogue."[26]

These bilateral negotiations, Yandarbiev relates, continued first in Moscow and then at a location outside the Russian capital from 25 to 28 May 1992. On this occasion, the Russian delegation behaved more truculently than it had in mid-March, insisting that the agreed-upon March protocol was no longer binding and that the current talks represented in effect a "blank slate." The Chechen delegation, headed by Yandarbiev, was also shown a document in which the so-called Popular Council of Ingushetiya asked the Supreme Soviet of the Russian Federation "to demarcate the border between Chechnya and Ingushetiya."[27] Realizing that this "request" could serve as a pretext for a Russian incursion into Chechnya, Yandarbiev and his Chechen colleagues insisted that the Chechen Republic and Ingushetiya alone would decide the issue of their common border. Yandarbiev achieved a victory of sorts when the official signed protocol of the 25–28 May meetings specifically confirmed the protocol of the earlier 14 March meeting, which, it will be recalled, had recognized Chechen "independence and sovereignty."[28]

One Russian who came to the North Caucasus region in the autumn of 1992 to see whether or not an agreement could be reached between Russia and Chechnya was A. M. Ivanov, who subsequently published an account of his discussions with Chechen leaders in the newspaper *Russkii vestnik*. Musa Temishev, who was chief editor of the pro-independence newspaper, *Ichkeriya*, was quoted by Ivanov as declaring in that Chechen publication on 22 October: "I have said, do say, and will say that we [Chechens] must be together with Russia. I repeat: 'with' but not 'in.' There is an essential difference in this. I am for one economic, cultural, ruble, and military space with Russia. I am for

---

[25] Yandarbiev, *Checheniya*, pp. 132–33.
[26] Ibid., pp. 134–35,   [27] Ibid., p. 142.
[28] For the text of the 28 May protocol, see ibid., pp. 142–43.

Chechnya being an organic part of a Russian commonwealth. I repeat, a commonwealth [sodruzhestvo]. A commonwealth exists only among equals."[29]

Temishev's views, Ivanov discovered, were typical of those held by leading Chechens. Thus, Movladi Udugov, the republic's information minister, told him on 24 October: "We are for one defense and financial space with Russia," while General Dudaev affirmed: "I am for one economic and military space." These statements induced Ivanov to ask: "On the basis of such principles, why not enter into negotiations with Dudaev?" "One conclusion," he added, "must be made with all clarity and certainty: it is necessary to recognize the independence [nezavisimost'] of the Chechen Republic."[30] Unfortunately, Ivanov's flexibility with regard to the "Chechen problem" turned out to be a rare quality among Russian elites.

Threat of a Russian invasion through Dagestan

On the evening of 6 September, Udugov announced from a district of Dagestan which bordered on Chechnya that Chechen security had established the presence in that region of two battalions of Russian MVD "crimson beret" *spetsnaz*, supported by sixty-seven armored vehicles.[31] The national guard of Chechnya was hastily brought to full battle readiness. The cover story being used by the Russian MVD soldiers was that they were in the area to suppress possible "bread riots." Once it became clear, however, that the "crimson berets" were in fact pursuing a direct route into Chechnya – i.e., were apparently planning an armed invasion of that republic – the local inhabitants of that region of Dagestan (Chechens, Avars, and Kumyks) physically blocked the movement of the MVD forces and simultaneously took two of their officers hostage. On the evening of 7 September, the two MVD battalions began a retreat from the town of Khasavyurt, Dagestan; the local inhabitants pledged to release their MVD hostages as soon as they had received a telegram with the news that the "crimson berets" had returned to their home base in Novocherkassk. This aborted incursion seems to have been a serious, if somewhat tentative, effort by the Russian leadership to remove Dudaev from power.

---

[29] A. M. Ivanov, "Vid na Rossiyu iz Chechni," *Russkii vestnik*, 41–44 (1992), 9.
[30] Ibid.
[31] "Moskva poslala voiska v Dagestan," *Nezavisimaya gazeta*, 9 September 1992, p. 3. For Yandarbiev's comments on this episode, see Yandarbiev, *Checheniya*, p. 201.

The negotiations continue

As now seemed to be the pattern in Moscow's relations with Chechnya, threats to invade would alternate with offers to negotiate. During the autumn of 1992, the Russian vice president, Aleksandr Rutskoi, unexpectedly involved himself in the negotiations, holding talks in Moscow with leading Chechen figures Yusup Soslambekov and Aslambek Akbulatov. This was, it should be noted, the first time that a representative of the Russian executive branch had joined the negotiations; in point of fact, however, Rutskoi was at this juncture much closer politically to parliamentary speaker Khasbulatov than he was to President Yeltsin.

The Russian and Chechen sides agreed to revive the work of the joint commission, which had apparently last met in May. It was decided to open an official representation of the Chechen Republic in Moscow and one of the Russian Federation in Groznyi. Another decision taken was to lift the "economic, financial, and air blockade" of Chechnya.[32]

On 25 September, another high-level meeting of the two sides was held in Chishki; the leader of the Russian side on this occasion was Yurii Yarov, first deputy chairman of the Russian Supreme Soviet, and of the Chechen side, Bektimar (Bek) Mezhidov, first deputy chairman of the Chechen parliament. A moment of tension occurred at these meetings when the Russian delegation tried to seat an outspoken anti-Dudaev Chechen, Isa Aliroev, as a member of the Russian representation; the Chechen side "declared a protest" and demanded that Aliroev be removed, which was done. The gathering accepted the protocols of the March and May Russian–Chechen meetings and, thus, implicitly continued to recognize the independence and sovereignty of Chechnya.[33]

November 1992 – again to the brink of war

By November 1992, the Russian leadership had apparently grown weary of Chechnya's secessionist obstinacy. As in November 1991, a military and police solution to the Chechen problem appeared to be both feasible and achievable. A sharp territorial and ethnic dispute had broken out between North Ossetiya (the traditional ally of Russia in the North Caucasus region) and newly independent Ingushetiya, Chechnya's neighbor to the west. The Russian leadership evidently decided to exploit this crisis in order to crack down hard not only on the Ingush, but also on their Vainakh brethren, the Chechens, as well. A state of emergency was declared by the Russian government on 2 November in

[32] Ibid., pp. 199–200.   [33] Ibid., pp. 201–02.

both North Ossetiya and Ingushetiya. On 10 November, Russian troops entered Ingushetiya in order to enforce the state of emergency.

Ostensibly for the purpose of halting a flow of arms coming from Chechnya into Ingushetiya, as well as to prevent Chechens from coming to the aid of the Ingush, Russian forces on 10 November moved rapidly eastward across Ingush territory toward the as-yet-unmarked border with Chechnya. That same day, General Dudaev threatened retaliation against the Russian troops if they failed to withdraw from land histori-cally claimed by Chechnya (the Russian forces had taken up positions in three districts which were inhabited largely by Ingush but had belonged to Chechnya before Chechnya and Ingushetiya had been merged by Stalin in 1934). Dudaev gave the Russians until the morning of 11 November to withdraw; if they did not do so, he threatened, "the Chechen people will rise up in war."[34]

This threatened Russian invasion led also to the mobilization of the Confederation of the Peoples of the Caucasus (KNK) under Yusup Soslambekov, chairman of the confederation's parliament and an ethnic Chechen. The KNK threatened to send 500,000 volunteers against the Russian forces if they did not immediately withdraw from Chechen territory.[35] (The number of a half million KNK adherents was clearly exaggerated, but the threat from the Confederation was a real one.)

The moment was an exceptionally tense one, fraught with consider-able danger for the Russian Federation. As Caucasus specialist Sergei Arutyunov has recalled: "[T]here was a moment when two tank regiments, the Russian and Chechen ones, stood face to face . . . on the undemarcated Ingush–Chechen border." This tense standoff, Arutyu-nov believes, could have resulted in "an outbreak of a new Caucasian war, which would have involved all Caucasus mountaineers in a fight against Russians, Cossacks, and perhaps Ossetians." There was, at the end of 1992 and in 1993, he contends, the threat of an outbreak of a new Caucasus war, such as the one which had torn the region apart from 1817 to 1864. This new war, he believes, would likely have been ignited by the KNK attacking the Russian troops.[36] Such a war, in

---

[34] Radio Liberty–Radio Free Europe, *RFE–RL Daily Report*, 11 November 1992.

[35] Fiona Hill, *"Russia's Tinderbox": Conflict in the North Caucasus and Its Implications for the Future of the Russian Federation* (Cambridge, MA: John F. Kennedy School of Government, Harvard University, Strengthening Democratic Institutions Project, September 1995), pp. 50–51, and *RFE–RL Daily Report*, 12 November 1992. In his published volume of memoirs, Soslambekov does not discuss his activities in the KNK.

[36] S. A. Arutyunov, "Possible Consequences of the Chechenian [sic] War for the General Situation in the Caucasus Area," Conference on the War in Chechnya: Implications for Russian Security Policy, 7–8 November 1995, sponsored by the Department of National Security Affairs, Naval Postgraduate School, Monterey, California, un-published paper.

Arutyunov's opinion, would have been far more devastating than the conflict which actually erupted two years later, in December 1994. By late 1994, Russia was no longer being riven by internal *dvoevlastie*, while other autonomous republics of the North Caucasus region had essentially lost interest in political secession from Russia.

The Tishkov group has noted that, in testimony before the Govorukhin Commission, former acting prime minister Egor Gaidar confirmed that, in November 1992, "the intention of the Russian leadership [was to] finish with the Dudaev leadership." Russian minister of nationalities Sergei Shakhrai is seen by the Tishkov group as one of those who were arguing for "a coercive resolution of the crisis."[37] A key role in resolving the crisis, on the other hand, was played by Egor Gaidar and by the first deputy prime minister of Chechnya, Yaragi Mamodaev, who agreed upon a separation of the forces. Both of these peacemakers would, however, shortly be removed from their posts by Presidents Yeltsin and Dudaev.[38]

Unfortunately, the agreement brokered by Gaidar and Mamodaev did not hold, and at least some Russian forces remained on, or perhaps over, the unmarked Ingush border with Chechnya. In its issue of 18 November, the Russian army newspaper *Krasnaya zvezda* reported indignantly that armed Chechens, led personally by General Dudaev, had disarmed a Russian outpost located near the town of Sernovodsk (a settlement which today is located within the borders of Chechnya): "At the order of the president of Chechnya," *Krasnaya zvezda* angrily recounted, "his personal guard, having arrived in eight automobiles, seized the post, whose senior officer was Major Kokorin. In the presence of the Chechen leader, ropes with slip-knots were thrown over the necks of Russian officers . . . who were beaten and then taken along with the remaining soldiers to Chechnya."[39]

General Aslakhanov's account of the November crisis

In his 1994 book on the Chechen crisis, retired MVD major general Aslambek Aslakhanov, a Chechen and an elected RSFSR people's deputy (and also the chairman of the Russian Supreme Soviet's influential Committee on Questions of Legality, Law and Order, and the Struggle with Crime, as well as being a member of the elite Presidium of

---

[37] V. A. Tishkov, E. L. Belyaeva, and G. V. Marchenko, *Chechenskii krizis* (Moscow: Tsentr kompleksnykh sotsial'nykh issledovanii i marketinga, 1995), p. 26.

[38] On this, see Emil' Pain and Arkadii Popov, "Rossiiskaya politika v Chechne," *Izvestiya*, 9 February 1995, p. 4.

[39] "Otvetsvennost' lozhitsya na Dzhokhara Dudaeva," *Krasnaya zvezda*, 18 November 1992, p. 1.

the Supreme Soviet), has written in detail concerning the November events. While future historians will want to check his account carefully, it would seem useful to summarize it here.

On 10 November, Aslakhanov recalls, he received an urgent call on a secret government telephone from Ruslan Aushev, the acting head of the Ingush Temporary Administration (elected president of Ingushetiya in February 1993), who warned him that "a thrust of [Russian] military units in the direction of the Chechen Republic" was just then taking place on Ingush territory.[40] Aushev asked that Aslakhanov immediately contact Yeltsin, Khasbulatov, and acting prime minister Egor Gaidar.

Learning that Gaidar, armed with "special powers" granted to him by Yeltsin, planned shortly to fly to Vladikavkaz in North Ossetiya, Aslakhanov managed to get himself included as a member of Gaidar's party. During the flight from Moscow to Vladikavkaz, he and Gaidar had "a substantive conversation during which I succeeded in communicating to the acting prime minister the true situation in the Ossetian–Ingush drama and in the region as a whole." Another issue – of great concern to Aslakhanov – which the two of them discussed was "the possible positioning of [Russian military] forces directed toward implementing a regime of 'emergency rule' on Chechen territory."

After landing in Vladikavkaz, Aslakhanov traveled to Nazran', the capital of Ingushetiya, where he met with Ruslan Aushev in an attempt to resolve what both regarded as an exceptionally dangerous crisis. The two were cheered by the fortuitous appearance in Nazran' of two leaders of the Chechen Republic, First Deputy Prime Minister Yaragi Mamodaev and Kh. Maraev. These two leaders joined Aushev and Aslakhanov in seeking to separate the Russian and the Chechen forces confronting each other on the unmarked Ingush–Chechen border. A welcome moment occurred early in the morning, when Gaidar telephoned Mamodaev from Vladikavkaz with the heartening news that "the forces had been separated."

Shortly thereafter, Aslakhanov remembers, Gaidar was replaced as chief Russian negotiator by Sergei Shakhrai, accompanied by his first deputy, General Aleksandr Kotenkov. Shakhrai expressed agreement over the telephone with Aslakhanov's view that "the beginning of military actions throughout the whole North Caucasus" was possible if the crisis were mismanaged. Mamodaev, Aushev, and Aslakhanov then traveled to Vladikavkaz, where they met with Shakhrai and Kotenkov, "and came to agreement on all questions." The situation, however,

---

[40] For Aslakhanov's account, see Aslambek Aslakhanov, *Demokratiya prestupnoi ne byvaet* (Moscow: author publication, 1994), pp. 176–81. All quotations in this section are taken from these pages.

Aslakhanov recalls, remained exceedingly tense: "We had no doubt that on both sides [i.e., Russia and Chechnya] there were those who wished to flex their muscles and unleash a fratricidal war."

On 15 November, the signing of an agreement between Russia and the Chechen Republic on the separation of forces took place in the village of Ordzhonikidzevskaya. Present were an Ingush delegation headed by Ruslan Aushev; a group of Russian generals led by General Kotenkov; a Chechen delegation headed by Mamodaev; and Aslakhanov, who was representing himself (but also, in effect, the Russian Supreme Soviet). The assembled officials signed the agreement ending the armed standoff between Russian and Chechen forces.

Following this signing ceremony, Mamodaev, Aslakhanov, and others were being driven by car when they were halted by an unit of angry Russian paratroopers. The paratroopers said, according to Aslakhanov, that only an hour before General Dudaev and a group of armed Chechens had appeared at their post. "He had asked if they knew who he was and [said] that they were located on Chechen territory. The commander of the paratroops had responded that the Russian soldiers were there in accord with an agreement concluded with the Chechen Republic. Following these words, Dudaev had ordered that they be arrested. A major and a sergeant who refused to surrender their weapons had been beaten. After having ordered that they be shot, Dudaev then left." Fortunately, Aslakhanov adds, the Chechen soldiers had the good sense not to carry out this "insane order," and the Russian military men were freed and their weapons were returned to them. (It should be noted here that, to my knowledge, no other account exists which claims that Dudaev actually gave an order to execute the Russian soldiers – indeed, this incident is probably the same one as is described in the above-cited 18 November issue of *Krasnaya zvezda*.)

On the following day, 16 November, according to Aslakhanov, Dudaev declared publicly that "he had not given Mamodaev the authority to carry out negotiations or to sign an agreement." This statement infuriated Sergei Shakhrai, who threatened that, "if there is no mandate from Dudaev concerning the delegation of powers to the representative of Chechnya, then the agreement is annulled." Undaunted, Dudaev then began to assemble a new team of negotiators from among his closest entourage.

At this point, Aslakhanov relates, he decided that he had to take matters into his own hands. Accompanied by Kh. Maraev, he went to see Dudaev in person. "For the first time," he remembers, "I addressed this man with a request that he act in the name of compassion toward the people and that he permit Mamodaev to complete the negotiations.

To Dzhokhar's honor, he did not create a spectacle." The crisis was over, and the previously negotiated agreement was allowed to stand.

What Aslakhanov has to say about his meeting with Dudaev has the ring of truth. An outspoken opponent of the Chechen president and a strong supporter of one of his chief rivals, Ruslan Khasbulatov, Aslakhanov nonetheless bears witness that, when approached directly as a moral being, Dudaev did not behave wildly but rather consented to do the reasonable thing and sanctioned a negotiated settlement.

Yandarbiev's account

In his second volume of memoirs, Zelimkhan Yandarbiev has provided a version of events which differs in significant ways from that of General Aslakhanov. He writes that, before the Russian thrust toward the Chechen border had begun, Russian military units had been heavily concentrated in Stavropol' krai, North Ossetiya, and Dagestan, as well as in Ingushetiya. On 13 November, General Dudaev had written to the North Ossetian government about this question, and, on 14 November, a similar letter had been sent to the government of Dagestan. By the middle of September, Russian MVD troops, Yandarbiev adds, had been "almost entirely replaced by regular army units, and artillery had been brought up."[41]

Concerning the events covered in the account of General Aslakhanov, Yandarbiev writes: "Aslambek Aslakhanov and other Moscow politicians arrived in Checheniya. And here there took place an intrigue. A delegation of the parliament and of the Cabinet of Ministers was conducting negotiations with the Russian military and representatives of the Russian state in Nazran' [Ingushetiya] . . . At that time, Dudaev was conducting an inspection of the territory along the line where the two forces met, and he came upon a Russian post and disarmed it. After a short while, the Russian military, acting out of revenge, arrested the delegation of Mamodaev–Aslakahanov and demanded the return of their weapons. This was done. But our delegation, straight from Russian captivity, went on television at 12:00 midnight and attacked D. Dudaev, accusing him of attempting to provoke a war."[42]

The Security Council launches the "half-force" variant

In December 1992, the Russian Security Council took a decision and approved supporting documents actively to bolster pro-Russian forces

---

[41] Yandarbiev, *Checheniya*, pp. 211–15. On 10 November, Dudaev had also sent a letter to US president Bill Clinton concerning the threatened Russian invasion (p. 214).
[42] Ibid., p. 213.

in the North Caucasus region. This decision provided a rationale for Russia's subsequent refusal to find a modus vivendi with Dudaev's leadership and for promoting Chechen movements in opposition to him.[43] Thus, the much-discussed "half-force" variant, launched in 1994, is present, in kernel form, in this Security Council decision of late 1992.

Soslambekov's account of meetings held in late 1992

Yusup Soslambekov, a close ally of Dzhokhar Dudaev until January 1992, when he broke sharply with the Chechen president over the issue of forming a Cabinet of Ministers, served as chairman of the Committee on Foreign Affairs of the Chechen parliament (elected in 1991). As chairman of this important committee, Soslambekov played a leading role in all negotiations with Russia which took place in late 1992 and early 1993. At the time of the tense November 1992 crisis, Soslambekov headed a Chechen delegation which met in Vladikavkaz with Russian deputy premier Sergei Shakhrai and the Russian minister of emergency situations, Sergei Shoigu. Later, Soslambekov traveled to Moscow for another talk with Shakhrai. At this meeting, it was agreed that Moscow would allocate 2.5 billion rubles for the payment of pensions and benefits in Chechnya and would also approve the resumption of flights between Groznyi and Moscow.

Also in late 1992, Soslambekov and the delegation he headed met in Moscow with Russian vice president Aleksandr Rutskoi, Russian "power ministers" Viktor Barannikov and Viktor Yerin, and Yurii Yarov, first deputy chairman of the Russian Supreme Soviet. These contacts were followed by the already-noted meeting in Groznyi between Yurii Yarov and the first deputy chairman of the Chechen parliament, Bektimar Mezhidov, at which "documents were signed defining the basis of a peaceful resolution of the question of the mutual relations of the Russian Federation and the Chechen Republic."[44]

A key problem with this negotiation process at this point was, of course, that it completely omitted any participation by the Chechen president.

Negotiations during 1993

In December 1992, Sergei Shakhrai had succeeded in securing agreement from the leading Chechen politicians Yaragi Mamodaev and

[43] Hill, *"Russia's Tinderbox"*, pp. 84, 86.   [44] Soslambekov, *Chechnya*, pp. 17–19.

Yusup Soslambekov to a draft document with the cumbersome title "Treaty on the Separation of Power and Authorities Between the State Governing Bodies of the Russian Federation and the Governing Bodies of the Chechen Republic." This draft treaty built upon the earlier efforts of Egor Gaidar and Mamodaev, who, in November 1992, had signed a preliminary memorandum for a treaty on a division of powers, a document which "later became the basis of the [so-called] Tatarstan model."[45] General Dudaev, however, decisively repudiated this draft treaty and dismissed the negotiations which had taken place as representing a mere "private initiative."[46]

Negotiations on a treaty nonetheless continued on 14 January 1993, when Russian deputy prime minister Shakhrai and Ramazan Abdulatipov, chairman of the Council of Nationalities of the Russian Supreme Soviet and an ethnic Avar from Dagestan, arrived in Groznyi for talks. Representing the Chechen side were leading parliamentarians Khusein Akhmadov, Bektimar Mezhidov, and Yusup Soslambekov, as well as Sherip Yusupov (the Chechen representative, i.e., ambassador, in Moscow). During the meeting, a decision was reached to create working groups to prepare a "Treaty on the Delimitation and Mutual Delegation of Powers." On 19 January, this draft treaty was published in the Chechen press (but those responsible for printing it soon lost their positions).[47]

Dudaev's fierce opposition to this January visit by Shakhrai and Abdulatipov soon became evident. On the 15th of January, the Chechen president sharply criticized the protocol which had been signed on the previous day. On the 17th, the chairman of the Chechen parliament, Khusein Akhmadov, revealed that Dudaev "in all ways had attempted to break off the negotiations with Russia and had even wanted to hinder the landing of the airplane in which the representatives of Russia, Sergei Shakhrai and Ramazan Abdulatipov, had arrived in Chechnya." And Akhmadov added: "The parliament succeeded in organizing the guard of the Russian delegation despite . . . the refusal of the minister of security of Chechnya to carry out the order to protect the Russian

[45] Emil Payin, "Understanding the Conflict in Chechnya," in Fred Wehling, ed., *Ethnic Conflict and Russian Intervention in the Caucasus* (San Diego, CA: Institute on Global Conflict and Cooperation, University of California, 1995), p. 24.

[46] Emil A. Payin and Arkady A. Popov, "Chechnya," in Jeremy R. Azrael and Emil A. Payin, eds., *US and Russian Policymaking with Respect to the Use of Force*, Part I (Santa Monica, CA: RAND, 1996), posted on Discussion List about Chechnya, 6 November 1996, Chechnya@Plearn.EDU.PL.

[47] Shakhrai address to the Constitutional Court in *Rossiiskie vesti*, 13 July 1995, 3. For the text of a draft treaty written by Yusup Soslambekov, see Soslambekov, *Chechnya*, pp. 58–62.

delegation."[48] Yusup Soslambekov has gone further and claimed that Dudaev sent Chechen *spetsnaz* in armored vehicles to the parliament building to "arrest the members of the Russian delegation," but this version is not borne out by other sources that I have seen.[49] Most likely, the *spetsnaz* were sent to intimidate the negotiators and to induce the Russian delegation to leave the republic.

On 18 January, Dudaev declared publicly that, "while, on the whole, he supports the conducting of Chechen–Russian negotiations, he does not agree with a number of the formulas of the protocol signed by the Russian delegation and the representatives of the Chechen parliament on 14 January." In particular, Dudaev took exception to the term "delimitation of powers," which he saw as impinging upon the sovereignty of Chechnya.[50] Dudaev's acting vice president, Yandarbiev, has contended that the January talks "sharply lowered the level of agreement between the Chechen Republic and Russian Federation" reflected in the signed protocols of 12–14 March and 25–28 May 1992.[51]

It should be noted here that Dudaev's treatment of Russian deputy premier Shakhrai during his visit to the Chechen capital served to deepen an animus against the general on Shakhrai's part, one which had already become apparent to journalists in late 1992 when, "as administrative head in the Ossetian–Ingush conflict zone, on one occasion, [Shakhrai] barely escaped arrest when he arrived in Groznyi to conduct negotiations with Dudaev."[52] Suspecting Shakhrai of being hostile to Chechnya's sovereignty, and to him personally, Dudaev declared after breaking off negotiations with Russia in January 1993 that he had "a lack of desire to see Shakhrai as the chief representative of Russian power" in the future.[53]

One reason for Dudaev's suspicion of Shakhrai was presumably the latter's open support for the cause of the Russian Cossacks. In January 1992, Shakhrai had held meetings in Moscow with representatives of the Union of Cossack Armies of Russia after which a Union of Cossacks of Southern Russia had been established. In 1992, seemingly influenced by Shakhrai's pro-Cossack views, Yeltsin had issued a decree formally rehabilitating the Cossacks, while, in March 1993, another decree of Yeltsin's essentially restored the Cossacks' former status under the

[48] Timur Muzaev, "V Groznom net edinodushiya po otnosheniyu k Moskve," *Nezavisimaya gazeta*, 20 January 1993, p. 1.
[49] Soslambekov, *Chechnya*, p. 23.   [50] Muzaev, "V Groznom."
[51] Yandarbiev, *Checheniya*, p. 222.
[52] Maria Eismont, "The Chechen War: How It All Began," *Prism*, Part IV, 8 March 1996
[53] Tishkov, et al., *Chechenskii krizis*, p. 26.

tsarist Russian Empire as territorially based paramilitary units in the North Caucasus region.[54]

President versus parliament in Chechnya

As specialists Emil' Pain and Arkadii Popov have noted, the Constitution of the Chechen Republic, which had been adopted in 1992, officially accorded (Part 3, Article 62) the determining of domestic and international policy in the republic to the parliament. Negotiating a treaty with Russia was therefore to be the responsibility of the parliament, not the president.[55] By late 1992 and early 1993, however, a sharp power struggle was already taking place between the Chechen president and parliament, similar to what was occurring in the Russian Federation, where the *dvoevlastie* conflict between the Yeltsin presidency and the Khasbulatov-led parliament had commenced in earnest in December 1992, at the time of the Seventh Congress of People's Deputies.[56]

In mid- to late January 1993, Dudaev decided once again to take control of the Chechen side of the negotiation process, which had for the past six months been in the hands of ambitious rivals like Mamodaev and Soslambekov, whom he did not trust. A large Chechen government delegation, headed by Yandarbiev, was therefore sent to Moscow; among those included in the delegation were the Chechen minister of economics, the minister of finance, the minister of internal affairs, the chief of the Central Bank, and the head of the petrochemical industry. The titular head of the Russian delegation with whom they were to negotiate was Nikolai Ryabov, a deputy chairman of the Russian Supreme Soviet. The meetings were led de facto by people's deputy Vladimir Lysenko, a former deputy chairman of Goskomnats.[57]

According to Yandarbiev, "The process itself of the negotiations inspired hope. Having discussed the political aspect of the question . . .

[54] Hill, *"Russia's Tinderbox"*, pp. 36–37, 70.
[55] Payin and Popov, "Chechnya," n. 20. For the text of the Chechen constitution in Russian and in English translation, see Diane Curran, Fiona Hill, and Elena Kostritsyna, *The Search for Peace in Chechnya: A Sourcebook, 1994–1996* (Cambridge, MA: John F. Kennedy School of Government, Harvard University, Strengthening Democratic Institutions Project, March 1997), pp. 99–141.
[56] On the Russian *dvoevlastie* struggle from December 1992 through October 1993, see John B. Dunlop, *The Rise of Russia and the Fall of the Soviet Union*, 2nd edn. (Princeton, NJ: Princeton University Press, 1995), pp. 303–23. For a useful collection of documents on this crisis assembled by Yeltsin supporters, see *Moskva, osen' 93: khronika protivostoyaniya* (Moscow: Respublika, 1994). See also R. I. Khasbulatov, *Velikaya rossiiskaya tragediya*, 2 vols. (Moscow: TOO SIMS, 1994), and Aleksandr Rutskoi, *Lefortovskie protokoly* (Moscow: Paleya, 1994), and Rutskoi, *Krovavaya osen'* (Moscow: author publication, 1995).
[57] Yandarbiev, *Checheniya*, p. 224.

we agreed to change the tactic of the negotiations: it was decided to establish trade and economic relations first. Then, proceeding from what had been achieved on this issue, we would also resolve the political part of the problem. For two days, we worked in this direction. The principles of trade and economic relations were worked out, as was the cooperation of the power structures in the sphere of the struggle with crime."[58]

This focus on economic relations appeared to be a promising approach. When the time came for the delegates to sign a communiqué summing up the results of their two days of talks, however, the head of the Russian delegation, Nikolai Ryabov, according to Yandarbiev, unexpectedly "declared that he had to consult with the chairman of the Supreme Soviet, Khasbulatov." Returning from his meeting with Khasbulatov, Ryabov then announced that "the Russian side does not consider the continuation of negotiations possible, since the Chechen delegation has repudiated what was agreed in Groznyi [by Mamodaev and Soslambekov] concerning the working out of an agreement on the delimitation of powers."[59] Yandarbiev and his fellow Chechen delegates then issued a sharp protest and left Moscow. Perhaps the most promising development in the Russian–Chechen negotiation process had come to an abrupt end.

On the eve of the critical 25 April 1993 Russia-wide referendum – which asked voters whether they supported the Russian president and his social and economic policies – General Dudaev sent Yeltsin a letter in which he advised him to disband the Russian Supreme Soviet and to set new parliamentary elections and to hold a referendum on a new Russian constitution.[60] Yeltsin did not reciprocate this expression of sympathy and ignored Dudaev's letter (though in effect he followed Dudaev's strategic advice!).

Summing up what might be termed the Yeltsin–Shakhrai strategy for dealing with Dudaev, Emil' Pain and Arkadii Popov have written: "[P]rior to summer 1994, the Russian leaders relied on the possibility that Chechnya would peacefully adopt a more pragmatic policy. They were apparently waiting for the blatant failures of Dudaev's adventurist economic, social, and diplomatic policies to discredit his regime in the eyes of the Chechen people. The leadership in Moscow hoped that at that point the implacable 'General-President' would be removed by a domestic opponent [who] would be more inclined to compromise with

---

[58] Ibid., p. 225.   [59] Ibid.
[60] Pain and Popov, "Rossiiskaya politika v Chechne," *Izvestiya*, 9 February 1995, p. 4. For the text of this letter and of two other letters which Dudaev sent to Yeltsin in 1993, see *Komissiya Govorukhina*, pp. 146–51.

Moscow. Since the Kremlin did not want to increase Dudaev's authority or his popular legitimacy, the Russian government opted not to negotiate with Dudaev directly, but with other influential persons (including his rivals) within the Chechen leadership." This policy of "excluding Dudaev from the process of negotiation in advance," Pain and Popov note, "produced only deadlock."[61]

The strategy of excluding Dudaev

As we have seen, the cornerstone of the Yeltsin–Shakhrai strategy for managing the Chechen crisis was to avoid all personal contact with Dudaev. A number of Russian and North Caucasian commentators have focused upon this as a critical error in judgment. Thus, for example, Makhmud Esambaev, a member of the Public Council of the Government of the Russian Federation to Regulate the Chechen Crisis, recalled in 1995: "I have long been well acquainted with the President of Russia. I said to him: 'Boris Nikolaevich, don't let war happen. No matter who is president of Chechnya, invite him in and speak with him.'" And Esambaev continued: "I said to Dudaev: 'Dzhokhar, why do you want to separate from Russia?' He answered me: 'Makhmud, they don't want to take account of me [schitat'sya so mnoi]. We are *rossiyane* [i.e., Russian citizens without regard to ethnicity], and I am a *rossiiskii* general.' If they had invited him to participate in talks, there would not be war today."[62]

The Tishkov group has noted that Dudaev repeatedly insisted that the chief negotiations on the future of Russian–Chechen relations had to be conducted between himself and "the president or, possibly, the prime minister [of Russia]."[63] Tishkov believes that, for the sake of a successful settlement, and for the avoidance of war, Yeltsin should have been willing to talk with Dudaev, no matter how painful it was for him personally.[64] Pain and Popov, however, have argued that, "If such a meeting had taken place, it would only have strengthened Dudaev," whom they dismiss as "a person completely without principle."[65] In my opinion, Tishkov is right here, while Pain and Popov are wrong. Russia during Yeltsin's first presidential term was, as we have repeatedly noted, a state wracked by political turmoil and economic dislocations; the last thing such a country needed was a major war. Its president therefore should have been prepared to go the extra mile for peace.

[61] Payin and Popov, "Chechnya."   [62] In *Chechnya: tragediya Rossii*, p. 153.
[63] Tishkov, et al., *Chechenskii krizis*, p. 26.
[64] Tishkov in *Novoe vremya*, 15 (1995), 22–23.
[65] In "Rossiiskaya politika v Chechne," *Izvestiya*, 9 February 1995, p. 4.

The attempt of the Russian leadership to exclude Dudaev from negotiations resulted, predictably, in an impasse. As Sergei Shakhrai noted in his presentation to the Russian Constitutional Court in July 1995, talks between Chechen delegations and Russian representatives continued in Moscow during January–May 1993 but "once again Dudaev broke off the negotiations." "The second half of 1993," he added, "did not bring any constructive results in the process of political regulation [of the conflict]."[66]

By the summer of 1993, the Russian leadership had decided upon a more aggressive approach to the Chechen problem. At that point, the Russian government invited "all inhabitants of Chechnya to travel to Stavropol' krai to receive their pensions."[67] According to Vladimir Lysenko, about 10,000 Russians, Ingush, and Chechens took the government up on this offer despite a prohibition from the Dudaev regime. By offering pensions to those living in Chechnya, the Kremlin was apparently seeking to pursue a "divide and rule" policy.

According to Zelimkhan Yandarbiev, Dudaev continued to exhibit a willingness to negotiate with the Moscow leadership during the latter part of 1993. Thus a Chechen representative, M. Mugadaev, was sent to the Russian capital for talks with Prime Minister Viktor Chernomyrdin, while the Chechen foreign minister, Shamsudin Yusef, conferred in Moscow with Yurii Yarov, first deputy chairman of the Russian Supreme Soviet. "From this," Yandarbiev complains, "there was created an impression that a change in relations had taken place. But it was only an impression and nothing more."[68]

In December 1993, following the decisive defeat by Yeltsin of Rutskoi, Khasbulatov, and their supporters in the bloody "October events," a new Russian constitution was adopted in a Russia-wide referendum.[69] Like the earlier Federation Treaty of 1992, this document necessarily had an impact over the full range of Russo-Chechen relations. A detailed discussion of the constitution and its relation to Chechen secessionism will appear in the forthcoming second volume of my study on the war.[70]

---

[66] In *Rossiiskie vesti*, 13 July 1995, p. 3.

[67] Vladimir Lysenko, *Ot Tatarstana do Chechni: stanovlenie novogo rossiiskogo federalizma* (Moscow: Institut sovremennoi politiki, 1995), p. 164.

[68] Yandarbiev, *Checheniya*, p. 284. On Yusef, see Muzaev, *Chechenskaya respublika*, p. 92.

[69] For the text of the new Russian constitution, see Vladimir V. Belyakov and Walter J. Raymond, eds., *Constitution of the Russian Federation* (Lawrenceville, VA: Brunswick, 1994).

[70] For a useful discussion of the constitutional and legal issues raised by Chechen separatism, see *Pravovye aspekty chechenskogo krizisa* (Moscow: Memorial, 1995). See also Edward W. Walker, "Constitutional Obstacles to Peace in Chechnya," *East European Constitutional Review*, Winter 1997, pp. 55–60.

Also in December 1993, Yeltsin, accompanied by his three "power ministers," paid a visit to the North Caucasus region during which a number of hard-line decisions were taken affecting both the North Ossetian–Ingush dispute and Chechnya. With regard to the Chechen Republic, a decision was made to tighten controls over Chechen borders and to take control of the railway leading into Chechnya. Dudaev and his military commanders then declared publicly that these moves constituted a veiled declaration of war. An unnamed aide to Yeltsin who had accompanied him on his trip (most likely Sergei Shakhrai) noted that "[S]teps were also being taken to prevent Dudaev making any more of the foreign trips which he has so far been able to make at will."[71]

Another dimension of the political deadlock obtaining between Russia and Chechnya during 1992–93 deserves to be briefly noted: namely, economic self-interest. As Emil' Pain and Arkadii Popov have observed: "While there were no influential advocates in either the Russian government or parliament of granting Chechnya official independence, a number of senior [Russian] officials were interested in preserving the status quo in the 'quasi-separated,' crime-ridden, Chechen Republic – a status quo which made it possible for them to make fortunes through bank fraud and illegal oil and arms deals."[72]

The Govorukhin Commission of the Russian State Duma has drawn attention to the fact that Chechnya received billions of US dollars from the sale abroad of oil and petroproducts during 1992–93. "Only the direct complicity of Russian government structures," the commission concluded, "could have ensured the arrival of enormous amounts of oil into Chechnya [from the Russian Federation] as well as the sending of processed oil-products abroad through Russian pipelines and the receipt of petrodollars by the Dudaev regime."[73] The practice of sending Russian oil into Chechnya from Stavropol' krai, the commission noted, was stopped only in August 1993, while Russian oil continued to be sent in through Dagestan until November 1994, i.e., until just one month before the Russian invasion.

Negotiations in 1994

In January 1994, there was a brief flicker of hope that negotiations between the Russian and Chechen militaries might possibly lead to a settlement. A draft agreement was reached in which "a single defense space" for Russia and Chechnya was foreseen. According to the

[71] In *RFE–RL Daily Report*, 9 December 1993, p. 2. See also *Nezavisimaya gazeta*, 7 December 1993, pp. 1, 3.
[72] Payin and Popov, "Chechnya."   [73] In *Pravda*, 28 February 1996, p. 2.

Chechen representative to the talks, Colonel Mirzhuev, the Russian side pledged to provide the armed forces of Chechnya with weapons, hardware, and ammunition, and to repair Chechen military equipment at its plants; in addition, the Russian side agreed to help prepare Chechen officer cadres and stated explicitly that it would not use its armed forces against the Chechen Republic.

For its part, Chechnya agreed to participate in a common system of defense with Russia in order to repel external aggression and, in time of war, to provide the Russian air force with bases on its territory. Chechnya also consented in the draft agreement to participate in joint maneuvers with Russian forces and pledged that it would not enter into any military unions or blocs directed against Russia. In peacetime, it was agreed, Chechnya's army would not exceed 1.5 percent of the republic's population.[74] Unfortunately, this most promising draft agreement was not pursued further.

Tatarstan strikes a deal with Russia

On 15 February 1994, recalcitrant Tatarstan signed a bilateral treaty with Russia. The treaty affirmed that Tatarstan was united with Russia on the basis of the new treaty and of the constitutions of the two states (there existed, it should be noted, contradictions between the two constitutions, and the new treaty was not submitted, as required, for approval by the Federation Council). As part of the agreement which had been reached between the two sides, Tatarstan gained a right to conduct its own international and economic relations with foreign states, and the right to decide questions of ownership, use, and distribution of land and natural resources located on its territory.[75] The return of Tatarstan to the fold left secessionist Chechnya as the sole holdout among the eighty-nine "subjects" of the Russian Federation.

Commenting on Chechnya's status as the lone holdout republic, deputy premier Sergei Shakhrai declared at the time: "My position is the following. The situation in which 1,200,000 *rossiyane* live there outside the Constitution of the Russian Federation and outside the

---

[74] See Radio Mayak, 9 January 1994, in RFE–RL, *Russia & CIS Today*, 10 January 1994, p. 016/17.

[75] For the text of the treaty, see *Rossiiskaya gazeta*, 17 February 1994, p. 6. For a discussion of the treaty and its significance, see Gail W. Lapidus and Edward W. Walker, "Nationalism, Regionalism, and Federalism: Center–Periphery Relations in Post-Communist Russia," in Gail W. Lapidus, ed., *The New Russia: Troubled Transformation* (Boulder, CO: Westview Press, 1995), pp. 107–08, and Edward W. Walker, "The Dog That Didn't Bark: Tatarstan and Asymmetrical Federalism in Russia," *Harriman Review*, Winter 1996, pp. 1–35.

framework of Russian laws is no longer tolerable. The raging of criminality is such that neither the life nor the future of a man is safeguarded. Thousands of families are forced to abandon their homes. Naturally the federal authorities cannot remain indifferent."[76]

According to Zelimkhan Yandarbiev, in his second volume of memoirs, the signing by Russia of a treaty with Tatarstan prompted the Russian government, acting in Yeltsin's name, to send Dudaev the following ultimatum: "Cease accusing Russia of imperial ambitions, and take the treaty signed with Tatarstan as the basis for a possible Moscow meeting." Since Dudaev was willing to participate in such a meeting, Yandarbiev continues, the prospects at this point for a meeting of Yeltsin and Dudaev "looked fully realizable." And his account continues: "There were even [positive] signals from Moscow. But then the Shakhrais and Filatovs, placing their bets on Zavgaev and Khadzhiev, were able to talk the president out of his intentions." A "new escalation of tensions" therefore occurred rather than "a meeting at the top."[77]

In early September 1994, Vladimir Lysenko, a deputy chairman of the State Committee on Nationality Affairs under Valerii Tishkov and, subsequently, chairman of the subcommittee of the State Duma on the development of federal relations, made the apposite comment that the conclusion of the treaty with Tatarstan, as well as other successes in the nationalities area, had made the Russian leadership "dizzy with success." Rather than pursuing a patient policy and waiting for Dudaev's weak government to fall over the next two years, Shakhrai and his colleagues succumbed "to a very great temptation," namely, "to interfere in the [Chechen] conflict on the side of the opposition, helping it to smash Dudaev." And Lysenko warned prophetically: "But God forbid that they should do this. As soon as Russian troops appear on the territory of Chechnya, the *gazavat* will be transformed from a threat into a reality and the opposition will be transformed into a [Russian] fifth column."[78]

Shakhrai diminishes chances of a settlement with Dudaev

During February and March 1994, Russian deputy premier Sergei Shakhrai took actions which effectively reduced the chances of reaching a settlement between Russia and Chechnya. In February, he inserted a section into Yeltsin's annual presidential address to the Russian Federal

[76] In *Rossiiskaya gazeta*, 17 February 1994, p. 1.
[77] Yandarbiev, *Checheniya*, pp. 294–95.
[78] Lysenko, *Ot Tatarstana do Chechni*, p. 165.

Assembly, delivered on 24 February, that underlined the illegitimate nature of the existing government bodies in Chechnya and demanded new elections in that republic, as well as the initiation of negotiations with Russia on the delimiting of powers which would leave no room for Chechnya's independence.[79] Shakhrai went on to affirm that a treaty between Russia and Chechnya on the delimitation of powers was possible, but that, as a precondition, new Chechen elections would need to be held first.

On 25 March, the Russian State Duma "adopted a decree by which it is recommended to the president and to the government, first, that they carry out consultations on the question of future negotiations with all political forces of the Chechen Republic (and not only with Dudaev), and, the main thing, it insisted that a preliminary condition for the concluding of the proposed Russian–Chechen treaty on the delimitation of powers be the holding of elections in the Chechen Republic to the republican organs of power and to the Federal Assembly of the Russian Federation."[80]

As Emil' Pain and Arkadii Popov have underscored, this last stipulation – i.e., that new elections be conducted in Chechnya to the Russian Federation parliament – "already completely excluded negotiations with Dudaev, because he considered himself the lawful president of an independent state and could not conceive of conducting elections to the organs of 'neighboring' Russia."[81] It, thus, seemed clear that, as far as the Russian State Duma was concerned, it no longer made sense to attempt to negotiate with Dudaev; Russia should reach out to his rivals and opponents within Chechnya.

Pain and Popov, Valerii Tishkov, and other commentators have identified deputy premier Sergei Shakhrai as being the driving force behind the adoption of this Duma decree. Sergei Yushenkov, the chairman of the defense committee of the State Duma, has noted the ways in which Shakhrai successfully managed to use the Duma as a club against Dudaev. "At one point," Yushenkov recalls, "it seemed that an agreement satisfactory to everyone (on the model of the Treaty with Tatarstan) had been achieved, but Moscow, in the person of Shakhrai, became obstinate. The chief [Russian] 'nationalist' at that time demanded that the State Duma revoke the decision of the [1991] Supreme Soviet of the RSFSR concerning the deeming of the elections of Dudaev

---

[79] For the text of the address, see *Rossiiskaya gazeta*, 25 February 1994, pp. 1–7. For a discussion of the address, see Payin and Popov, "Chechnya."

[80] Pain and Popov, "Rossiiskaya politika v Chechne," *Izvestiya*, 9 February 1995, p. 4. For the text of the decree, see *Rossiiskaya gazeta*, 29 March 1994, p. 1

[81] Pain and Popov, "Rossiiskaya politika v Chechne," *Izvestiya*, 9 February 1995, p. 4.

as illegitimate. The explanation for this was the following: if the decision of that legislative branch were revoked, then one could sign a new treaty with Dudaev; if not, then Moscow would not sign any documents with the illegitimate Dudaev."[82]

Shakhrai obviously understood that the rightist-leaning Russian State Duma that had been elected in December 1993 would never agree to revoke the 1991 RSFSR Supreme Soviet's decision concerning the much-detested Dudaev. The result of this intrigue by Shakhrai was that "the variant of a peaceful resolution of the question [of Russian–Chechen relations] was missed." And Sergei Yushenkov concludes: "S. Shakhrai was incapable of overcoming or did not want to overcome his personal animosity toward Dudaev."[83] Journalist Maria Eismont, in a similar vein, has observed: "Before the spring of 1994, only two persons in the Russian political establishment called for the Dudaev regime to be overthrown: the former communist leader in the Chechen–Ingush Republic, Doku Zavgaev . . . and Sergei Shakhrai."[84]

One could argue in hindsight that this belligerent stance by the Russian official in charge of nationality and regional affairs in the Russian Federation rendered the December 1994 military invasion of Chechnya a likely outcome. The period from March through May 1994 witnessed increasing efforts by Russia to adopt the so-called half-force strategy, sponsored by Shakhrai, under which anti-Dudaev Chechens were to be encouraged and assisted in ousting Dudaev from power. There was also a well-planned attempt, most likely approved at the top levels of the Russian government, to assassinate the Chechen president in late May. Certain actions of the Russian leadership during April and May 1994 can plausibly be seen as preparing the way for such "direct action."

During the period between late March and mid-April 1994, various high-ranking Russian officials gave out mixed signals on how to resolve the Russian–Chechen political standoff. On 25 March, for example, during talks in Moscow with Chechen state secretary Aslambek Akbulatov, Yeltsin's chief of administration, Sergei Filatov, made three hard-line conditions for the beginning of negotiations: that Chechnya "stop slandering Russia"; that the talks be held on the basis of Chechnya being a republic of the Russian Federation; and that the Chechen side study the recent Russian–Tatarstan treaty as a basis for negotiations.

---

[82] S. N. Yushenkov, *Voina v Chechne i problemy rossiiskoi gosudarstvennosti i demokratii* (Moscow: author publication, 1995), p. 8.
[83] Ibid., p. 11.   [84] Eismont, "The Chechen War."

Akbulatov affirmed that Chechnya was open to compromise but noted that it would never surrender its sovereignty.[85]

Several days later, Vladimir Shumeiko, chairman of the upper house of the Russian parliament, the Federation Council, signaled a somewhat more flexible approach. As a basis for renewing negotiations with Chechnya, he suggested this schema: that the Chechen Republic remain within Russia, and that the Russian government recognize Dudaev as the president of Chechnya, since the decision of the RSFSR Congress of People's Deputies in 1991 concerning the illegality of Dudaev's election "has lost its juridical effect" following the dissolution of the congress itself.[86]

In mid-April, Russian deputy minister of economics Valerii Fateev suggested during an interview with the press agency Interfax that the Federation Council should recognize the legitimate character of Dudaev's rule, noting that the general had been in power for three years. Fateev, who had recently headed a parliamentary delegation which had visited North Ossetiya and Ingushetiya, had also during this trip, on his own initiative, held a meeting with General Dudaev. Fateev called for an urgent renewal of talks between Russia and Chechnya, and he termed attempts by the Russian leadership to negotiate with the Chechen opposition and to condition a future bilateral treaty with Chechnya on the holding of early parliamentary and presidential elections in that republic as "of no use to Russia."[87] Unfortunately, Fateev's counsel had no noticeable effect on the Russian side.

On 14 April, Yeltsin unexpectedly gave an order to his government to begin negotiations with Groznyi and, on the basis of those talks, to conclude a treaty of the "Tatarstan type." One must ask whether this new tack represented a serious effort to initiate negotiations with Dudaev or whether it was a smokescreen for other kinds of solutions. As Pain and Popov have written: "From May [1994], they began the formation of a Russian delegation to carry out consultations . . . [But] the make-up of the delegation wavered for three months (!) and Shakhrai was named as its head . . . a person already declared by Dudaev to be 'an enemy of the Chechen people' and, in addition, since he was the minister of the affairs of the Russian regions [and not the Russian foreign minister] Shakhrai was unacceptable to the president of the Chechen Republic for that reason as well . . . Shakhrai was the most consistent opponent of the legitimization of Dudaev and therefore of a possible meeting of Yeltsin with him."[88]

[85] In *RFE–RL Daily Report*, 29 March 1994, p. 2.
[86] See *Izvestiya*, 1 April 1994, p. 2.   [87] In *RFE–RL Daily Report*, 17 April 1994, p. 2.
[88] Pain and Popov, "Rossiiskaya politika v Chechne," *Izvestiya*, 9 February 1995, p. 4.

Dudaev is nearly assassinated

In the middle of May 1994, the leadership of the Russian Federation for the first time began to signal a serious desire to initiate negotiations with Dudaev personally. On 19 May, during a press briefing held at the Kremlin, Yeltsin's official spokesman, Vyacheslav Kostikov, stated that the Russian president "does not see any insuperable obstacles to negotiations with Groznyi," and noted that Nikolai Egorov, the former chief of administration of Krasnodar krai, had just been appointed chairman of the Ministry of Nationality Affairs "to activate work in this direction." "In the Kremlin," Kostikov declared in a complete about-face of Russian policy, "they are inclined to recognize Dudaev as the legal president of Chechnya and to conduct negotiations precisely with him."[89] Such negotiations, he noted, could result in a personal meeting between Yeltsin and Dudaev.

Two days later, Yeltsin's chief of administration, Sergei Filatov, confirmed that Yeltsin would shortly be meeting with Chechen president Dzhokhar Dudaev. Filatov noted that Sergei Shakhrai had been released from the post of minister of nationality affairs "in part because of the need to improve relations with Chechnya."[90] A new plenipotentiary representative, he said, would be appointed to conduct bilateral talks with Chechnya.

Had the Yeltsin leadership decided upon a radical change of course in its dealings with separatist Chechnya? Or was it, instead, seeking to lull Dudaev and his entourage into a false sense of security? On 27 May, as was noted in chapter 4 (pp. 154–55), a powerful and sophisticated remote-control car bomb was set off in Groznyi which would have killed Dudaev had he been in his usual position in the automobile procession. Instead, the Chechen minister of interior and one of his deputies died in the blast. Though angered by the attack, Dudaev nonetheless expressed a continued willingness to negotiate a settlement with Russia. "If they think that they can break us here by terroristic acts," he warned, "then the hour is not far away when the same misfortune will come to Russia. If Yeltsin wants to meet, then let's meet and resolve this at the state level."[91]

But, while the Russian leadership had only several days previously expressed a keen interest in holding such a meeting, it now, apparently, completely lost interest in having one. Deputy Premier Sergei Shakhrai reemerged from the shadows and, once again, de facto took over the

---

[89] In *Izvestiya*, 20 May 1994, p. 2.
[90] ITAR-TASS report, summarized in *RFE–RL Daily Report*, 24 May 1994.
[91] NTV, 5 June 1994, in RFE–RL, *Russia & CIS Today*, 6 June 1994, p. 0403/32.

supervision of Russian nationality and regional affairs (although Nikolai Egorov, a militant Cossack from a Cossack village in Krasnodar krai, southern Russia, remained as titular minister of nationality affairs).[92]

Activating the "half-force" variant

As Pavel Fel'gengauer, military correspondent for the newspaper *Segodnya*, has remarked: "By mid-1994 it was decided to begin a covert operation to overthrow Dudaev, using the same tactics that were so successful in Abkhaziya in 1993, where the Russian army unofficially supported the Abkhaz rebels by providing them with quantities of arms and also firepower, air power, and logistical support."

And Fel'gengauer continues: "Originally, the idea to use the Chechen opposition to overthrow Chechen President Dzhokhar Dudaev came from Deputy Prime Minister Sergei Shakhrai. General Aleksandr Kotenkov, deputy nationalities minister and a senior member of Shakhrai's political faction, was the one who took on the practical task of supplying money and weapons to the opposition. Obviously, Shakhrai and Kotenkov had been given the go-ahead by President Boris Yeltsin."[93]

As was noted in chapter 4 (pp. 154–56), a Provisional Council of the Chechen Republic had been brought into existence in December 1993, chaired by former MVD official Umar Avturkhanov, the leading anti-Dudaev figure in the northern Nadterechnyi district (which was also the home district of Yeltsin adviser Doku Zavgaev). On 3–4 June 1994, i.e., just one week after the failed attempt on Dudaev's life, the Provisional Council held a Congress of the Peoples of Chechnya, attended by more than 2,000 delegates, in the village of Znamenskoe, Nadterechnyi district; this Congress represented a key step forward in the attempt by Chechen opposition forces to overthrow Dudaev. The Provisional Council voiced a lack of trust in Dudaev and declared itself to be "the sole legitimate organ on the territory of the Chechen Republic."[94]

Beginning in the summer of 1994, two deputy chairmen of the newly named minister for nationality affairs, Nikolai Egorov, both of whom held the rank of general – Aleksandr Kotenkov, a close aide to Deputy Premier Shakhrai, and Kim Tsagalov, a North Ossetian – took up

---

[92] For Egorov's biography, see Muzaev, *Chechenskaya respublika*, pp. 69–70, and *Moscow News*, 16–22 December 1994, p. 4.

[93] Dr. Pavel Felgenhauer, "The Chechen Campaign," Conference on the War in Chechnya: Implications for Russian Security Policy, 7–8 November 1995, sponsored by the Department of National Security Affairs, Naval Postgraduate School, Monterey, California, unpublished paper.

[94] Muzaev, *Chechenskaya respublika*, p. 44.

residence on the border with Chechnya and began to prepare the overthrow of Dudaev "under the cover of the opposition, with the participation of Russian military personnel recruited by the FSK." In Moscow, the coordinators of this "black" operation were Sergei Shakhrai, Sergei Filatov, Yeltsin's chief-of-staff, and Minister of Nationalities Egorov.[95] At some point during the late summer or autumn of 1994, General Tsagalov appears to have been replaced by FSK colonel Khromchenko. According to journalist Maria Eismont, it was General Kotenkov and Colonel Khromchenko who were responsible "not only for the arms supplies from Russia to Chechnya, but also for the recruitment of Russian servicemen to take part in the military operations in Chechnya under FSK patronage."[96]

Also serving as a key figure in the operation directed against the Dudaev regime was Vladimir Lozovoi, head of the North Ossetian and Ingushetian Interim Administration, a body operating under the supervision of Sergei Filatov.[97] According to Stephen J. Blank and Earl H. Tilford of the US Army War College, at some point during the summer of 1994, "Yeltsin signed an 'instruction' releasing 150 billion rubles of state funds for action against Chechnya."[98]

In mid-July 1994, anti-Dudaev Chechen leaders present in Moscow were invited by the "Daimokhk" Chechen–Ingush Cultural Center to attend a meeting at the Hotel Peking. "[T]he leaders of the so-called 'opposition,'" Yusup Soslambekov recalls, "were present . . . [T]hey announced that financing, arms, information, and political support had already been guaranteed by the Government of the Russian Federation; in this regard, they cited the support and guarantees of Deputy Premier S. Shakhrai and the head of the [presidential] administration, S. Filatov . . . They called upon those assembled in the room to support the armed overthrow of the Dudaev regime." Among those in the room who advocated this position, Soslambekov remembers, were General Vakha Ibragimov, Abdula Bugaev, and Isa Aliroev. Convinced that "we should not involve Russian structures and their special services in the internal affairs [of Chechnya]," Soslambekov maintains that he argued forcefully against the plan.[99]

[95] Tishkov, et al., *Chechenskii krizis*, p. 28. On Kim Tsagalov, see Muzaev, *Chechenskaya respublika*, p. 90.
[96] Eismont, "The Chechen War."
[97] Stephen J. Blank and Earl H. Tilford, Jr., *Russia's Invasion of Chechnya: A Preliminary Assessment* (Carlisle, PA: US Army War College, 1995), pp. 11–12.
[98] Ibid., p. 11.   [99] Soslambekov, *Chechnya*, pp. 28–29.

Dudaev reaches out to Russian rightists

Understandably anxious over the activities taking place on the border of Chechnya, Dudaev appears to have conceived the idea of seeking help from hard-line elements in the Russian Federation who wished to reconstitute the USSR. During the summer of 1994, he invited a delegation of the Russian National Assembly, headed by former KGB major general Aleksandr Sterligov, to Groznyi to discuss a proposal to hold a meeting of the former Presidium of the USSR Supreme Soviet in the Chechen capital "to denounce the Belevozhskii Treaty [of December 1991, which sanctioned the breakup of the Soviet Union] and to recreate the USSR."[100]

In late July 1994, it was reported that Dudaev had sent a letter to former USSR procurator general Sukharev, urging him to "investigate the legality of the Belovezhskaya Pushcha agreements." Dudaev maintained that the USSR had been dissolved against the will of a majority of its citizens.[101] As has been noted, the Chechen leadership was consistently willing to see Chechnya become a union republic within a larger supra-ethnic entity such as a revived USSR. Be that as it may, Dudaev's overtures to the politically weak Russian right were doomed from the start and may well have served further to antagonize Boris Yeltsin.[102]

Accelerating the "half-force" variant

By mid-July 1994, it began to become apparent that the Yeltsin leadership had arrived at a firm decision to overthrow Dudaev in a "black" operation. As Emil' Pain and Arkadii Popov have commented, the idea for such an operation was familiar, "since during 1992 alone it had been successfully tried in the Caucasus on two occasions. All of the details of the overthrow of Presidents Gamsakhurdia (in Georgia) and El'chibei (in Azerbaijan) were known to the Russian Secret Services so well that it is doubtful that they would have looked for outside expertise in formulating scenarios to overthrow Dudaev."[103]

Future historians of the Russian–Chechen conflict will be indebted to M. A. Smith of the Royal Military Academy at Sandhurst, Britain, for his most useful "Chronology of the Chechen Conflict," the first part of which traces developments on an almost daily basis from 4 July 1994

---

[100] Payin and Popov, "Chechnya," n. 13. On the contacts between Dudaev and General Sterligov, see Yandarbiev, *Checheniya*, pp. 303, 309.
[101] *RFE–RL Daily Report*, 26 July 1994, p. 1.
[102] See Payin and Popov, "Chechnya," n. 13.   [103] Ibid.

through 23 May 1995.[104] As Smith's chronology shows, there was a
kind of internal logic at work behind the activities of the Russian
leadership in the period from July to December 1994. The "half-force"
variant served steadily to push the Russian leadership in the direction of
a "full-force" military invasion in December.

The following recitation of some of the events which took place
during the period from late July through late August 1994 shows how
the Russian side began, in effect, to take largely irreversible steps toward
an armed conflict with Chechnya. On 23 July, the Provisional Council
under anti-Dudaev opposition leader Umar Avturkhanov appealed to
Yeltsin for recognition as the sole body of state authority in Chechnya.
Two days later, on 25 July, Yeltsin's chief-of-staff, Sergei Filatov, is
reported to have met in Moscow with Avturkhanov.

On 29 July, the Russian government issued a declaration on Chechnya
in which it claimed that the situation in that republic was effectively
"out of control." "The ambitious policy of Dudaev," the declaration
asserted, "which attempts to depict Russia as an 'aggressor' and 'enemy'
of the Chechen people, has brought the Chechen Republic to isolation
from the Russian Federation." "The policies of the present leadership of
the Chechen Republic," the declaration went on, "have become the
chief destabilizing factor in the North Caucasus, hindering the regular-
izing of the Ossetian–Ingush conflict."[105]

The following day, 30 July, Yeltsin's chief-of-staff, Filatov, accused
the Dudaev regime of carrying out public decapitations and voiced his
opinion that only "healthy forces" in the republic, such as Avturkhanov's
Provisional Council, could restore order.[106] On 1 August, the Provi-
sional Council under Avturkhanov announced that it had deposed
Dudaev and had taken power in Chechnya. It also affirmed that it
intended to hold new elections in May–June 1995. The next day, 2
August, Russian deputy premier Sergei Shakhrai warmly welcomed the
Provisional Council's statement. On that same day, however, Dudaev
issued a strong denial that he had been overthrown and charged the
FSK with training Russian units for action in Chechnya disguised as
Chechen opposition forces.

[104] Dr. M. A. Smith, "A Chronology of the Chechen Conflict," Conflict Studies Research
Center (CSRC), RMA Sandhurst, Part I, July 1995, available from Postmaster
@csrc.demon.co.uk. Part II, issued by the CSRC in April 1996, continues the
coverage of events through 31 December 1995.
[105] For the text of the declaration, see Rossiiskaya gazeta, 2 August 1994, p. 1.
[106] From Smith, "Chronology." Yandarbiev claims that the beheadings were carried out
as vendettas by the families of persons who had been victimized by the criminal
activities of "opposition" leader Ruslan Labazanov and his followers. See Yandarbiev,
Checheniya, p. 303.

On 11 August, Yeltsin was interviewed on television as he departed on a working tour of the Volga. On the subject of Chechnya, Yeltsin stated that intervention by force in that republic was "impermissible and must not be done." But he then added with a sly smile: "However, the situation in Chechnya is now changing. The role of the opposition to Dudaev is increasing. So I would not say that we are not having any influence at all."[107]

General Dudaev reacted instantly to Yeltsin's public suggestion that he had already reached a meeting of the minds with the Chechen opposition headed by Avturkhanov. "The declaration of President Yeltsin concerning the situation in the Chechen Republic of Ichkeriya," Dudaev declared, "bears witness that he personally is directing this unprecedented provocation. Evidently the methods of the political leadership of Russia have not only not changed, but they have become even more aggressive and inhuman . . . We will interpret the introduction of troops onto the territory of Ichkeriya as aggression . . . The [Chechen] National Congress has delegated to me the right to declare *gazavat*. It is a very high responsibility and a difficult task."[108] On the same day on which Yeltsin made his remarks, 11 August, Dudaev signed a decree initiating a military mobilization within the republic.

As Russian journalist Lyudmila Leont'eva underscored on the pages of *Literaturnaya gazeta*, Dudaev had, up until that time, been careful to exempt Yeltsin from responsibility for the subversive actions of the Russian special services. In mid-August, however, she concluded sadly, "the idea of a meeting of the two presidents . . . has burst [like a bubble]."[109] War had therefore become more likely.

According to investigative journalist Maria Eismont, on 25 August, the Russian government adopted a secret (i.e., unconstitutional, according to the 1993 Russian constitution) resolution under which the Chechen Provisional Council of Umar Avturkhanov was recognized as the "only legitimate power structure in Chechnya."[110] Simultaneously with the adoption of this secret resolution, Avturkhanov was promised all possible support in both the military and economic spheres, and the Russian government stepped up the payment of wages and pensions to the populace of the Nadterechnyi and Urus-Martan districts of Chechnya.

On 26 August, Russian deputy premier Shakhrai stated categorically that "[T]he possibility of a political dialogue with Dzhokhar Dudaev has been exhausted." Shakhrai went on to claim that Dudaev controlled de

---

[107] Smith, "Chronology."   [108] In *Obshchaya gazeta*, 19 August 1994, pp. 2–3.
[109] In *Literaturnaya gazeta*, no. 33, 17 August 1994, p. 1.
[110] Eismont, "The Chechen War."

facto only "the center of Groznyi," and he noted that the Russian government was "carrying out consultations with the Provisional Government [under Avturkhanov] in Chechnya, which controls a significant part of the territory."[111]

On 28 August, Dudaev claimed publicly that the Chechen leadership had in its hands a signed statement from a captured FSK colonel in which that officer asserted that Yeltsin had signed an instruction allocating 150 billion rubles from the Russian budget for subversion activities against Chechnya. Three days later, on 31 August, fighting began to intensify between the Dudaev and opposition forces. The Provisional Council announced that it had sealed off the city of Groznyi and gave Dudaev until 6 September to surrender. On the same day, the Provisional Council also announced that it had set up authorities in six of the eleven districts of Chechnya.

As can be seen, the fast-moving events which took place between late July and the end of August 1994 had brought Russia and Chechnya to the edge of war. In accord with a secret decision that had been adopted, Russia was now financially underwriting and militarily assisting the Avturkhanov-led opposition to the extent that the conflict between the two sides could, in the future, be seen by Chechens as a struggle between an elected Chechen president and puppets being manipulated by a foreign power, Russia.

The proxy war heats up – September–November 1994

In the charged period extending from the beginning of September to the failed invasion of Groznyi on 26 November, the Russian government gave no indication that it was prepared to negotiate with the Dudaev leadership. In an appeal issued to the Chechen people, published on 6 September, the Russian government warned Chechens "not to succumb to any provocations of Dudaev and his entourage concerning the need for a withdrawal of Russian troops [from Chechnya]." "Not one military unit of the Russian Federation," the declaration pledged piously, "has crossed the administrative borders of the Chechen Republic."[112]

On 6 September, the FSK petitioned the Russian procurator general to begin criminal proceedings against Dudaev and his entourage in connection with alleged mass murders being carried out in Chechnya. Two days later, on 8 September, Yeltsin's chief-of-staff, Sergei Filatov, flatly ruled out a future Yeltsin–Dudaev meeting but added that the

[111] In *Rossiiskaya gazeta*, 27 August 1994, p. 1.
[112] In *Rossiiskaya gazeta*, 6 September 1994, pp. 1–2.

conflict between Russia and Chechnya ought to be resolved by peaceful means.[113]

On 9 September, the chairman of the FSK, Sergei Stepashin, arrived in the North Caucasus for consultations. He visited the towns of Vladikavkaz and Mozdok and met with Vladimir Lozovoi, head of the provisional administration in North Ossetiya and Ingushetiya, as well as with the North Ossetian political leadership. The next day, 10 September, the Russian procurator general drew the attention of the Federal Assembly and the Russian federal government to the need immediately to restore law and order in the Chechen Republic.

On 16 September, Deputy Premier Shakhrai affirmed unequivocally that Chechnya was part of the Russian Federation and stated that all methods which were lawful in Russia, including crisis methods, could be used to administer that territory. Shakhrai offered his opinion that the army should not be drawn into the conflict but said that the Ministry of Internal Affairs possessed the necessary structures to defend the internal integrity of the Russian state. He also stated that the FSK was working against criminal structures in Chechnya. Like Filatov, Shakhrai firmly rejected the idea of holding talks with Dudaev.

On 30 September, Deputy Premier Shakhrai stated flatly that the institution of the presidency had to be abolished in Chechnya. A week later, on 8 October, he asserted that a free criminal zone had been formed in Chechnya as a result of the actions of the Dudaev regime and predicted that the use of Russian MVD forces might prove necessary, though it should be possible, he added, to avoid employing the army.

In late October 1994, General Dudaev wrote what was apparently his last appeal to Yeltsin, in which he insisted that the Russian president was being given bad advice on Chechnya by his entourage and drew attention to the fact that both he and Yeltsin shared a dangerous opponent: Khasbulatov. Dudaev noted that less than a year remained of his own presidential term, adding, "I have the intention to strictly observe the set date and the order of carrying out the [next] elections." This letter by Dudaev, Yandarbiev recalls, "elicited no response in Moscow."[114]

A fortnight later, on 11 November, Shakhrai was continuing to deny that the Russian leadership should hold talks with Dudaev. The Russian government, he said, would talk with Groznyi only once Dudaev had resigned, and once new elections had taken place in Chechnya.

---

[113] From Smith, "Chronology."
[114] Yandarbiev, *Checheniya*, pp. 319–20. Yandarbiev provides the text of the letter but does not supply a date for it. Sanobar Shermatova in "Chetvertaya popytka?" dates the letter as late October 1994.

Four days later, on 15 November, Shakhrai was unexpectedly removed by Yeltsin as chief Russian negotiator for the Russian–Chechen dispute (though he retained his post as deputy premier). It was bruited that he would soon be replaced as negotiator by Nikolai Egorov, minister for nationalities and regional policy (the appointment of Egorov as Russian plenipotentiary representative in Chechnya was announced on 30 November). It soon became evident that Shakhrai, a "hawk" as far as relations with Chechnya were concerned, had been replaced by a "super-hawk," Egorov.

As this brief chronicle of events has shown, there were no peace overtures nor any offers to negotiate with Dudaev made by the Russian government in the critical period between 1 September and 26 November 1994. While Russian government spokesmen, such as Shakhrai and the procurator general, were taking an unyielding hard line toward secessionist Chechnya, the Russian special forces were consistently (and at times farcically) denying any involvement in the militarized activities of the Chechen opposition. To take one example, on 31 August 1994, the FSK demanded that one of its officers who had been seized in Chechnya (Colonel Stanislav Krylov) be released by the Chechens. On 5 September, however, the same FSK denied that it had any officers in Chechnya. (Later that same day, the Chechen minister of internal affairs, Ayub Satuev, showed Russian journalists a second captured FSK officer, Sergei Terekhov, who publicly – and undoubtedly under duress – confirmed that he had come to Chechnya to coordinate the work of opposition groups.)

On 3 October, the Provisional Council under Avturkhanov launched a helicopter attack (using Russian military helicopters) on the Groznyi suburbs. Later that same day, the Russian Ministry of Defense denied that its forces were operating in Chechnya. On 22 November, the Russian Ministry of Defense once again denied that its troops were taking part in military operations against Chechnya. (Apart from the military helicopters, the Ministry of Defense could, in a legalistic sense, have been telling the truth – Russian military personnel aiding the Chechen opposition had been hired as independent "contract workers" by the FSK.)

Alternative strategies for dealing with Chechnya

In the period between September and November 1994, it became clear to many observers of the Russian political scene that the Russian Federation and the Chechen Republic could be heading toward an armed confrontation. There was also general agreement among observers that Dudaev and his leadership had been severely weakened both by a bankrupt economy and by the emergence of a significant political opposition. As specialist Sergei Arutyunov has noted: "By September 1994, perhaps no more than 20 percent of the total population were supporting [Dudaev]; and any strong support was limited practically exclusively to his own clan and other groups related to him either by clan ties or by business."[115]

Dudaev thus seemed to be on the ropes politically. But how was he to be finished off? In early 1994, the Analytical Center of the President of the Russian Federation had been created in order to bring some intellectual firepower to bear on the problems facing the beleaguered executive branch. Two of the scholars at the new center were Emil' Pain, at the time head of the Working Group on National Policy of the Presidential Council, and Arkadii Popov, a consultant to the Center. In May 1994, a group of experts at the Center, including Pain and Popov, submitted their "Proposals for Conducting Negotiations with the 'Chechen Republic.'" The nub of their counsel was: "[I]t makes sense to conduct *official negotiations* precisely with the current president of the Chechen Republic," but also "[I]t is desirable to conduct *consultations* with the opposition – in a semi-official capacity." It was emphasized in these proposals that the slightest threat to introduce federal troops into Chechnya always played directly into the hands of Dudaev.[116]

Unfortunately, Pain and Popov subsequently concluded, the analysts at the Center turned out to be "victims of a certain political game." Powerful elements within the Kremlin were not interested in holding real negotiations with the Chechens, but merely wanted to project the "semblance of a negotiation process."[117]

On 7 September 1994, the Analytical Center submitted to the Expert Analytical Council of the President of the Russian Federation a report entitled "On the Political Situation in the Chechen Republic." On 9 and 10 September, the gist of this report was made public by Pain and Popov on the pages of the newspapers *Rossiiskie vesti* and *Izvestiya*.[118] In explaining the Center's views to *Izvestiya*, Pain stressed that "Moscow must strive to localize it [Chechnya] and to create a status quo out of those persons who recognize its laws. The departure from the political scene of El'chibei [in Azerbaijan] and Gamsakhurdia [in Georgia] bears

---

[115] Arutyunov, "Possible Consequences."
[116] In "Rossiiskaya politika v Chechne," *Izvestiya*, 9 February 1995, p. 4. Emphasis in original.
[117] Ibid.
[118] Ibid. On the report, see also *Rossiiskie vesti*, 9 September 1994, p. 1, and *Izvestiya*, 10 September 1994, p. 1.

witness to the fact that an incapable, nationalistic, and isolated regime will force people all the more quickly to come to self-definition."[119]

What, then, was the best strategy for the Russian Federation to pursue? "Strengthen the [rail, air, highway] blockade of the Chechen Republic," the Analytical Center's report advised, "and do not permit the penetration onto its territory of armed groups from neighboring republics." "Strengthen," it went on, "the attractiveness of the image of those districts of Chechnya which voluntarily reestablish the jurisdiction of Russia (by paying pensions and supporting the health system, both of which have been destroyed in recent years)." "Strengthen the Russian law enforcement structures in the region." And finally: "Carry out consultations with representatives of various political forces in the Chechen opposition." Such policies, featuring a peaceful competition of two systems, Pain believed, would shortly lead to the fall of the Dudaev regime.[120]

Once again, the Analytical Center's advice was disregarded by the Kremlin leadership. Moreover, beginning in September 1994, the Center "ceased to receive any commissions whatever" from the presidential apparatus, while the channels of information coming to it also "narrowed." A competing analytical center, created by Yeltsin's powerful chief bodyguard, General Aleksandr Korzhakov, and headed by former KGB general Georgii Rogozin, had seemingly begun to call the shots on how to solve the Chechen problem.[121]

Two difficulties connected with the program advocated by Emil' Pain and his colleagues at the Center should be briefly noted. In contrast to what he had earlier been saying, by September 1994, Pain was arguing against conducting negotiations with President Dudaev. "Today," he stressed during an interview with the newspaper Izvestiya, "negotiations with Dudaev are excluded, since there are now many Dudaevs in Chechnya. No one controls the entire territory of the republic, and many districts are alienated from the [Dudaev] regime. Therefore, one has either to talk to everyone or wait until the Chechens become tired of instability and make their choice."[122]

As we saw in chapter 4 (pp. 158–60), the sole Chechen politician with a realistic chance to replace Dudaev was Ruslan Khasbulatov. But, in the Izvestiya interview, Pain rejected Khasbulatov's candidacy: "The

[119] Izvestiya, 10 September 1994, p. 1.
[120] Ibid. A similar approach was advocated in both April and September 1994 by Vladimir Lysenko. See Lysenko, Ot Tatarstana do Chechni, pp. 84, 164–65.
[121] In "Rossiiskaya politika v Chechne," Izvestiya, 9 February 1995, p. 4. On Korzhakov's think tank, see Izvestiya, 24 January 1995, and "Merlin's Tower," Moscow News, 16, 17, and 18 (1995).
[122] Izvestiya, 10 September 1994, p. 1.

candidacy of Khasbulatov for the role of the national leader of Chechnya," he pronounced, "seems to be unlikely . . . He has become a marginal, transitional figure."[123] Given Pain's rejection of holding negotiations with Dudaev, and of having any dealings with Khasbulatov, his proposals, even if they had been accepted by the Kremlin, would have been unlikely to assist the cause of a negotiated peace.

The rise of the "party of war"

During September–October 1994, a surge in the influence of hard-liners within the Yeltsin leadership became apparent. The new prominence of "hawks" at the top of the Russian leadership impacted the growing conflict with secessionist Chechnya.[124] The leading members of this rising militant group were: General Aleksandr Korzhakov (b. 1950), head of the Presidential Security Service; Oleg Soskovets (b. 1949), first deputy prime minister; Nikolai Egorov (b. 1951), minister for national-ities and regional affairs (also named a deputy prime minister on 7 December); General Mikhail Barsukov (b. 1947), head of the Chief Guards Administration of the Russian Federation; and, lastly, Oleg Lobov (b. 1937), secretary of the Russian Security Council. Supporting this group's orientation toward war with Chechnya were the three Russian "power ministers": Pavel Grachev (b. 1948), minister of defense; Sergei Stepashin (b. 1952), minister of security; and Viktor Yerin (b. 1944), minister of internal affairs.

Concerning the rise of this "party of war," the Tishkov group has aptly commented: "Several reasons which were, in the first place, of a domestic Russian character were pushing the federal forces toward a broad-scale military involvement in Chechnya . . . After the December elections of 1993, when liberal ideology and practice as the basis for the politics of the authorities received a serious blow from great power-nationalistic aims and moods, it was precisely the motifs of strength-ening statehood which began more and more strongly to acquire weight in Russian politics. In the opinion of certain experts, during 1994 the vector of mass moods of *rossiyane* began noticeably to tilt in the direction of traditional Russian and imperial values . . . The president and his entourage began to lose support both among the people and among a part of the political and economic elite of the country . . . A group of conservatively inclined politicians, who were closest to the president, and also the 'power' ministers, activated their efforts in order to turn the

---

[123] Ibid.
[124] On the rise of this group, see John B. Dunlop, "The 'Party of War' and Russian Imperial Nationalism," *Problems of Post-Communism*, March–April (1996), 29–34.

president in the direction of great power and state preservationist principles and actions."[125]

And the Tishkov group continued: "In the midst of these tendencies, there took place efforts to take the mass media under state control . . . ; to alter the course of privatization; to neutralize the 'democratic lobby'; . . . and to frighten certain liberal-oriented financial groups. But the main thing in this turning process was to be an action against the rebellious region of the country [Chechnya]. A rapid 'expedition' into Chechnya was to become . . . the beginning of a 'great change,' and its chief political goal was to consist in 'a demonstration of the effectiveness of the regime.'"[126]

The debacle of 26 November

As we saw in chapter 4 (pp. 161–63), the anti-Dudaev opposition had, in an almost bloodless operation, succeeded in taking the city of Groznyi on 15 October. Inexplicably, the Kremlin had then ordered the opposition forces to quit the city. The most likely reason for this seemingly irrational decision was a fear that Ruslan Khasbulatov would have benefited from this development and might conceivably have emerged as a new president of Chechnya. Once this extraordinary opportunity was allowed to pass, the Russian leadership was forced to rely ever more heavily on Russian military personnel secretly recruited by the FSK. This "Russianization" of the conflict, in turn, ran the considerable risk of further alienating the Chechen populace.

The culmination of the strategies which were adopted in the wake of the failed operation of 15 October was, of course, the catastrophic failed invasion of 26 November. On that day, a major Russian invasion force launched a concerted attack on Groznyi. "Nowhere in the world," General Dudaev commented acidly, "is there an opposition with assault aircraft, tank armadas, and mercenary troops. This is intervention pure and simple, under the guidance of Russia's top leadership."[127] A number of the tanks pouring into the city were, as has been noted, manned by Russian crews who had been recruited as contract workers for a "black" operation by the FSK. According to investigations carried out by the newspaper *Izvestiya*, there were seventy-eight Russian contract workers among the attacking force. Twenty-one of them were soon captured by Dudaev's forces (along with seventy-four opposition

[125] Tishkov, et al., *Chechenskii krizis*, p. 28.   [126] Ibid.
[127] In *Moscow News*, 48, 2–8 December 1994, pp. 1–2.

Chechens).[128] Twenty-six Russian soldiers reportedly eluded capture, which suggests that the remaining thirty-one were either killed or went missing.[129]

According to the testimony of three of the captured contract workers: "Recruiters came to their unit from the FSK. They offered the officers and soldiers a contract to carry out a secret task on the territory of Russia. The pay was to be: 3 million rubles to prepare the equipment, and 3 million for the operation. Those who signed contracts were given a vacation and then sent to Mozdok [in North Ossetiya]. There they asked them not to shave so they would be physically similar to Chechens. At the Mozdok base they prepared thirty-four tanks."[130]

The FSK recruiters explained to the men that the invasion would be a cakewalk: "They explained to everyone: Dudaev has fled, his forces are demoralized, the people [i.e., the Chechens] are prepared to meet the liberation of the city with flowers." Instead, the contract workers found themselves, on 26 November, in the midst of a living hell, as their Chechen infantry support melted away while Dudaev's men moved in with grenade-launchers and hand grenades to pick off the tanks and armored vehicles one by one. Many of the Russians were killed when they refused to surrender and tried to effect a breakout back to their own forces.[131]

Commenting on this Russian debacle, Sergei Yushenkov, chairman of the Duma's defense committee, has remarked: "It is stupid to count on Chechens to shoot at other Chechens on a mass scale. But I think that this was precisely what was dreamed up by the FSK or by some other structures. Of course, the collapse of the opposition operation became obvious despite gigantic support from Russia . . . The tanks were accompanied by 'infantry,' which consisted of Chechen opposition, but, of course, they were not trained. Our military specialists became agitated over the fact that, as soon as they entered Groznyi, the opposition [forces] melted away . . . And our [Russian] lads had been assured that only a small Dudaev band was ensconced there. Your task, they were told, is only to bring in the tanks and, if necessary, to fire your guns to frighten people."[132]

In his second volume of memoirs, Zelimkhan Yandarbiev writes that "discord" among the leading Chechen opposition figures was a key factor behind the failure of the 26 November attack upon Groznyi:

---

[128] *Izvestiya*, 10 December 1994, pp. 1, 4. According to another account, eighty-two Russian military contract employees participated in the operation. See *Moscow Times*, 11 December 1994, p. 34. For the number of Chechens captured on 26 November, see *Moscow Times*, 4 December 1994, p. 9.
[129] Khasbulatov, *Chechnya*, p. 44.   [130] *Izvestiya*, 10 December 1994, pp. 1, 4.
[131] Ibid.   [132] Yushenkov, *Voina v Chechne*, pp. 63–64.

"Avturkhanov and Khasbulatov, as well as Zavgaev sitting in Moscow, were unhappy that the city was to be taken in the name of S. Khadzhiev. But the Kremlin had made its choice."[133]

Yandarbiev also asserts that, two days before the Russian incursion, Dudaev had sent a representative to Ingushetiya asking the secretary of that republic's security council to supply him with "anti-tank weapons and grenade launchers." The Ingush, he intimates, responded affirmatively to this request.[134]

A number of commentators have observed that the debacle of 26 November made the 11 December invasion of Chechnya almost inevitable. "After that [the failure of 26 November]," Pavel Fel'gengauer, military correspondent for the newspaper *Segodnya*, has observed, "Yeltsin was left with no choice but to send the regular army into Chechnya."[135] If there were to be no new invasion, Fel'gengauer pointed out, then the Yeltsin leadership would have to explain to the parliament and to the Russian public why there had been a "black" operation in Chechnya and why that operation had failed so abysmally. The twenty-one military contract personnel being held by Dudaev were, in this regard, an acute embarrassment. General Boris Polyakov, commander of the Kantemir Tank Division, angrily resigned his position on 4 December "when he learned that his soldiers had been recruited as mercenaries [by the FSK] without his knowledge."[136]

"I think that the plan of war," Valerii Tishkov has commented, "arose after the dramatic showing on television . . . of captured and humiliated Russian officers and soldiers. The aides and advisers of the president tried to direct his attention to that reportage. The decision was taken by Yeltsin himself."[137]

For the Chechen populace, the 26 November invasion also represented a key turning point. "On 26 November," Ruslan Khasbulatov has noted, Dudaev's forces "now became not bandit formations but rather the armed opposition of a people to [foreign] occupation." "[T]he pride of the Chechen-mountaineer," he concluded, "had come awake."[138]

The Security Council adopts a secret decision to invade

On 28 November, just two days after the debacle in Groznyi, the Russian Security Council convened behind closed doors to discuss the

---

[133] Yandarbiev, *Checheniya*, p. 342.   [134] Ibid.
[135] Felgenhauer, "Chechen Campaign."
[136] In Kronid Lyubarskii, "Proigrannaya voina," *Novoe vremya*, 49 (1994), 12–14, and Smith, "Chronology."
[137] In *Novoe vremya*, 15 (1995), 22–23.   [138] Khasbulatov, *Chechnya*, pp. 40–41.

Chechen crisis. This first meeting appears not to have included the full membership of the council; that plenary session took place on the following day, 29 November.[139] What, it might be asked, is the Security Council, and what is its constitutional function? "The fact that all major decisions connected with Russia's military actions in Chechnya were made by the Russian Security Council," Emil' Pain and Arkadii Popov have written, "necessitates a thorough examination of its decision-making role. First, it is necessary to keep in mind that the Security Council, despite its important appearance, is not an independent decision-making organ. All decisions by the Security Council acquire executive standing only after the president, who is simultaneously the chairman of the Security Council, signs an appropriate decree. From both a legal and practical standpoint, the Security Council is an advisory body to the President."

And they conclude: "Therefore, the proper question is not how the Security Council readied its 'decision' but what its various members, beginning with the 'power ministers,' advised President Yeltsin and whose advice he heeded. Since the Security Council's proceedings [on 29 November] were conducted behind tightly closed doors, however, this is an almost impossible question to answer."[140]

The veil of secrecy surrounding the 29 November session has been lifted in part by Yurii Kalmykov, at the time justice minister of the Russian Federation, an ethnic Circassian from the North Caucasus region. "When the official Security Council session was held," he recalled in an interview with the newspaper *Komsomol'skaya pravda*, "all the documents had already been prepared, and the Security Council members only had to vote – to either adopt or reject the 'force option.' This very much surprised me. I said – let's discuss things first, I want to speak. But I was told that we would vote first. I again tried to put my view. The president said again – let's vote on it. I had to agree . . . And I voted in favor. So did everyone. And then we started discussing it."[141]

As can be seen, Yeltsin had made up his mind to adopt the "force

[139] Smith, "Chronology." The members of the Security Council were: President Boris Yeltsin, chairman; Viktor Chernomyrdin, prime minister; Oleg Lobov, secretary of the Security Council; Vladimir Shumeiko, speaker of the Federation Council; Ivan Rybkin, speaker of the State Duma; Defense Minister Pavel Grachev; Interior Minister Viktor Yerin; FSK Chairman Sergei Stepashin; Evgenii Primakov, chairman of the Foreign Intelligence Service; Finance Minister Vladimir Panskov; Foreign Minister Andrei Kozyrev; Chief of the Border Guards General Andrei Nikolaev; Sergei Shoigu, minister for emergency situations; and Sergei Shakhrai, deputy prime minister. (See *Moscow Times*, 22 January 1995, pp. 14–15.)
[140] Payin and Popov, "Chechnya."
[141] In *Komsomol'skaya pravda*, 20 December 1994, p. 3; English translation: FBIS-SOV 94-245, 21 December 1994, pp. 11–13.

option" before the beginning of this meeting. He was clearly not interested in receiving advice from the full membership of his Security Council. "Some Security Council members," Kalmykov remembers, "advocated talks with the Chechen Republic leadership. [Evgenii] Primakov, for instance. [Vladimir] Shumeiko spoke on this subject . . . I was essentially the only one who categorically opposed the force option. I said that strong-arm action in Chechnya would lead to a partisan war, that a one-day victory might be won but that a long war would then begin and would result in protracted hostilities – after all, the Caucasus is a special region. The president's reaction to this was – that's your personal opinion . . . After this I was forced to resign."[142]

Once again, from Kalmykov's account, it emerges that Yeltsin himself had, at this point, become a driving force behind the approaching invasion. The two Security Council members other than Kalmykov who urged caution were individuals who had had at least some contact with the Muslim world. Evgenii Primakov, chairman of the Foreign Intelligence Service (SVR), was a specialist in Middle Eastern politics, while Vladimir Shumeiko served as chairman of the upper chamber of the Russian parliament, the Federation Council, which included influential representatives from the North Caucasus region.

According to former foreign minister Andrei Kozyrev, who was a participant in the 29 November meeting, "[T]he military people convinced us in the Security Council meeting that it was going to be a 'bloodless blitzkrieg' and would not last longer than 20 December."[143] In similar vein, Aleksandr Zhilin, military correspondent for the weekly *Moscow News*, has reported: "Those near Yeltsin assert that the Russian president had no doubt that the war in Chechnya would be a short one. Deputy Premier Sergei Shakhrai and Defense Minister Grachev convinced him of this, Yeltsin's aides say now."[144]

On 30 November, Yeltsin took another portentous step, issuing a secret (i.e., unconstitutional) decree embodying the decisions which had been rammed through during the Security Council meeting held on the previous day.[145] On 11 December, the day of the Russian invasion, this secret decree (No. 2137c) was superseded by another secret presidential decree (No. 2169c).[146]

---

[142] Ibid. The *Financial Times* reported Kalmykov's resignation in its 20 December 1994 issue, p. 14.
[143] Cited by Payin and Popov, "Chechnya," n. 30.
[144] Aleksandr Zhilin, "Chechnya's Spreading Impact on Kremlin Politics," *Prism*, Part II, 21 July 1995.
[145] The text of this secret decree was subsequently published by the pro-democracy weekly *Novoe vremya*, 14 (1995), 6–9.
[146] On this, see Kronid Lyubarskii, "Shemyakin sud," *Novoe vremya*, 32 (1995), 8–10.

Russia moves toward war

On 28 November, the date on which the initial Security Council meeting was held, Russian military aviation, in a well-planned assault, had eliminated all of the aircraft available to the Dudaev government, both military and civilian, and had closed the runways of the two airfields located near Groznyi.[147]

On 29 November, the day on which the second and key Security Council session had occurred, Yeltsin issued a public appeal "to the participants of the armed conflict in the Chechen Republic." "Despite all the efforts of the federal organs of state power," Yeltsin declared, "it has not been possible to stop the internal conflict in Chechnya, and its scale is widening." "Expressing the will of our multinational people, and in accordance with the powers given to me by the Constitution of the Russian Federation and by Article 7 of the Law 'On Emergency Situations,'" Yeltsin affirmed, "I appeal to all participants in the armed conflict in the Chechen Republic with a warning and a demand that in the course of forty-eight hours . . . a cease-fire be enacted, that all firearms be laid down, and that all armed formations be disbanded." If this were not done, Yeltsin threatened, "then emergency rule will be introduced onto the territory of the Chechen Republic."[148]

As can be seen, this appeal by Yeltsin embodied what was in fact an untruth: namely, that Russia was serving as a neutral, peacemaking force seeking to solve an internal Chechen conflict. In reality, Russia was doing everything in its power to bring the anti-Dudaev opposition to power.

On the morning of 11 December, Russian Ministry of Defense and Ministry of Interior units entered Chechnya. The invasion force consisted of 23,700 men, supported by 80 tanks and 208 armored vehicles. The force divided into three columns, which then moved into Chechnya from Ingushetiya, North Ossetiya, and Dagestan.[149] As he had in November 1991, Yeltsin disappeared from view, allegedly to undergo a minor nose operation. A full-fledged war with Chechnya had begun.

[147] Maria Eismont, "The Chechen War."
[148] In *Rossiiskaya gazeta*, 30 November 1994, p. 1.
[149] Felgenhauer, "Chechen Campaign," and Smith, "Chronology."

Conclusion

> [W]ar was not inevitable. There are all grounds to stipulate that the direct reason for the war was an incompetent decision by the [Russian] Security Council.
>
> Sergei Yushenkov, chairman of the State Duma Defense Committee[1]

> Moscow invaded [Chechnya] out of pique.
>
> Stephen J. Blank and Earl H. Tilford, Jr., *Russia's Invasion of Chechnya*[2]

At the end of November 1994 – just two weeks before the Russian military invasion of Chechnya – two colonels from the Russian General Staff visited the State Military Historical Archive in Moscow with an official request from the Ministry of Defense to learn more about the historical context of armed conflict in the North Caucasus. The archival staff were eager to help, but it turned out that the two colonels were interested only in "general information which they could have found in any pre-Soviet encyclopedia."[3]

As this episode demonstrates, the Russian Ministry of Defense had little notion of the historical experience of the people whose lands they were about to invade. The Russian military – and, evidently, the Russian government as well – had contracted a case of historical amnesia, and this amnesia, in turn, constituted an intelligence failure of immense proportions.

In his short book on the Chechen crisis, Sergei Yushenkov, chairman of the State Duma Defense Committee and a retired military officer, recalls how he exerted himself in vain to forestall the invasion of Chechnya in the period following the military debacle of 26 November

---

[1] Sergei Yushenkov, *Voina v Chechne i problemy rossiiskoi gosudarstvennosti i demokratii* (Moscow: author publication, 1995), p. 14.

[2] Stephen J. Blank and Earl H. Tilford, Jr., *Russia's Invasion of Chechnya: A Preliminary Assessment* (Carlisle, PA: US Army War College, 1995), p. 11.

[3] Alexander A. Belkin, major (retired), "War in Chechnya: Impact on Civil-Military Relations in Russia," Conference on the War in Chechnya: Implications for Russian Security Policy, 7–8 November 1995, sponsored by the Department of National Security Affairs, Naval Postgraduate School, Monterey, California, unpublished paper.

1994. "Those who attacked our tanks," he tried to explain to leading figures in the Kremlin, "are not bandits, although there were some bandits among them. But, on the whole, they are a people with their own customs, which are perhaps strange and incomprehensible for us . . . I said to those who raised objections, 'At least read [Lev Tolstoi's] *Hadji Murat*.'" "Why can't we carry out an operation in our country like the United States did in Haiti?," Oleg Lobov, secretary of the Russian Security Council, retorted haughtily, "It is time for us to show that we can do it. Enough is enough!"[4] For Oleg Lobov, an ahistorical man, there was no essential difference between the Caribbean Haitians and the North Caucasian Chechens.

If the Russian military and the Russian political leadership had little notion of who the Chechens were, the Chechens, for their part, were keenly and painfully aware of who they were as a people, and what their historical relationship with Russia had been. "For a Chechen," Caucasus specialist Sergei Arutyunov has observed, "to be a man is to remember the names of seven generations of paternal ancestors . . . and not only their names, but the circumstances of their deaths and the places of their tombstones. This constitutes an enormous depth of historic memory, and in many cases the remembered deaths occurred at the hands of Russian soldiers – under Catherine the Great, under Nicholas the First, under Stalin."[5] "[E]ven the smallest Chechen boy," Arutyunov has noted, "already knows well the whole history of the deportations [of 1944] and the entire history of the sufferings of his people."[6]

As Arutyunov has remarked elsewhere, Chechnya is best seen as representing a "military democracy," a comparatively rare form of political and social organization. "[L]ike any other military democracy, e.g., like the Iroquois in America or Zulu in South Africa," he writes, "Chechens retained an institution of supreme military chief. In peacetime, that chief would have no power at all. No sovereign authority was recognized, and the nation might be fragmented in a hundred rival clans. However, in time of danger, when confronted with an aggressor,

---

[4] Yushenkov, *Voina v Chechne*, p. 64.
[5] Sergei Arutiunov, "Ethnicity and Conflict in the Caucasus," in Fred Wehling, ed., *Ethnic Conflict and Russian Intervention in the Caucasus*, Policy Paper no. 16 (San Diego, CA: Institute on Global Conflict and Cooperation, University of California, August 1995), pp. 16–17.
[6] From Arutyunov's comments on Chechen historical memory, delivered before the Russian Constitutional Court on 13 July 1995: "Istoricheskaya pamyat' Chechni," *Novoe vremya*, 29 (1995), 12–15.

the rival clans would unite and elect a military leader. While the war was going on, this leader would be obeyed."[7]

The tumultuous events occurring in Chechnya during the years 1991–94 tend to confirm Arutyunov's analysis. Confronted by the chaos and political uncertainty accompanying the collapse of the USSR, Chechens, as it were, instinctively selected a general as their first president (though the election, as we have seen, did not correspond to international standards). During the times when Russia appeared seriously to be contemplating an invasion (November 1991, March 1992, November 1992, November–December 1994), the Chechens would, to a notable extent, rally around their supreme military chief in order to repel a potential foreign aggressor. When tensions would subside, Chechen society would once again "fragment" into its constituent clans, and Dudaev's power would visibly dissipate. The Russian political and military leaderships appear to have been ignorant of this key dynamic.

Commenting upon the historical experience of the Chechens under both the tsars and communists, Valerii Tishkov noted in testimony before the Russian Constitutional Court in 1995: "Former regimes, and not only the Soviet, but the tsarist as well, committed a great many crimes against the Chechen people. The most tragic episode is the Stalin deportation."[8] In a similar vein, Sergei Arutyunov has underscored that the Chechens have "suffered from the tsarist colonialist and Stalinist neo-imperialist policies more than any other nation in the Caucasus, and, probably, next only to the Crimean Tatars, on the all-Russian [and all-USSR] scale."[9] It seems clear that a post-communist Russian democratic leadership should have been alert to this factor of past crimes (and genocide) committed against the Chechens. Visiting new crimes upon such a "punished people" would obviously mesh poorly with a professed system of political democracy and respect for human rights.

In addition to being manifestly the victims of past "crimes," the Chechens during the tsarist period after 1859, and – especially, as we saw in chapter 3 (pp. 85–88), in the Soviet period – were not accorded an equitable "slice of the pie" with regards to economic well-being and social services. Whether it was rate of employment, level of housing and educational benefits, or quality of health and human services, the Chechens invariably placed at or close to the bottom among the peoples

---

[7] S. A. Arutyunov, "Possible Consequences of the Chechenian [sic] War for the General Situation in the Caucasus Area," Conference on the War in Chechnya: Implications for Russian Security Policy, 7–8 November 1995, sponsored by the Department of National Security Affairs, Naval Postgraduate School, Monterey, California, unpublished paper.
[8] In *Novoe vremya*, 15 (1995), 22–23.   [9] Arutyunov, "Possible Consequences."

of the Russian Federation. As Sergei Arutyunov has underscored: "[T]he whole system of the traditional education of the Chechens makes them potentially first-rate partisans . . . but it does not make them potential criminals. It is unemployment which most of all makes people criminals, and unemployment was higher in Chechnya than in other regions of the Caucasus and, in general, in a majority of the other regions of Russia."[10] The high unemployment prevalent among Chechens stemmed from the indifference and the discriminatory policies and practices of the Soviet regime.

In addition to grossly underestimating the motivation and military potential of the Dudaev-led Chechens, the Yeltsin leadership (as will be demonstrated in detail in volume II of this study) seemed to be unaware of or indifferent to clear-cut major weaknesses of the Russian state: its structural semi-collapse; acute economic and administrative dislocations; and, most significantly, the demoralization, corruption, and rampant inefficiency of the Russian military and of other "power structures." A war with well-armed and highly motivated Chechens would predictably serve to strain the rickety structures of the Russian state to the utmost.

At this point, we have arrived at the period upon which this study has been concentrating, the years 1989–94, which witnessed the "Chechen Revolution"; the election of Dudaev as Chechen president in 1991; the collapse of the Soviet Union in December 1991; and then two and a half years of sputtering negotiations between Russia and Chechnya, followed by the "half-force" variant of August–November 1994, and then the "full-force" Russian invasion of 11 December.

The recurrent clashes which took place during 1990 and 1991 between the Gorbachev-led USSR and Yeltsin-led RSFSR directly impacted the Chechens. Both sides in this struggle sought to get the Russian autonomous republics on their side, and engaged in a kind of bidding war for their support. Gorbachev, as we have seen, held out the prospect of upgrading Checheno-Ingushetiya to union republic status. Shortly after being elected chairman of the Russian Supreme Soviet in 1990, Yeltsin began to urge the autonomies to "take that amount of power which you yourselves can ingest."[11] This bidding war, not surprisingly, triggered an upsurge in nationalist and secessionist sentiment among the Chechens. In November 1990 – more than a year before the collapse of the Soviet Union – the republican Supreme Soviet

---

[10] In *Novoe vremya*, 29 (1995), 12–15.
[11] "Vremya," Central Television, 12 August 1990, in Radio Free Europe–Radio Liberty (RFE–RL), *USSR Today*, 12 August 1990, p. 656/03.

declared the Chechen–Ingush Republic to be a sovereign state. A year later – and still before the collapse of the USSR – the full independence of Chechnya was decreed by Dudaev.

While the leadership of the Russian Federation adopted a conscious decision to invade Chechnya in both November 1991 and November 1992 (and there was, in addition, a tentative coup launched in Groznyi in late March 1992, while an invasion of sorts seems to have been attempted by MVD "crimson berets" in September 1992), Yeltsin and his entourage were, in hindsight, fortunate that all of these earlier incursions had to be aborted. The devastation and loss of life occurring during the Russo-Chechen war of 1994–96 would, one suspects, have been quite small in comparison with what might have happened if, say, a war had broken out with Chechnya and the Confederation of Peoples of the Caucasus (KNK) in late 1992. By late 1994, a "gathering of the Russian lands," sponsored by Deputy Premier Shakhrai, had succeeded in reducing separatist sentiment among most of the peoples of the North Caucasus. Indeed, if the problem of Chechnya had been handled in as skillful a fashion, this "gathering" process might have been completed by the end of 1994.

What, then, went wrong? Much of the blame for what went awry obviously attaches to Sergei Shakhrai, the gifted lawyer serving as minister for nationality and regional affairs of the Russian Federation. Appointed to his post in October 1992, Shakhrai appears to have soon concluded that no agreement was possible with the prickly and egotistical General Dudaev. Instead, he attempted to circumvent Dudaev and to negotiate a settlement with such leading (and ambitious) Chechen politicians as Yaragi Mamodaev, Khusein Akhmadov, and Yusup Soslambekov. To be sure, the Chechen constitution, adopted in 1992, assigned the conducting of such negotiations to the republic's parliament, but, by the beginning of 1993, Dudaev had already become embroiled in a *dvoevlastie* struggle with his parliament, mirroring the one taking place in Russia. For this reason, Dudaev insisted upon being the chief negotiator with Russia and, moreover, demanded that either Yeltsin or Prime Minister Chernomyrdin be his negotiation partner.

By mid-1993, Shakhrai seems to have decided that there was no further point in dealing with Dudaev even through proxies, and, by the spring of 1994, he began taking concrete steps to undermine him through supporting "opposition" Chechens, such as former MVD official Umar Avturkhanov (an ally of Yeltsin adviser and former Chechen–Ingush republican Communist Party boss Doku Zavgaev). In late May 1994, a carefully planned attempt was made to assassinate Dudaev; following this failure, the Russian leadership increasingly turned to "black" operations under which the FSK advised and armed the Chechen opposition.

But what if Shakhrai and the Kremlin had seriously attempted to negotiate with Dudaev? In their book, *The Chechen Crisis*, the Tishkov group points to a number of key mistakes made by the Russian leadership. "First," they emphasize (as many others have also done) that, "during the whole time of this crisis, no one among the first persons of the state entered into contact with President Dudaev to hear him out and discuss his position."[12] One can readily agree that this was indeed, in retrospect, a cardinal error.

Elsewhere Tishkov has stressed his opinion that "military intervention was not necessary, because Dudaev had been willing to negotiate with the Russian government on the eve of the [December 1994] attack."[13] This point has also been made by former Russian justice minister Yurii Kalmykov, who, it will be remembered, had resigned his post following the 29 November 1994 Security Council meeting. "After resigning," he has recalled, "I met with Dudaev in Groznyi. He stated: 'I am ready to meet with Chernomyrdin today and discuss problems without preconditions.'" And Kalmykov added: "Those who believe that political means have been exhausted in Chechnya should leave politics."[14]

The available evidence suggests that Tishkov and Kalmykov are correct here; by 1994, Dudaev had been forced by circumstance to give up his dream of forming a Caucasus-wide "Mountain Republic," while general economic collapse and a restive populace in Chechnya were sapping his resolution not to strike a deal with the Kremlin. A "Tatarstan-plus" type of agreement could therefore likely have been negotiated with the Russian government in 1994.

The chief reason that the Russian leadership refrained from such negotiations seems to have been that Sergei Shakhrai (and Yeltsin as well, as we shall see) harbored a deep-seated personal animus, even hatred, for Dudaev. In June 1995, State Duma deputy Valerii Borshchev, a well-known "democrat," was witness to a revealing exchange between Yeltsin and Shakhrai. Borshchev had asked for a meeting with Yeltsin to brief him on the details of his visit to Budennovsk, the site of a bloody 1995 clash between Russians and Chechens. Shakhrai, who was present at the meeting, tried to interject a point into the conversation,

---

[12] V. A. Tishkov, E. L. Belyaeva, and G. V. Marchenko, *Chechenskii krizis* (Moscow: Tsentr kompleksnykh sotsial'nykh issledovanii i marketinga, 1995), p. 51.
[13] In Open Media Research Institute (OMRI), *Daily Report*, 21 February 1995.
[14] In *Komsomol'skaya pravda*, 20 December 1994, p. 3, in FBIS-SOV-94-245, 21 December 1994, pp. 11–13.

but Yeltsin "cut him off abruptly and reminded him that he, Shakhrai, was one of the initiators of the war in Chechnya."[15]

Indeed, Yeltsin appears to have been correct in making this assertion. As another Duma deputy, Sergei Yushenkov, has noted: "S. Shakhrai was incapable of overcoming or did not want to overcome his personal enmity toward Dudaev."[16] "How did we arrive at a point where war has begun in the Chechen Republic?," Ruslan Aushev, the president of Ingushetiya, asked during the 16–17 December 1994 debates in the Federation Council concerning the just-launched Russian invasion: "I recall the statements of S. M. Shakhrai concerning the fact that this problem [Chechnya] was uninteresting to him, that Dudaev himself was uninteresting, and that all of this was uninteresting."[17] Other commentators have pointed to Shakhrai's inability to overlook slights he had received from Dudaev during late 1992 and early 1993 and to the fact that, as a Terek Cossack, he appeared to share that group's corporate historical animosity toward the Chechens.

But what about President Yeltsin himself? It is he, clearly, who must bear the final responsibility for the invasion. "The decision concerning the Chechen war," Fedor Burlatskii has concluded, "judging from everything, was prepared by the closest entourage of the president. But the president himself took the decision: after all, the Security Council is only a consultative organ."[18]

A number of Russian commentators have noted that Yeltsin in his relationship with Dudaev (or, rather, in his lack thereof) permitted himself to give way to strong emotion and to pique. For the president of a major power to permit himself such an indulgence in dealing with an ethnic minority must inevitably be self-defeating. "[T]he decisive escalation of the conflict," the Tishkov group has noted, "took place under conditions of a personalization of the clash." In this connection, they cite a revealing statement made by Mintimer Shaimiev, the president of Tatarstan: "Yeltsin was almost certainly ready for negotiations with Dudaev on the Tatar model, but then they [his entourage] told him that Dudaev had spoken negatively about him." The Tishkov group concludes: "Evidently, from a certain moment on, B. Yeltsin (under the unquestionable influence of his aides and of certain members of the Government) crossed Dudaev off the list of Russian [rossiiskie] poli-

---

[15] *Vechernyaya Moskva*, 10 July 1995.   [16] Yushenkov, *Voina v Chechne*, p. 11.
[17] In *Chechnya: tragediya Rossii* (Moscow: Izdanie Soveta Federatsii, 1995), p. 34.
[18] Fedor Burlatskii, "Uroki kavkazkoi kampanii," *Nezavisimaya gazeta*, 31 January 1995, p. 2.

ticians with whom it was permissible to have any dealings, and he then raised him to the rank of chief enemy."[19]

A striking similarity between the characters of Yeltsin and his arch-rival Dudaev has been pointed to by some commentators. "In my view," Major Aleksandr Belkin has written, "it is essential for further under-standing the inevitability of the armed conflict in Chechnya to compre-hend why President Yeltsin declined any possibility of a personal meeting with Dudaev as a last hope for a peaceful solution of the crisis. As I see it, certain individual features of Yeltsin's character made it psychologically difficult if not impossible (though not excusable) to meet his twin brother from Chechnya. Like Yeltsin himself, Dudaev strove for political power; as Dudaev was ready to sacrifice the unity of the Russian Federation for his own independent rule in Chechnya, so Yeltsin was prepared to facilitate the disintegration of the Soviet Union in order to win power from Gorbachev."[20]

In similar fashion, the Tishkov group has underscored their view that the clash between Yeltsin and Dudaev "was a conflict between extra-ordinarily ambitious, egocentric, and willful leaders, inclined toward coercive improvisations in politics."[21] Journalist Galina Koval'skaya, writing in the weekly *Novoe vremya*, has referred to a "battle of the iron presidents [Yeltsin and Dudaev]."[22]

Critics of the Yeltsin leadership's policies toward Chechnya have argued that an imaginative approach to the issues in dispute between Russia and Chechnya could quite feasibly have resulted in a treaty, such as that which was reached between Russia and Tatarstan in February 1994. In a statement entitled "It Would Have Been Worthwhile for Yeltsin to Pick up the Phone and Call Dudaev," Valerii Tishkov has argued that the ingredients of such an agreement with Chechnya were present all along. The Chechen constitution, adopted in March 1992, he noted, should have been fully acceptable to the Russian government, "with the exception of the preamble, which I would have make a subject of negotiations."[23]

And Tishkov went on: "I think that to dictate the harsh phrase that 'Chechnya is a subject of the [Russian] Federation' is simply counter-

[19] Tishkov, et al., *Chechenskii krizis*, pp. 29, 33.
[20] Belkin, "War in Chechnya." I have introduced some minor changes into Belkin's English text to make it grammatical.
[21] Tishkov, et al., *Chechenskii krizis*, p. 29.   [22] In *Novoe vremya*, 1 (1995), 6–9.
[23] For the text of the Chechen constitution, see *Konstitutsiya Chechenskoi Respubliki* (Groznyi: Parlament Chechenskoi Respubliki, 1992). For Russian and English versions of the Chechen constitution, see also Diane Curran, Fiona Hill, and Elena Kostritsyna, *The Search for Peace in Chechnya: A Sourcebook, 1994–1996* (Cambridge, MA: John F. Kennedy School of Government, Harvard University, Strengthening Democratic Institutions Project, March 1997), pp. 99–141.

productive. If it is not present in regard to Tatarstan, then why should Chechnya after so many losses . . . be forced into that kind of relationship? The variant of a state associated with the Russian state, with a high degree of external ties, is, in my view, fully acceptable."[24]

In a similar vein, Vladimir Lysenko, chairman of the Russian State Duma's Subcommittee on the Development of Federal Relations, has observed that the "idea of a confederative union" linking Russia and Chechnya was a potentially fertile and workable one. "De facto," Lysenko noted at the end of 1994, "according to the treaty signed between Moscow and Kazan', Tatarstan is in such a [confederative] position. Such a non-standard approach could also have been applied to Chechnya. I would remind you that even in the [pre-revolutionary] Russian Empire its various parts had different statuses."[25]

As we saw in chapter 5 (pp. 187–88), the contours of a "Tatarstan-plus" type of agreement were visible to intelligent observers as early as in 1992. Chechnya would receive sovereignty and independence (*nezavisimost'*) from the Russian Federation but would agree, in turn, to form "a single economic and military space" with Russia. Chechnya, further, would agree not to enter into any military unions or blocs directed at Russia. Chechen military cadres would be trained at Russian military academies, while Chechen military hardware would be repaired at Russian facilities.

Such an agreement would have involved painful concessions on the part of the Russian Federation. But compared to the widespread human and economic devastation which would result from war, it was a relatively small price to have to pay. Concessions to an ethnic group which had lost at least a quarter of its populace to Stalin-era genocide and which had been a "punished people" throughout the Khrushchev and Brezhnev periods were both called for and necessary.

As we saw in chapter 5 (pp. 188–91), Deputy Premier Shakhrai did everything that he could in the wake of the signing of the Russia–Tatarstan treaty in February 1994 to ensure that Chechnya would face a harsher bargaining position on Russia's part than Tatarstan had been confronted with.[26] A perusal of the text of the Russia–Tatarstan treaty impresses with the flexibility and looseness of its language, and with its

[24] In *Novoe vremya*, 15 (1995), 22–23.
[25] Vladimir Lysenko, *Ot Tatarstana do Chechni: stanovlenie novogo rossiiskogo federalizma* (Moscow: Institut sovremennoi politiki, 1995), p. 188.
[26] For the text of the Russia–Tatarstan treaty, see *Rossiiskaya gazeta*, 17 February 1994, p. 6. See also *Sbornik dogovorov i soglashenii mezhdu organami gosudarstvennoi vlasti Rossiiskoi Federatsii i organami gosudarstvennoi vlasti sub"ektov Rossiiskoi Federatsii o razgranichenii predmetov vedeniya i polnomochii* (Moscow: Izdanie Gosudarstvennoi Dumy, 1997), pp. 212–18.

conceptual "wriggle room." As Valerii Tishkov has underscored, this treaty nowhere explicitly states that Tatarstan is a "subject of the Russian Federation."

What Shakhrai and Yeltsin were prepared to do for Tatarstan, they were apparently unwilling to do for Chechnya, presumably because of their personal detestation of Dudaev. As was shown in chapter 5 (pp. 188–90), a precondition stipulated by Shakhrai for the drawing up of a treaty with Chechnya was the prior holding of new elections to both the organs of power within the Chechen Republic and to the two chambers of the Russian Federal Assembly. Shakhrai got the Russian State Duma to adopt a decree embodying such a harsh bargaining position toward Chechnya in late March 1994.

"The Russian political-military leadership," Major Aleksandr Belkin has concluded, "did not use all the peaceful means available to resolve the problem. Instead, its civilian part represented by so-called intellectuals . . . unsuccessfully exercised the policy of 'carrots' and 'sticks.' They failed to propose to Dudaev a 'carrot' big enough so that he could not reject it (as they had done in the case of Tatarstan)."[27]

Another key flaw in the Russian leadership's approach to negotiations with Chechnya was its simultaneous dealings with and clear-cut preference for the so-called Chechen opposition. As Timothy Lee Thomas, an analyst with the US military, has commented: "A final factor working against any Russian attempt at mediation was the fact that, while talking to Dudaev's people, Russia simultaneously held separate talks with the Dudaev opposition, the group it had supported with arms, training, and men in the November [1994] attack on Groznyi. As a result, Russian mediation was not considered impartial or credible by the Chechens but rather condescending. Thus the stage was set for a bloody confrontation."[28]

If, as Major Aleksandr Belkin has noted, the Russian leadership did not, on the whole, skillfully employ the "carrots" available to it in dealing with Chechnya, it also notably failed to employ available "sticks." The Tishkov group has pointed out that, "a number of necessary measures were not taken [by the Russian Federation] in the sphere of the economy and controls over the borders and air space which are usually taken by a state in the case of the appearance of a rebellious region." The Russian Foreign Ministry, they note, did not announce to the international community that "an internal crisis was taking place."

[27] Belkin, "War in Chechnya."
[28] Timothy Lee Thomas, *The Caucasus Conflict and Russian Security: The Russian Armed Forces Confront Chechnya* (January 1995, US Army, Foreign Military Studies Office, Fort Leavenworth, KS).

And, lastly, corrupt Russian officials behaved "extremely unprofession-ally" in permitting Dudaev "to create a network of support in [Russian] federal structures."[29]

The plan for the resolution of the Chechen crisis elaborated in 1994 by the Analytical Center of the President of the Russian Federation (i.e., by Emil' Pain, Arkadii Popov, and their colleagues) advocated a similar, but more aggressive approach. The Analytical Center, as we saw in chapter 5 (pp. 200–03), urged that all rail, air, and road connections to the republic be blockaded; that customs, tax, and police controls be established on Chechnya's borders; and that those regions of the republic (Nadterechnyi and Urus-Martan districts) which recognized Russian laws be transformed into showcase districts through the payment by Russia of pensions and other benefits ("a peaceful competi-tion of two systems"). The idea was to isolate Chechnya, to show the Chechens the economic and social benefits of cooperating with Russia, and to wait for the scheduled 1995 elections in Chechnya which would likely bring a new leadership to power.[30] This was an aggressive approach, but it might conceivably have worked.

The so-called half-force variant sponsored by Deputy Premier Shakhrai and by others in the Kremlin, which employed the FSK to train and assist Chechen opposition forces, might also have produced results, but only if the Russian leadership had been prepared to acquiesce to Ruslan Khasbulatov's accession to the position of Chechen head of state. The Govorukhin Commission has drawn attention to the opinion of General Aleksandr Kotenkov, first deputy chairman of the Ministry of Nationalities under Sergei Shakhrai, who believes that, in the summer of 1994, "none of the active leaders of opposition groups could compare with R. Khasbulatov, who had come to Chechnya with his 'peacemaking' mission; if the Moscow politicians had risked staking their cards on him, then power could have been taken."[31]

General Kotenkov would seem to be right. A prickly and obstinate leader with a penchant for ruthlessness and intrigue, Ruslan Khasbu-latov should, nonetheless, from the Kremlin's perspective, have been preferable to Dudaev, because, unlike Dudaev, he was not a military general but, rather, an experienced, professional politician who almost certainly would have been able, and would have wanted, to conclude a

---

[29] Tishkov, et al., *Chechenskii krizis*, p. 51.
[30] For the Analytical Center's program, see *Rossiiskie vesti*, 9 September 1994, p. 1; *Izvestiya*, 10 September 1994, p. 1; and Emil A. Payin and Arkady A. Popov, "Chechnya," in Jeremy R. Azrael and Emil A. Payin, eds., *US and Russian Policymaking with Respect to the Use of Force*, Part I (Santa Monica, CA: RAND, 1996), posted on Discussion List about Chechnya, 6 November 1996, Chechnya@Plearn.EDU.PL.
[31] In *Komissiya Govorukhina* (Moscow: Laventa, 1995), pp. 59–60.

Tatarstan-type treaty with Russia. The fact that Khasbulatov was manifestly not a "Moscow stooge" could have helped him immensely in persuading his fellow Chechens to agree to such a treaty.

In point of fact, as we saw in chapter 4 (pp. 161–63), the "half-force" variant actually seems to have worked. On 15 October 1994, opposition forces allied with Khasbulatov took the city of Groznyi with a minimal loss of life (seven persons on both sides). But Moscow apparently bridled at the prospect of a Khasbulatov accession to power and ordered Bislan Gantamirov's opposition forces out of the city. Moscow clearly wanted "puppet" Chechens to rule Chechnya and not the largely uncontrollable Khasbulatov. This significant miscalculation on Moscow's part rendered a transition from a "half-force" to a "full-force" variant virtually certain. Beginning on 26 November 1994, the threatened Russian invasion was transformed in the minds of a majority of Chechens into a clear-cut national threat.

As Sergei Arutyunov has noted, the Russian–Chechen conflict of 1991–94 is, in a number of ways, reminiscent of the charged political situation obtaining in Central Europe and the Balkans in the years preceding the Great War. "As we all know," he writes, "although World War I was triggered by a fanatic nationalist intellectual, the basic responsibility for the war lies with the designs of the great powers – Germany, Austria-Hungary, and others as well – to establish their domination over ever-larger territories. The same is true of the conflicts in the Caucasus today. They are all *triggered* by extremist statements and irresponsible actions of local ethnic minority patriots, but the basic responsibility for them lies with the central governments and ruling elites of larger nations such as Russia, who still hope to solve their problems by force. And in the end, most will probably be defeated [by the secessionist regions]."[32]

A chief reason that the expansionist designs of Russia (and of Georgia and Azerbaijan) in the Caucasus region will likely fail, Arutyunov believes, is that "Georgian, Azeri, and Russian troops hate to fight for their governments' domination on lands which are very far from most soldiers' own homes." And Arutyunov concludes on an optimistic note: "[T]here are all reasons to believe that the already shrunken territory of Russia is not going to shrink any more. When real democracy finally wins in Russia, there will be room for all minorities and autonomies, as there is room for them in modern Germany or Spain . . . But the way toward this relative democratic stability in Russia may be even more prolonged and painful than it was in Germany or Spain."[33]

[32] Arutiunov, "Ethnicity and Conflict," pp. 16–18. Emphasis in the original.
[33] Ibid.

One can concur with Arutyunov's assertion that the "basic responsibility for the war" between Russia and Chechnya which broke out in December 1994 lies with the outbreak of a virulent form of Russian neo-imperialism. As we have seen, the Russian "black" operations carried out in Chechnya were modeled on earlier secret operations conducted by the FSK and the Russian military in Georgia, Azerbaijan, and Moldova. The aim behind these secret operations was, it seems, to reassemble the "space" of the former Soviet Union into a single state or, failing that, to create a coerced Russian "sphere of influence" in which the newly independent states would be forced to do Russia's political and economic bidding. A concomitant goal was to ensure that Russia obtained a major share of the oil and gas riches of the Caspian region. Since obdurate Chechnya sat athwart Russia's neo-imperial thrust southwards – and, moreover, since, when the Soviet Union collapsed in 1991, Chechnya had, by historical accident, found itself within the internationally recognized boundaries of the Russian Federation – the republic's desire for independence had to be swiftly crushed by force of arms.

Summing up

The December 1994 Russian military invasion of Chechnya was the result of a massive intelligence failure and of an egregious miscalculation. The Dudaev-led Chechens constituted a martial people – highly motivated, courageous, and skillful in battle – who nourished burning grievances against the Russian state. It should have been self-evident to the Russian leadership that the Chechens would fight long and hard against a perceived foreign invader. But the Yeltsin leadership had little inkling of who the Chechens were. The Russian "party of war" likewise had little apparent understanding of the pronounced weaknesses of the Russian state and of its military and "power" structures. A rickety, corrupt, and collapsing military machine was to be pitted against a keenly motivated and well-armed warrior people adept at guerrilla tactics. The results should have been predictable.

Unfortunately, the Yeltsin leadership, when confronted with a Chechnya bent on secession, elected not to conduct serious negotiations with President Dudaev. A "Tatarstan-plus" type of agreement could, in my opinion, have been reached. But the Russian leadership chose instead to resort to Brezhnev (and even Stalin)-era practices: "black" operations, destabilization campaigns, assassinations, and the installation of "puppet" regimes. The Yeltsin regime, however, lacked the will and the ability to utilize such coercive tools successfully. Moreover, a relatively free press and other structures of emerging semi-democracy rendered a reversion to communist-era practices difficult and in many ways unfeasible.

Behind the decision to invade Chechnya lay the arrogance and hubris of the Russian "party of war." A "great power," it was believed, must swat aside its enemies and opponents like so many flies. A disturbing ethnic dimension also seems to have played a role in the invasion. Nationality ministers Sergei Shakhrai and Nikolai Egorov were both by background Russian Cossacks who seem to have internalized that community's historic animus against the Chechens. The results of their apparent inability or unwillingness to be dispassionate and fair-minded toward the pro-secession Chechens were unfortunate, even catastrophic.

War broke out because of a conviction on the part of a significant segment of the Russian leadership that ethnic grievances can be resolved through the use of force and through "black" operations rather than through patient negotiation. With the invasion of Chechnya in December 1994, Russia's new "Time of Troubles" deepened and became increasingly murky.

Index